HOUSING MARKET POLICY OPTIONS

HOUSING ISSUES, LAWS AND PROGRAMS

Additional books in this series can be found on Nova's website
under the Series tab.

Additional e-books in this series can be found on Nova's website
under the e-book tab.

ECONOMIC ISSUES, PROBLEMS AND PERSPECTIVES

Additional books in this series can be found on Nova's website
under the Series tab.

Additional e-books in this series can be found on Nova's website
under the e-book tab.

HOUSING MARKET POLICY OPTIONS

MELISSA O. MURRAY
AND
WILLIE T. COLE
EDITORS

nova publishers
New York

NOTICE TO THE READER

The Publisher has taken reasonable care in the preparation of this book, but makes no expressed or implied warranty of any kind and assumes no responsibility for any errors or omissions. No liability is assumed for incidental or consequential damages in connection with or arising out of information contained in this book. The Publisher shall not be liable for any special, consequential, or exemplary damages resulting, in whole or in part, from the readers' use of, or reliance upon, this material. Any parts of this book based on government reports are so indicated and copyright is claimed for those parts to the extent applicable to compilations of such works.

Independent verification should be sought for any data, advice or recommendations contained in this book. In addition, no responsibility is assumed by the publisher for any injury and/or damage to persons or property arising from any methods, products, instructions, ideas or otherwise contained in this publication.

This publication is designed to provide accurate and authoritative information with regard to the subject matter covered herein. It is sold with the clear understanding that the Publisher is not engaged in rendering legal or any other professional services. If legal or any other expert assistance is required, the services of a competent person should be sought. FROM A DECLARATION OF PARTICIPANTS JOINTLY ADOPTED BY A COMMITTEE OF THE AMERICAN BAR ASSOCIATION AND A COMMITTEE OF PUBLISHERS.

Additional color graphics may be available in the e-book version of this book.

LIBRARY OF CONGRESS CATALOGING-IN-PUBLICATION DATA

ISBN: 978-1-62257-294-6

Published by Nova Science Publishers, Inc. † New York

CONTENTS

Preface		**vii**
Chapter 1	Reduce, Refinance, and Rent? The Economic Incentives, Risks, and Ramifications of Housing Market Policy Options *Sean M. Hoskins and Matthew Kurlanzik*	**1**
Chapter 2	The U.S. Housing Market: Current Conditions and Policy Considerations *Board of Governors of the Federal Reserve System*	**37**
Chapter 3	Testimony of Mark Zandi, Chief Economist and Co-Founder of Moody's Analytics. Hearing on "State of the Housing Market: Removing Barriers to Economic Recovery"	**63**
Chapter 4	Testimony of Philip L. Swagel, Professor of International Economic Policy, University of Maryland School of Public Policy. Hearing on "State of the Housing Market: Removing Barriers to Economic Recovery"	**81**
Chapter 5	Preserving Homeownership: Foreclosure Prevention Initiatives *Katie Jones*	**93**
Chapter 6	National Mortgage Servicing Standards: Legislation in the 112th Congress *Sean M. Hoskins*	**141**
Index		**159**

PREFACE

The ongoing problems in the U.S. housing market continue to impede the economic recovery. House prices have fallen an average of about 33 percent from their 2006 peak, resulting in about $7 trillion in household wealth losses and an associated ratcheting down of aggregate consumption. At the same time, an unprecedented number of households have lost, or are on the verge of losing, their homes. The extraordinary problems plaguing the housing market reflect in part the effect of weak demand due to high unemployment and heightened uncertainty. But the problems also reflect three key forces originating from within the housing market itself: a persistent excess supply of vacant homes on the market, many of which stem from foreclosures; a marked and potentially long-term downshift in the supply of mortgage credit; and the costs that an often unwieldy an inefficient foreclosure process imposes on homeowners, lenders, and communities. This book provides a framework for thinking about directions policymakers might take to help the housing market.

Chapter 1 – The bursting of the housing bubble in 2006 precipitated the December 2007 - June 2009 recession and a financial panic in September 2008. With the housing market seen as a locus for many of the economic problems that emerged, some Members of Congress propose intervening in the housing market as a means of improving not only the housing market itself but also the financial sector and the broader economy. Critics are concerned that further intervention could prolong the housing slump, delay recovery, and affect outcomes based on the government's preferences.

Three frequently discussed proposals for the housing market are (1) reducing mortgage principal for borrowers who owe more than their homes are worth, (2) refinancing mortgages for borrowers shut out of traditional financing methods, and (3) renting out foreclosed homes.

Principal reductions have the potential to improve the housing market by minimizing disruptive defaults and foreclosures. However, by shifting the debt burden from the borrower to the lender, principal reduction may negatively impact financial institutions that would have their investments' principal balances reduced. Principal reduction, nonetheless, might improve the broader economy if it stimulates consumer spending, diverting income from debt repayment to spending on other goods and services.

Legislation introduced in the 112th Congress to reduce mortgage principal includes H.R. 1587, H.R. 3841, H.R. 4058, and S. 2093. Principal reduction is also part of the settlement reached between several mortgage servicers and 49 state attorneys general and the federal government.

Large-scale refinancing helps borrowers who are current on mortgage payments to refinance into a new mortgage with a lower interest rate. Because refinancing generally helps borrowers who are current, it is unlikely to have a major effect on the housing market, but it may prevent some foreclosures that could occur in the absence of a refinance. In addition, refinancing has the potential to have a larger effect on the economy by stimulating consumer spending. A mortgage refinance could lower a borrower's monthly payment, freeing up more income for non-housingrelated spending. Some of the additional spending of borrowers may come at the cost of the financial sector. Although some financial institutions may lose investment income from refinancing, others could benefit from the increased business associated with refinancing.

President Obama, in his 2012 State of the Union address, proposed streamlining the existing program to refinance Fannie Mae and Freddie Mac loans and establishing a new mass refinancing plan for non-Fannie Mae and non-Freddie Mac loans. Congressional proposals for large-scale refinancing of Fannie Mae and Freddie Mac loans include H.R. 363 and S. 170.

Renting out foreclosed homes currently held by banks and other financial institutions has the potential to stabilize housing prices by reducing the supply of homes on the "for sale" market. However, this policy depends on house prices increasing in the future such that, when the rented properties are eventually sold, they are sold in a healthier market. Unlike principal reductions and mass refinancing, renting foreclosed homes does not reduce existing homeowners' payments or increase their disposable income. Any impact on consumer spending is likely to be indirect through stabilizing house prices and preserving neighboring homeowners' equity.

The Federal Housing Finance Agency (FHFA), the regulator of Fannie Mae and Freddie Mac, has started a pilot project to convert foreclosed homes into rentals. Congressional proposals to expand the renting of foreclosed properties include H.R. 1548, H.R. 2636, and S. 2080.

Chapter 2 – The ongoing problems in the US housing market continue to impede the economic recovery. House prices have fallen an average of about 33 percent from their 2006 peak, resulting in about $7 trillion in household wealth losses and an associated ratcheting down of aggregate consumption. At the same time, an unprecedented number of households have lost, or are on the verge of losing, their homes. The extraordinary problems plaguing the housing market reflect in part the effect of weak demand due to high unemployment and heightened uncertainty. But the problems also reflect three key forces originating from within the housing market itself: a persistent excess supply of vacant homes on the market, many of which stem from foreclosures; a marked and potentially long-term downshift in the supply of mortgage credit; and the costs that an often unwieldy and inefficient foreclosure process imposes on homeowners, lenders, and communities.

Looking forward, continued weakness in the housing market poses a significant barrier to a more vigorous economic recovery. Of course, some of the weakness is related to poor labor market conditions, which will take time to be resolved. At the same time, there is scope for policymakers to take action along three dimensions that could ease some of the pressures afflicting the housing market. In particular, policies could be considered that would help moderate the inflow of properties into the large inventory of unsold homes, remove some of the obstacles preventing creditworthy borrowers from accessing mortgage credit, and limit the number of homeowners who find themselves pushed into an inefficient and overburdened foreclosure pipeline. Some steps already being taken or proposed in these areas will be discussed below.

Taking these issues in turn, the large inventory of foreclosed or surrendered properties is contributing to excess supply in the for-sale market, placing downward pressure on house prices and exacerbating the loss in aggregate housing wealth. At the same time, rental markets are strengthening in some areas of the country, reflecting in part a decline in the homeownership rate. Reducing some of the barriers to converting foreclosed properties to rental units will help redeploy the existing stock of houses in a more efficient way. Such conversions might also increase lenders' eventual recoveries on foreclosed and surrendered properties.

Chapter 3 – This is Testimony of Mark Zandi, Chief Economist and Co-Founder of Moody's Analytics. Hearing on "State of the Housing Market: Removing Barriers to Economic Recovery"

Chapter 4 – This is Testimony of Philip L. Swagel, Professor of International Economic Policy, University of Maryland School of Public Policy. Hearing on "State of the Housing Market: Removing Barriers to Economic Recovery"

Chapter 5 – The foreclosure rate in the United States began to rise rapidly beginning around the middle of 2006. Losing a home to foreclosure can hurt homeowners in many ways; for example, homeowners who have been through a foreclosure may have difficulty finding a new place to live or obtaining a loan in the future. Furthermore, concentrated foreclosures can drag down nearby home prices, and large numbers of abandoned properties can negatively affect communities. Finally, the increase in foreclosures may destabilize the housing market, which could in turn negatively impact the economy as a whole.

There is a broad consensus that there are many negative consequences associated with rising foreclosure rates. Both Congress and the Bush and Obama Administrations have initiated efforts aimed at preventing further increases in foreclosures and helping more families preserve homeownership. These efforts currently include the Making Home Affordable program, which includes both the Home Affordable Refinance Program (HARP) and the Home Affordable Modification Program (HAMP); the Hardest Hit Fund; the Federal Housing Administration (FHA) Short Refinance Program; and the National Foreclosure Mitigation Counseling Program (NFMCP), which provides funding for foreclosure mitigation counseling and is administered by NeighborWorks America. Two other initiatives, Hope for Homeowners and the Emergency Homeowners Loan Program (EHLP), expired at the end of FY2011. Several states and localities have also initiated their own foreclosure prevention efforts, as have private companies. A voluntary alliance of mortgage lenders, servicers, investors, and housing counselors has also formed the HOPE NOW Alliance to reach out to troubled borrowers.

In March 2011, the House of Representatives passed a series of bills that, if enacted, would terminate the Home Affordable Modification Program (H.R. 839), the FHA Short Refinance Program (H.R. 830), and the Emergency Homeowners Loan Program (H.R. 836), as well as the Neighborhood Stabilization Program (H.R. 861), which is not a foreclosure prevention program but is intended to address the effects of foreclosures on communities. While many observers agree that slowing the pace of foreclosures is an important policy goal, there are several challenges associated with foreclosure prevention plans. These challenges include implementation issues, such as deciding who has the authority to make mortgage modifications, developing the capacity to complete widespread modifications, and assessing the possibility that homeowners with modified loans will default again in the future. Other challenges are related to the perception of unfairness, the problem of inadvertently providing incentives for borrowers to default, and the possibility of setting an unwanted precedent for future mortgage lending.

This report describes the consequences of foreclosure on homeowners; outlines recent foreclosure prevention initiatives, largely focusing on initiatives implemented by the federal government; and discusses the challenges associated with foreclosure prevention.

Chapter 6 – The United States single-family housing market has $10.5 trillion of mortgage debt outstanding. Servicers play an important role in this market. The owner of a mortgage loan or mortgage-backed security typically hires a servicer to act on its behalf. When loans are current, a mortgage servicer collects payments from borrowers and forwards them to the mortgage holders. If the borrower becomes delinquent, a servicer may offer the borrower an option that could allow the borrower to stay in his or her home, or the servicer may pursue foreclosure.

Following high foreclosure rates and recent allegations of abuse, mortgage servicing has attracted attention from Congress. In addition to hearings and congressional investigations, some in Congress have called for national servicing standards. The most comprehensive proposal, S. 824, the Foreclosure Fraud and Homeowner Abuse Prevention Act of 2011 (Senator Sherrod Brown et al.), and its companion bill in the House, H.R. 1783 (Representative Brad Miller et al.), contain provisions intended to protect investors and borrowers from improper servicing practices. S. 967, the Regulation of Mortgage Servicing Act of 2011 (Senator Jeff Merkley et al.), includes borrower protections in addition to those offered by S. 824 and H.R. 1783.

The servicing standards proposed in S. 824 and H.R. 1783 include provisions intended to ensure that servicers act in the best interest of investors who hold mortgage loans. The proposals would adjust the servicing compensation structure to better align servicer incentives with the incentives of the mortgage holder. Servicers would also be prohibited from purchasing services offered by their affiliates at inflated costs and passing the costs on to investors. In addition, servicers would be prohibited from choosing a loss mitigation option that would benefit their affiliates at the expense of other investors.

S. 824, H.R. 1783, and S. 967 have three major components for borrower protection. First, the three bills would require servicers to establish a single point of contact with the borrower. The single point of contact would be a case manager who is assigned to each delinquent borrower and would manage communications with the borrower. Second, the three bills would prohibit servicers from dual tracking, which means initiating foreclosure on a borrower while simultaneously pursuing a loan modification. Servicers would instead be required to determine whether the borrower is eligible for an alternative to foreclosure before initiating foreclosure. Third, S. 824 and H.R. 1783 would set minimum experience, education, and training levels for loan modification staff and limit caseload levels for individual employees.

Legislation is not the only avenue to setting servicing standards. Regulatory agencies, such as the Consumer Financial Protection Bureau, the Board of Governors of the Federal Reserve System, and the Federal Deposit Insurance Corporation, may include some or all of the proposed standards in their rules on securitization and qualified residential mortgages pursuant to the Dodd-Frank Wall Street Reform and Consumer Protection Act (P.L. 111-203).

Servicing standards could also be adopted through legal settlements between the servicers and the state attorneys general, as well as through enforcement actions taken by federal regulators in response to deficient servicing practices by some banks. If servicing standards are implemented by rule or by settlement agreements, they would apply only to those servicers under the regulators' purview or those who entered into the settlement agreements.

In: Melissa O. Murray and Willie T. Cole
Editors: Melissa O. Murray and Willie T. Cole

ISBN: 978-1-62257-294-6
© 2012 Nova Science Publishers, Inc.

Chapter 1

REDUCE, REFINANCE, AND RENT? THE ECONOMIC INCENTIVES, RISKS, AND RAMIFICATIONS OF HOUSING MARKET POLICY OPTIONS[*]

Sean M. Hoskins and Matthew Kurlanzik

SUMMARY

The bursting of the housing bubble in 2006 precipitated the December 2007 - June 2009 recession and a financial panic in September 2008. With the housing market seen as a locus for many of the economic problems that emerged, some Members of Congress propose intervening in the housing market as a means of improving not only the housing market itself but also the financial sector and the broader economy. Critics are concerned that further intervention could prolong the housing slump, delay recovery, and affect outcomes based on the government's preferences.

Three frequently discussed proposals for the housing market are (1) reducing mortgage principal for borrowers who owe more than their homes are worth, (2) refinancing mortgages for borrowers shut out of traditional financing methods, and (3) renting out foreclosed homes.

Principal reductions have the potential to improve the housing market by minimizing disruptive defaults and foreclosures. However, by shifting the debt burden from the borrower to the lender, principal reduction may negatively impact financial institutions that would have their investments' principal balances reduced. Principal reduction, nonetheless, might improve the broader economy if it stimulates consumer spending, diverting income from debt repayment to spending on other goods and services.

Legislation introduced in the 112th Congress to reduce mortgage principal includes H.R. 1587, H.R. 3841, H.R. 4058, and S. 2093. Principal reduction is also part of the settlement reached between several mortgage servicers and 49 state attorneys general and the federal government.

Large-scale refinancing helps borrowers who are current on mortgage payments to refinance into a new mortgage with a lower interest rate. Because refinancing generally

---

[*] This is an edited, reformatted and augmented version of a Congressional Research Service publication, CRS Report for Congress R42480, prepared for Members and Committees of Congress, from www.crs.gov, dated April 12, 2012.

helps borrowers who are current, it is unlikely to have a major effect on the housing market, but it may prevent some foreclosures that could occur in the absence of a refinance. In addition, refinancing has the potential to have a larger effect on the economy by stimulating consumer spending. A mortgage refinance could lower a borrower's monthly payment, freeing up more income for non-housingrelated spending. Some of the additional spending of borrowers may come at the cost of the financial sector. Although some financial institutions may lose investment income from refinancing, others could benefit from the increased business associated with refinancing.

President Obama, in his 2012 State of the Union address, proposed streamlining the existing program to refinance Fannie Mae and Freddie Mac loans and establishing a new mass refinancing plan for non-Fannie Mae and non-Freddie Mac loans. Congressional proposals for large-scale refinancing of Fannie Mae and Freddie Mac loans include H.R. 363 and S. 170.

Renting out foreclosed homes currently held by banks and other financial institutions has the potential to stabilize housing prices by reducing the supply of homes on the "for sale" market. However, this policy depends on house prices increasing in the future such that, when the rented properties are eventually sold, they are sold in a healthier market. Unlike principal reductions and mass refinancing, renting foreclosed homes does not reduce existing homeowners' payments or increase their disposable income. Any impact on consumer spending is likely to be indirect through stabilizing house prices and preserving neighboring homeowners' equity.

The Federal Housing Finance Agency (FHFA), the regulator of Fannie Mae and Freddie Mac, has started a pilot project to convert foreclosed homes into rentals. Congressional proposals to expand the renting of foreclosed properties include H.R. 1548, H.R. 2636, and S. 2080.

INTRODUCTION

The bursting of the U.S. housing bubble in 2006 precipitated the December 2007 – June 2009 recession and a financial panic in September 2008. Falling house prices contributed to rising foreclosure rates and lower consumer spending. In addition, mortgage defaults and the rise in foreclosures hurt financial institutions that owned the loans on the foreclosed homes, triggering a much broader collapse of the financial system. As credit flows slowed, so did economic growth.

Because the housing market was a locus for many of the economic problems that emerged, some Members of Congress and other experts propose intervening in the housing market not only as a means of improving the housing market itself but also the financial sector and the broader economy. Supporters of housing market intervention argue that housing market weakness has a strong indirect negative effect on the balance sheets of households and banks, which dampens the recovery of the wider economy.[1] Skeptics, however, worry that further intervention could prolong the housing slump, delay economic recovery, and affect outcomes based on the government's preferences.

Since the housing bubble burst, the federal government has created multiple programs to aid homeowners, but their impact has been less than anticipated. Many measures have been proposed either to modify existing programs or to establish new efforts to improve the housing market. Three frequently discussed approaches are (1) reducing mortgage principal for borrowers who owe more than their homes are worth, (2) refinancing mortgages for borrowers who find themselves locked into paying high interest rates, and (3) renting out foreclosed homes. Principal reductions aim to improve the housing market by minimizing defaults and foreclosures, thus reducing collateral damage to the economy. However, principal reduction shifts the losses of borrowers to banks and other lenders. At the same time, principal reduction might improve the wider economy if it stimulates consumer spending, allowing borrowers to divert income from debt repayment to spending on other goods and services.

Members of the 112th Congress have introduced multiple bills that would reduce mortgage principal on certain loans. These include H.R. 1587, the Home Foreclosure Reduction Act of 2011 (Representative John Conyers et al.); H.R. 3841, the Principal Reduction Act of 2012 (Representative Maxine Waters et al.); H.R. 4058, the Bankruptcy Equity Act of 2012 (Representative Earl Blumenauer et al.); and S. 2093, the Preserving American Homeownership Act of 2012 (Senator Robert Menendez). Principal reduction is also a component of a settlement reached between several mortgage servicers and 49 state attorneys general and the federal government. All of these initiatives are discussed more fully in "Principal Reduction" below.

A second approach, large-scale refinancing, helps borrowers who are current on their mortgage to refinance into a new mortgage with a lower interest rate. Because refinancing generally helps borrowers who are current, it is unlikely to have a major effect on the housing market, but it may prevent some foreclosures that could occur in the absence of a refinance. Some argue that refinancing would stimulate consumer spending. For example, a mortgage refinance could lower a borrower's monthly payment, freeing up more income that can be used to pay down debt or for non-housing-related spending. Some of the additional spending of borrowers may be offset by reduced income for investors. In a refinance, the previous owner of the mortgage is repaid on the loan earlier than expected and now faces reinvesting in a lower interest rate environment. Although some investors (including banks) may lose investment income from refinancing, other banks and mortgage originators benefit from the increased business associated with refinancing. Similarly, mass refinancing might cause Fannie Mae and Freddie Mac, two housing government-sponsored enterprises (GSEs), to lose investment income but gain from the reduced likelihood of default. It is unclear which effect would be larger. In his 2012 State of the Union address, President Obama proposed streamlining the existing program to refinance Fannie Mae and Freddie Mac loans and establishing a new mass refinancing plan for non-Fannie Mae and non-Freddie Mac loans. Congressional proposals for large-scale refinancing in the 112th Congress include H.R. 363, the Housing Opportunity and Mortgage Equity Act of 2011 (Representative Dennis Cardoza et al.), and S. 170, the Helping Responsible Homeowners Act (Senator Barbara Boxer et al.). These proposals are discussed more fully in "Large-Scale Refinancing" below.

A third proposal, renting out foreclosed homes currently held by banks, GSEs, and other financial institutions, has the potential to stabilize housing prices by reducing the supply of homes on the "for sale" market. Current policy encourages lenders to sell foreclosed property quickly rather than rent out vacant homes. A successful rental program depends on house prices increasing in the future such that the rented properties can eventually be sold in a healthier market. In addition, renting foreclosed homes keeps the properties in use and reduces the collateral damage to communities. Unlike principal reductions and mass refinancing, renting foreclosed homes does not reduce existing homeowners' payments or increase their disposable income. Any impact on consumer spending is likely to be indirect through favorable effects on household net worth due to stabilizing house prices and preserving neighboring homeowners' equity. The program would only prevent foreclosure if, in lieu of foreclosure, it allowed delinquent homeowners to rent out their own homes.

The Federal Housing Finance Agency (FHFA), the regulator and conservator of Fannie Mae and Freddie Mac, has started a pilot project to convert GSE foreclosed homes into rentals. Congressional proposals in the 112th Congress to allow for renting foreclosed properties include H.R. 1548, the Right to Rent Act of 2011 (Representative Raúl Grijalva et al.); H.R. 2636, the Neighborhood Preservation Act of 2011 (Representative Gary Miller et al.); and S. 2080, the Keeping Families in their Home Act of 2012 (Senator Dean Heller). These initiatives are discussed more fully in "Renting Foreclosed Homes" below.

Table 1 summarizes the potential impact of these policies on three categories of households: delinquent borrowers, borrowers who are paying on time, and renters.

Table 1. Possible Impact on Households

	Delinquent Borrowers	Borrowers Paying on Time	Renters
Principal Reduction	Lowered re-default rate.	If eligible, lowered likelihood of default.	Fewer foreclosures means reduced house purchase opportunities.
Large-Scale Refinancing	Not Addressed.	Free up income to spend on other goods.	Not Addressed.
Renting Foreclosed Properties	Could have home rented out to existing delinquent borrower or could be rented to new individual.	May stabilize house prices due to fewer vacancies, but house prices could fall if renters do not maintain properties.	Reduced house purchase opportunities but would potentially lower rents.

Source: Compiled by the Congressional Research Service (CRS).
Notes: This table provides only an overview of potential impacts of these programs. The actual impacts will depend on the details and eligibility of particular programs.

Table 2. Additional Possible Policy Impacts

	House Prices	Financial Institution Balance Sheets	Consumer Spending
Principal Reduction	May support prices by lowering default rates.	Writing down principal would cause institutions to lose capital.	Principal reductions could stimulate consumer spending.
Large-Scale Refinancing	If refinancing for only current borrowers, may have minimal impact on house prices.	Refinancing could increase the prepayment losses of institutions.	Large-scale refinancing could increase consumer spending.
Renting Foreclosed Properties	Removing vacant homes from the "for sale" market may support prices.	Delay losses if rented by institution. Multiple possible outcomes if sell to investors to rent.	By not increasing disposable income, renting properties may have a minimal impact on consumer spending, though lower rents could increase spending.

Source: Compiled by CRS.
Notes: This table provides an overview of potential impacts of the programs. The actual impacts will depend on the details and eligibility of particular programs.

Table 2 summarizes the likely impacts on house prices, financial institutions' balance sheets, and the broader economy.

The remainder of this report will further analyze principal reduction, refinance, and rental proposals. First, however, the next section provides one estimate of the size of the housing market problem.

THE SIZE OF THE HOUSING PROBLEM

In her September 2011 congressional testimony, Laurie Goodman, a senior managing director at Amherst Securities Group, estimated that 8.3 million to 10.4 million homeowners, approximately 15%-19% of all homeowners with a mortgage, are at risk of losing their homes in the next six years.[2] Goodman's estimates are shown in *Table 3*. Of the approximately 80 million homes in the United States, nearly 55 million have a mortgage. Goodman divides the mortgages into five categories and assigns an estimated default rate for each category to calculate the number of homes in jeopardy of transitioning to default (i.e., being more than 60 days delinquent on the mortgage).

The five categories, in order of highest to lowest default rate, are

- loans that are currently non-performing because the borrowers are no longer making their monthly payments;
- loans that were non-performing but have become re-performing because the borrowers have resumed payment;
- loans that have always been performing but have severe negative equity, meaning the borrower owes more on their mortgage than the home is worth;
- loans that are always performing and the borrowers have moderate negative equity; and
- loans that are always performing and the borrowers have positive equity.

Goodman includes a "lower bound" and a "reasonable" estimated default rate for each of the loan categories based on current trends in the foreclosure rate and the pace of economic recovery.[3]

Goodman's analysis suggests two broad types of policy approaches for improving the housing market. First, policies could attempt to keep people in their homes by lowering the default rates. Principal reduction and large-scale refinancing are two frequently discussed proposals attempting to accomplish this goal. Principal reduction generally involves lowering the amount of the mortgage that is owed for borrowers who are delinquent, have negative equity, or are both delinquent and have negative equity. Large-scale refinance proposals generally target borrowers who are current on their loans but cannot refinance because of their negative equity. Both proposals attempt to lower monthly payments for borrowers as well as reduce default rates by stimulating the economy through reducing or redistributing the debt burden of the mortgage. The second approach implied by Goodman's analysis is to ease the transition of foreclosed homes into the market. Rather than flooding the market with foreclosed homes and potentially further lowering house prices, some have proposed converting the foreclosed homes into rental properties. Different proposals call for financial institutions either to rent the properties directly themselves or to sell properties in bulk to investors who would rent the vacant homes. The remainder of this report analyzes each of these three major policy proposals.

Table 3. Homes in Jeopardy of Default
(as of August 2011)

Status	Loans	Estimated Default Rate		Number of Homes in Jeopardy	
		Lower Bound	Reasonable	Lower Bound	Reasonable
Non- Performing Loans	4,517,820	80%	90%	3,614,256	4,066,038
Re-Performing Loans	3,863,756	50%	65%	1,931,878	2,511,411
Always Performing Loans >120 LTV	2,646,578	25%	40%	661,644	1,058,631
Always Performing Loans 100-120 LTV	5,351,340	10%	15%	535,134	802,701
(5) Always Performing Loans <= 100 LTV	38,574,077	4%	5%	1,542,963	1,928,704
Totals	54,953,570			8,285,875	10,367,515

Source: Testimony of Ms. Laurie F. Goodman, a senior managing director at Amherst Securities Group, in U.S. Congress, Senate Committee on Banking, Housing, and Urban Affairs, Subcommittee on Housing, Transportation and Community Development, New Ideas to Address the Glut of Foreclosed Properties, 112th Cong., 1st sess., September 20, 2011, available at http://banking. senate.gov.

Notes: The loan-to-value (LTV) ratio is the ratio of the amount that a borrower owes on his mortgage to the value of his house. An LTV of 100% means that a borrower owes the same amount as the value of the house. An LTV greater than 100% means that the borrower has negative equity, owing more than the house is worth. For more on the underlying analysis, see the Appendix of Goodman's Senate Testimony at http://banking.senate.gov.

PRINCIPAL REDUCTION

As a result of falling house prices, an estimated 11 million – 15 million homeowners owe more on their mortgage than their home is worth.[4] Borrowers in this situation are said to be "underwater" on their homes or in "negative equity." Negative equity may impair a borrower's labor mobility, making it more difficult to sell the house and move for a new job, or limit the ability to use the house as collateral to take out a loan for a small business.[5] Borrowers with negative equity are also more likely to default and enter foreclosure than borrowers with positive equity, partly because borrowers with negative equity are often unable to sell their home for enough to cover the amount owed if they are unable to make their monthly payments.[6] Foreclosures can drive down home prices, forcing some borrowers further underwater and continuing the cycle of foreclosure. *Figure 1* shows the rise and fall of a measure of home prices since 1987. To address these concerns, some Members of Congress have proposed reducing the mortgage principal for underwater borrowers.

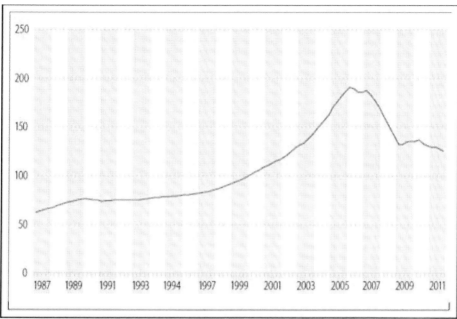

Source: S&P/Case-Shiller Home Price U.S. National Index, Seasonally Adjusted.
Notes: Index sets January 2000 equal to 100.

Figure 1. S&P/Case-Shiller Home Price Index, 1987 to 2011.

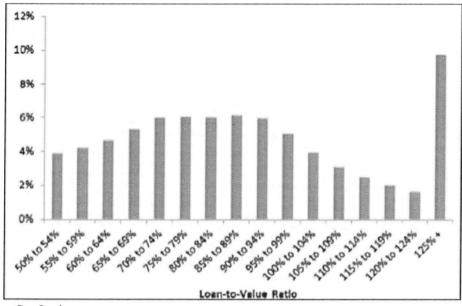

Source: CoreLogic.

Figure 2. Distribution of Homeowners by Home Equity (as of Fourth Quarter of 2011).

The amount that a borrower is underwater is often measured by the loan-to-value (LTV) ratio. The LTV ratio is the ratio of the amount that a borrower owes on the mortgage to the value of the house. An LTV of 100% means that a borrower owes the same amount as the value of the house. An LTV greater than 100% means that the borrower has negative equity, owing more than the house is worth. The more the LTV is above 100%, the more underwater the borrower is. Figure 2 shows the distribution of borrowers by the equity they have in their homes.

Homeowners with a mortgage can generally be divided into three groups: (1) those with a loan that is government-insured through the Federal Housing Administration (FHA), U.S. Department of Veterans Affairs, or other government agency; (2) those with a mortgage owned or guaranteed by Fannie Mae or Freddie Mac (the GSEs); and (3) those with a privately owned mortgage.

Most of the proposals discussed in this report focus on GSE loans and privately owned (non-GSE) mortgages.

A borrower with a privately owned mortgage could see principal reduced independent of any government assistance program if the mortgage holder (i.e., bank, credit union, or other investor) believed it is in its best interest. Non-GSE borrowers could also see their principal reduced through the federal government's Home Affordable Modification Program's (HAMP's) Principal Reduction Alternative (PRA). Borrowers with a GSE mortgage, on the other hand, are ineligible for principal reductions because of policies set by Fannie Mae's and Freddie Mac's regulator, the Federal Housing Finance Agency (FHFA).

Several bills have been introduced in the 112th Congress to reduce mortgage principal on some mortgages, including H.R. 1587, the Home Foreclosure Reduction Act of 2011 (Representative John Conyers et al.); H.R. 3841, the Principal Reduction Act of 2012 (Representative Maxine Waters et al.); H.R. 4058, the Bankruptcy Equity Act of 2012 (Representative Earl Blumenauer et al.); and S. 2093, the Preserving American Homeownership Act of 2012 (Senator Robert Menendez). Principal reduction is also a component of the settlement reached between several mortgage servicers and 49 state attorneys general and the federal government. The specifics of these proposals are discussed in "Legislative Proposals for Principal Reduction" below. The next section discusses some of the factors that influence whether a financial institution would offer a borrower a principal reduction.

Risks of Principal Reduction

Some argue that principal reductions are almost always in the best interests of a borrower and a financial institution if a borrower is near foreclosure. For example, a borrower may take out a $180,000 mortgage to buy a $200,000 house (giving the borrower a loan-to-value ratio of 90%). If the borrower is having trouble making the monthly mortgage payment and the value of the house falls to $150,000, the borrower could face foreclosure. If the value of the house was greater than the amount owed, potentially the borrower could sell the home to pay off the mortgage or borrower against the equity in the house to make the monthly payment; however, because the borrower has negative equity, selling the house may not cover the mortgage.[7] If the bank forecloses on the borrower and sells the house, it may only recover a fraction of what the house is worth, for example, $100,000.[8] Advocates of principal reduction state that it is in the best interest of the financial institution to reduce principal by less than the amount they would lose in foreclosure.

Multiple factors not captured by the above example may explain why principal reductions are not offered more frequently.[9] When a borrower is delinquent, he or she is likely to fall into one of four categories. The borrower

- could become current on his mortgage without any assistance (Type 1);
- could default on the loan even if a loan modification is offered (Type 2);
- could become current on the loan but only if a modification is received (Type 3); and
- does not receive a modification and ends up in foreclosure (Type 4).

When considering whether to offer a delinquent borrower a modification, the mortgage holder would prefer to only target the Type 3 borrower. No action by the mortgage holder changes the outcome for the first two types and is therefore not worth the expense associated with attempting to help.[10] The challenge for the holder is in determining which of the four types of borrower any given delinquent borrower is. All borrowers have the incentive to claim to be Type 3. When offering a modification, the mortgage servicer (the financial institution that is in contact with the borrower and is tasked with making decisions about loan modifications) is therefore exposed to two different types of risk: self-cure risk and re-default risk. Self-cure risk is the risk that the servicer will offer a modification to the Type 1 borrower who would have become current without any assistance. Re-default risk is the risk that the servicer modifies a loan for the Type 2 borrower who re-defaults in spite of the modification. In addition, if it becomes known that a servicer is willing to offer a significant loan modification, then current borrowers have an incentive to default in order to become eligible for the modification. This then creates a third type of risk for the servicer, strategic default risk,[11] which is the incentive created for borrowers to become delinquent even though they are current on their mortgage and can afford to pay. Principal reduction could, some argue, increase strategic default risk and create moral hazard.[12]

If the objective of a financial institution is to maximize profits, then it will only offer principal reductions if it is the option that best maximizes profits. For a principal reduction to maximize profits, the expected amount gained by helping the Type 3 borrower who would have failed without the assistance must be greater than the losses associated with helping those who may self-cure, re-default, or strategically default.

Self-cure risk, re-default risk, and strategic default risk are present for all types of loan modifications, including changes to the interest rate and the balance of the loan. All borrowers, regardless of whether they "need" the modification, would benefit from decreased monthly mortgage payments.

Other loss-mitigation strategies besides principal reduction may more effectively minimize the risks to the mortgage holder. For example, principal forbearance is the removal of a portion of the principal from the amount used to calculate monthly principal and interest payments for a limited period, but the forborne amount is due at the end of the loan term, potentially with interest. Borrowers who do not need the modification may find forbearance less appealing because it changes the timing on their payments but may not necessarily reduce the amount that they must ultimately pay. Alternatively, principal reduction can be paired with other approaches to minimize risk. For example, combining principal reduction with a shared appreciation mortgage, in which the borrower agrees to share some of the future gains when the house is sold with the lender, could minimize strategic default risk. These other loss-mitigation strategies are also discussed later in this report.

Potential Impact of Principal Reduction

Housing Market

As mentioned previously, borrowers with negative equity are more likely to default and enter foreclosure than borrowers with positive equity. This can contribute to a negative spiral in which falling home prices lead to negative equity, which causes more foreclosures and a further fall in house prices. *Figure 3* shows the monthly delinquency and foreclosure rates since 2001. Principal reduction could potentially interrupt this cycle by either reducing the amount of negative equity or increasing the amount of positive equity, depending on the amount of principal that is reduced and the types of borrowers a principal reduction program targets.

Principal reduction could allow borrowers experiencing "house lock," those unable to sell their home for enough to cover the balance of the mortgage, to sell their home if a principal reduction returns them to positive equity.[13]

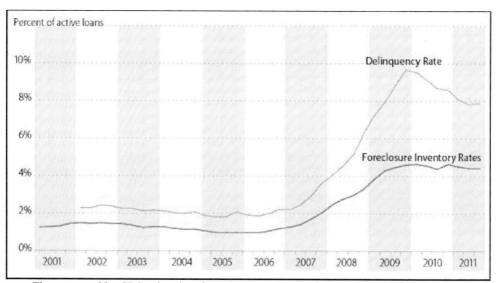

Source: Figure created by CRS using data from the Mortgage Bankers Association.
Notes: The Mortgage Bankers Association (MBA) is one of several organizations that reports delinquency and foreclosure data, but it does not represent all mortgages. MBA estimates that its data cover about 80% of outstanding first-lien mortgages on single-family properties. The delinquency rate includes borrowers who are more than 90 days delinquent as well as homes in the foreclosure inventory.

Figure 3. Total Delinquent and Foreclosure Percentage, by Month.

If the goal is to stabilize the housing market, then allowing more borrowers to sell may be counterproductive. In addition, some worry that principal reductions would be a windfall for those borrowers who sell immediately and would impose unfair losses on lenders. To address these concerns, some propose reducing principal incrementally over a period of years or requiring homeowners to share part of the house price appreciation with the lender when it is sold. Some opponents of principal reduction argue that, because negative equity is concentrated in a few states, principal reduction would therefore benefit some parts of the country at the expense of others. *Figure 4* shows the percentage of homeowners with negative equity by state. In that respect, a principal reduction policy may be similar to aid for natural disasters, which flows disproportionately to some geographic regions of the country.

Consumer Spending

By stabilizing the housing market, principal reduction could stimulate the economy by reducing borrowers' monthly mortgage payments, allowing them to spend more on other goods and services. However, the additional money available to consumers comes at the expense of the owners of the mortgages; involuntary principal reduction reduces the amount that the mortgage holder will receive. Although borrowers gain and investors may lose in a principal reduction, the amount is not necessarily zero-sum.[14] Given the potential additional spending by borrowers and decreased spending by investors, a net spending increase could occur through multiple channels.[15] First, if borrowers spend more of an additional dollar than investors would have spent of the same dollar, then principal reduction would increase spending. Second, a significant percentage of mortgage-backed securities (MBS) are held by foreign investors and the federal government. Reducing the investment income to those holders of MBS is unlikely to have a large negative impact on consumer spending in the United States.[16] Third, by reducing the number of foreclosures that would have occurred and stabilizing home prices, principal reduction would help the wider economy by preserving household wealth and building consumer confidence.[17]

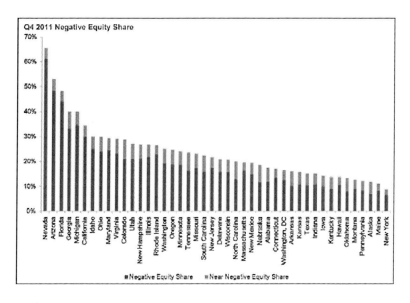

Source: CoreLogic.
Notes: Data are unavailable for Louisiana, Maine, Mississippi, South Dakota, Vermont, West Virginia, and Wyoming. Near negative equity includes borrowers with less than 5% of positive home equity.

Figure 4. Percentage of Homeowners with Negative Equity, by State. (as of Fourth Quarter of 2011)

Research has found a positive correlation between household wealth and consumer spending.[18]

Financial Sector

Assuming that the mortgage holders will reduce principal voluntarily when it is in their best interest, then a program requiring involuntary principal reductions would not be in the best interest of the mortgage holder. It would limit their choice set and potentially restrict their ability to maximize returns. If the mortgage holder is a bank or other lender, then the revenue that is lost by forgoing foreclosure and instead facing a less profitable option could cause the lender to curtail lending.

A widespread curtailment of lending could cause interest rates to rise. However, the Federal Reserve could potentially offset a possible credit contraction through open market operations or an expansion of its balance sheet.[19]

Although principal reductions could reduce their revenues, mortgage holders could, nonetheless, potentially benefit from a principal reduction program through two channels.

First, some experts argue that mortgage servicers[20] face a host of competing incentives, not all of which encourage the servicer to act in the best interest of the loan holder. These incentives, as well as shortcomings in a servicer's operational infrastructure, could encourage the servicer to pursue foreclosure when the investor would be best served by a loan modification, such as principal reduction.[21]

Mortgage holders could benefit from a principal reduction program if servicers' misaligned incentives prevented the optimal number of principal reductions from occurring.

Second, mortgage holders could suffer from coordination problems.[22] Foreclosure may be individually rational but collectively irrational. If mortgage holders think house prices will continue to fall, it may be in each individual mortgage holder's interest to pursue foreclosure and maximize its immediate return, but collectively—when all pursue foreclosure at the same time— each is made worse off. A large surge of foreclosures could further drive down house prices and reduce the mortgage holder's recovery when the property is eventually sold. Mandated principal reductions could alleviate the coordination problems by requiring all servicers to consider principal reduction prior to acting on foreclosure.

Current Principal Reduction Policies

Supporters of principal reduction argue that it has the potential to stabilize the housing market, support the recovery of lost household net worth, and stimulate the economy. Opponents of principal reduction, however, highlight its negative impact on financial institutions at a time when lending is still weak, and they raise issues of fairness associated with reducing the principal for some borrowers but not others.[23] This section of the report analyzes principal reduction by non-GSE financial institutions through the government's Home Affordable Modification Program (HAMP) and analyzes the GSE policy on principal reductions.

As *Figure 5* shows, the GSEs do not perform principal reductions, but non-GSEs—banks holding loans in their portfolio and private investors—do perform principal reductions (though, it was uncommon for private investors until 2011).[24] However, *Figure 6* shows that GSEs and non-GSEs use principal forbearance with similar frequency.

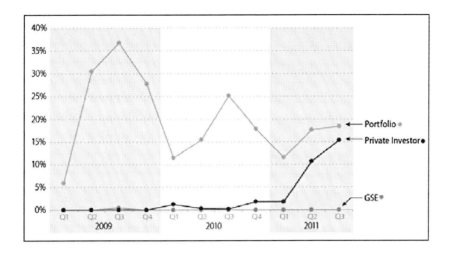

Source: OCC and OTS Mortgage Metrics Report.

Figure 5. Frequency of Principal Reduction.

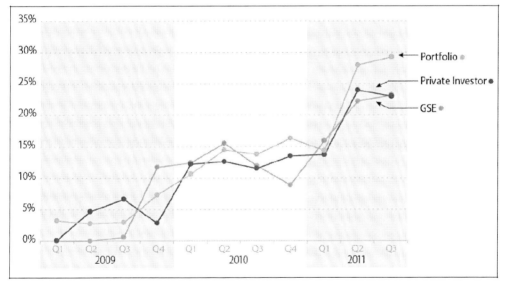

Source: OCC and OTS Mortgage Metrics Report.

Figure 6. Frequency of Principal Forbearance.

Non-GSE Loans: The Home Affordable Modification Program's Principal Reduction Alternative and the 2012 Mortgage Settlement

Non-GSE mortgage holders, such as banks, credit unions, thrifts, and other private investors, own approximately half of all the outstanding mortgage debt in the United States.[25] These mortgage holders may modify the terms of the mortgage (by reducing the interest rate or the principal, for example) independent of any government program if it is in the best interest of the borrower and the mortgage holder. This section analyzes one of the federal government's major initiatives to encourage non-GSE institutions to perform principal reductions, the Home Affordable Modification Program (HAMP).[26] Through HAMP's Principal Reduction Alternative (PRA), the federal government offers financial incentives to investors in non-Fannie and non-Freddie loans to reduce mortgage principal.

HAMP is part of President Obama's Making Home Affordable (MHA) program, which he announced on February 18, 2009. HAMP provides financial incentives to mortgage servicers to lower eligible troubled borrowers' monthly mortgage payments to more sustainable levels.[27] On March 26, 2010, HAMP announced the PRA.[28] Under the PRA, participating servicers are required to consider reducing principal balances as part of HAMP modifications for homeowners who owe at least 115% of the value of their home. Servicers run two net present value (NPV) tests[29] for these borrowers: the first is the standard NPV test, and the second includes principal reduction. If the NPV of the modification is higher under the test that includes principal reduction, servicers have the option to reduce principal. However, they are not required to do so. If the principal is reduced, the amount of the principal reduction will initially be treated as principal forbearance; the forborne amount will then be forgiven in three equal amounts over a three year period as long as the borrower remains current on his or her mortgage payments. The Administration offers financial incentives to servicers specifically for reducing principal. The PRA went into effect on October 1, 2010.[30] According to the Treasury Department, more than 60,000 PRA modifications were active as of January 2012. About 16,000 of these are active trial modifications, and about 44,000 are active permanent modifications.[31]

To encourage more principal reductions, the Treasury Department announced on January 27, 2012, that it would triple the incentive payments to investors.[32] Investors will now receive 18 cents to 63 cents for each dollar of principal reduced, depending on the borrower's loan-to-value ratio. As discussed in the next section, Treasury has offered to expand the PRA to include Fannie Mae and Freddie Mac loans by extending the incentive payments to them, but the Federal Housing Finance Agency (FHFA), the regulator and conservator of Fannie and Freddie, must agree to the policy before it can be implemented.

Some homeowners with non-Fannie and non-Freddie loans could also have their principal reduced as a result of the mortgage settlement between five banks and 49 state attorneys general and the federal government.[33] The settlement is expected to result in approximately $25 billion in monetary sanctions and relief.[34] Of the $25 billion, $17 billion is expected to be allocated to aiding homeowners who want to stay in their homes but cannot afford to at their current payment levels. Of the $17 billion, at least 60% must be allocated to principal reductions for borrowers who are in default or at risk of default.[35]

Fannie and Freddie's Position on Principal Reduction

Fannie Mae and Freddie Mac do not offer principal reductions on the loans they own or guarantee, which is approximately half of the $10.3 trillion U.S. mortgage market.[36] The decision not to offer principal reductions was made by Fannie Mae and Freddie Mac in consultation with FHFA.[37] Fannie Mae and Freddie Mac loans are eligible for modification under HAMP, but not for HAMP's PRA component.[38] GSE loans are also not covered for principal reduction under the terms of the mortgage settlement.

Congress established FHFA in 2008 in the Housing and Economic Recovery Act of 2008 (HERA; P.L. 110-289). The Acting Director of FHFA, Edward DeMarco, has interpreted FHFA's mandate to have three components:

> First, FHFA has a statutory responsibility as conservator to preserve and conserve the assets and property of the regulated entities. Second, the Enterprises have the same mission and obligations as they did prior to the conservatorship. Therefore, FHFA must ensure that Fannie Mae and Freddie Mac maintain liquidity in the housing market during this time of economic turbulence. Third, under the Emergency Economic Stabilization Act of 2008 (EESA), FHFA has a statutory responsibility to maximize assistance for homeowners to minimize foreclosures.39

Based on an analysis done by FHFA, DeMarco has decided that principal reductions are not the strategy that best fulfills the agency's mandates.[40]

Some Members of Congress have called for FHFA to perform principal reductions or at least make available its analysis justifying its decision. In response to these requests, FHFA released its analysis of principal reduction on January 20, 2012. The FHFA analysis consists of an introductory letter and three memos sent by FHFA staff to the acting director in December 2010, June 2011, and December 2011.

FHFA's analysis concludes that principal reduction is not the best method of minimizing taxpayer losses. Instead, FHFA offers other forms of loan modifications, including interest-rate reductions, loan-term extensions, and principal forbearance.[41] Principal reduction and forbearance can potentially lower a borrower's monthly payment to the same level, but, unlike principal reduction, FHFA notes that principal forbearance allows for future repayment and greater potential gains for investors and smaller potential losses for the taxpayer than principal reduction.

FHFA provided some but not all of the quantitative evidence it relied on in determining that principal forbearance better fulfilled its mandate than principal reduction. Of the approximately 30 million loans that the GSEs own or guarantee,[42] FHFA focused on the most underwater borrowers, the approximately 1.4 million that have an LTV ratio greater than 115% as of June 30, 2011. It calculated the expected losses of forbearing principal to an LTV of 115% and reducing principal to a 115% LTV. FHFA claims that reducing the principal on all 1.4 million loans to an LTV of 115% would require forgiving $42 billion. FHFA found that if it offered neither a principal forbearance nor a principal reduction, then the GSEs would experience losses of $101.8 billion. Based on FHFA's calculations, principal forbearance results in greater savings if offered to all borrowers, whereas principal reduction offers more savings if offered to only NPV positive borrowers. However, FHFA noted that there are added administrative costs associated with introducing principal reduction, which may reduce its potential benefit to Fannie Mae and Freddie Mac.[43] *Table 2* summarizes FHFA's results.

FHFA's analysis also includes results from research performed in June 2011 that provides two additional policy options to compare in addition to principal forgiveness and principal forbearance. FHFA estimated the cost of reducing principal to 115% LTV if the mortgage servicer contributed 33% and 50% of the forgiven amount. FHFA does not provide details on what a program involving servicer contributions would look like, but presumably the mortgage servicer for a pool of loans would share in the cost of reducing the principal, thereby lowering the cost of principal forgiveness assumed by Fannie and Freddie. FHFA's results are summarized in *Table 5*. Using earlier data, FHFA found that principal forgiveness would provide lower savings to Fannie Mae and Freddie Mac than principal forbearance, regardless of whether it is offered to all borrowers or only to NPV positive borrowers. However, both principal forgiveness options involving servicer contributions would produce greater savings than principal forbearance.

Table 4. FHFA Analysis I (as of June 30, 2011)

	Principal Forbearance	Principal Reduction
Losses reduced by offering to all borrowers	$24.0 billion	$20.0 billion
Losses reduced by only offering to NPV positive borrowers	$27.9 billion	$28.3 billion

Source: CRS calculations based on Table 3, p. 19, at http://www.fhfa.gov/ webfiles/ 23056/PrincipalForgivenessltr12312.pdf.

Notes: Numbers have been rounded and totals for Fannie Mae and Freddie Mac have been added together.

Table 5. FHFA Analysis II (as of June 30, 2010)

	Principal Forbearance	Principal Reduction	Reduction with 33% Servicer Contribution	Reduction with 50% Servicer Contribution
Losses reduced by offering to all borrowers	$17.8 billion	$14.9 billion	$24.0 billion	$28.6 billion
Losses reduced by only offering to NPV positive borrowers	$18.0 billion	$15.6 billion	$24.1 billion	$28.7 billion

Source: CRS calculations based on Table 3, p. 19, at http://www.fhfa.gov/webfiles /23056/Principal Forgivenessltr12312.pdf.

Notes: Numbers have been rounded and totals for Fannie Mae and Freddie Mac have been added together.

As mentioned previously, the Treasury Department announced that it was tripling the investor incentives under the HAMP PRA as well as offering the incentives to Fannie and Freddie loans.

Depending on how the program is structured, it may have parallels to the servicer contribution versions of principal reduction that FHFA previously analyzed, but, instead of the servicer bearing some of the cost of reducing principal, the Treasury Department would contribute to the principal reduction.

After the Treasury Department's announcement, FHFA Acting Director DeMarco released a statement stating that

> FHFA has been asked to consider the newly available HAMP incentives for principal reduction. FHFA recently released analysis concluding that principal forgiveness did not provide benefits that were greater than principal forbearance as a loss mitigation tool. FHFA's assessment of the investor incentives now being offered will follow its previous analysis, including consideration of the eligible universe, operational costs to implement such changes, and potential borrower incentive effects.44

As part of the explanation for why non-GSE loans have their principal reduced but FHFA does not reduce principal for GSE loans, the FHFA analysis compares the type of loans that the GSEs insure to non-GSE loans. In general, GSE loans have performed better than non-GSE loans since the bursting of the housing bubble in 2006 and 2007.[45] FHFA notes that, as of June 2011, fewer than 10% of borrowers with GSE loans had negative equity in their homes, but 35.5% of loans in private-label securities had negative equity.[46] In addition, FHFA argues that some mortgage servicers may have agreed to reduce principal for non-GSE loans because they had previously purchased the loans from a different bank or servicer at a discount, a practice not employed by the GSEs.[47] Lastly, FHFA notes that the GSEs' requirement of credit enhancement on high LTV loans, often in the form of mortgage insurance or a second lien, may lower the benefits received by the GSEs from a principal reduction.

As previously described, the analysis of loan modification options is sensitive to the underlying assumptions of re-default risk, self-cure risk, and strategic default risk. FHFA does not specifically address self-cure risk or strategic default risk in its analysis, but notes that it relies on Treasury's HAMP NPV model. The model may factor in these risks, although that information is not included in the FHFA analysis.[48] For re-default risk, FHFA provides evidence from HAMP modifications that the best predictor of re-default is the amount that a borrower's monthly payment is reduced and not the borrower's LTV ratio. Because principal forbearance and reduction both reduce monthly payments to the same level, they should have similar re-default rates. FHFA's model assumed that principal reduction reduced the re-default rate more than under principal forbearance but does not state what number or range was used for the re-default rate.

Other aspects of FHFA's methodology were not described in its analysis. For example, FHFA uses HAMP's NPV model, but does not adopt all of HAMP's other characteristics in its analysis. To be eligible for HAMP, a borrower must be either delinquent or in danger of falling behind on his or her payments.[49] FHFA analyzes a policy in which all borrowers with an LTV above 115% are eligible. Offering forbearance or forgiveness to only delinquent borrowers may reduce the cost of the program.[50] However, if only some borrowers receive assistance, then strategic default risk becomes a concern. HAMP also offers incentive payments to investors if principal is reduced to an LTV as low as 105%. It is unclear why FHFA assumed a reduction to an LTV of 115% in its analysis. Others have criticized the FHFA study for not differentiating loans with mortgage insurance from loans without mortgage insurance, for basing the analysis on the attributes of the loan at origination rather than borrowers' current attributes (such as credit scores), and for other potential shortcomings.[51]

Legislative Proposals for Principal Reduction

A principal reduction policy could target all borrowers, including those underwater, those underwater and delinquent, or some other subset, such as just GSE borrowers. Eligibility in a principal reduction proposal is likely to be determined by the underlying policy goal. Proposals to improve the housing market may be most effective by targeting delinquent borrowers who could afford a lower monthly payment though they cannot afford their current payment.

On the other hand, proposals to stimulate consumer spending by redistributing debt burdens may be more effective if eligibility for principal reduction is broader.

Members in the 112th Congress have introduced legislation to reduce mortgage principal. The bills address different subsets of homeowners as well as use different methods for reducing principal. H.R. 1587, the Home Foreclosure Reduction Act of 2011 (Representative John Conyers et al.) and H.R. 4058, the Bankruptcy Equity Act of 2012 (Representative Earl Blumenauer et al.) would allow for the cramdown of mortgage debt for principal residences in bankruptcy.[52]

Some believe that cramdown in bankruptcy would strengthen the negotiating position of borrowers prior to bankruptcy and would incentivize mortgage holders to modify more loans.

H.R. 3841, the Principal Reduction Act of 2012 (Representative Maxine Waters et al.), would require Fannie Mae and Freddie Mac to establish a principal reduction program for qualified mortgages. A qualified mortgage is a mortgage, regardless of whether the borrower is current or delinquent, that

- is owned or guaranteed by Fannie Mae or Freddie Mac;
- is the first mortgage on a single-family home that is the borrower's primary residence;
- was originated on or before the act would be enacted;
- has an LTV greater than 120%; and
- it has been determined that the net present value of reducing principal exceeds the net present value of foreclosing.

Under the program, qualified mortgages would see their principal reduced to an LTV not more than 90%.

If a borrower in the program eventually sells the home, at least one-third of the amount that the property appreciated would be given to the GSE that owns or guarantees the mortgage. If the property eventually enters foreclosure, then the borrower must pay Fannie or Freddie the difference between the sales price at foreclosure and the amount of the outstanding principal balance before the principal reduction.

S. 2093, the Preserving American Homeownership Act of 2012 (Senator Robert Menendez), requires the director of the FHFA and the Federal Housing Commissioner to establish shared appreciation mortgage modification pilot programs for FHFA and FHA loans. To be eligible, borrowers with Fannie Mae, Freddie Mac, or FHA loans must

- be at least 60 days delinquent or at risk of imminent default on their mortgage;
- have the mortgage on their primary residence;
- be underwater on their mortgage; and
- have a documented financial hardship that prevents or will prevent them from making their payments.

Under the pilot programs, loans would be reduced to an LTV of 95% within three years by reducing the principal by one-third of the necessary amount over each of the three years; the interest rate could also be reduced if necessary to achieve affordable payments; the homeowner would have to pay the investor at most 50% of any increase in the value of the house if the homeowner refinances or sells the home. Borrowers would be eligible only if the modification results in greater cash flows to investors than other loss mitigation activities.

LARGE-SCALE REFINANCING

With mortgage rates at historic lows, some have proposed establishing a large-scale refinancing program that would help borrowers who are current on their mortgage refinance into a new mortgage with a lower interest rate. Unlike a principal reduction, the principal balance of the loan does not change with a mortgage refinancing. A borrower prepays the existing loan with a new loan, presumably with more favorable terms. Refinancing allows borrowers to potentially lower their monthly payments. To refinance, a borrower typically must be current on his or her mortgage loan.

Example of a Mortgage Refinance

- A borrower took out a $200,000 mortgage in 2006 with a 6.5% fixed interest rate to be paid over 30 years. The borrower's monthly payments are about $1,264.
- Part of each monthly payment goes to paying down the principal and the interest. In 2012, the outstanding balance is $184,396.
- By refinancing the remaining $184,396 into a new 30 year loan with a 4% interest rate, the new monthly payments are $880. To refinance, the borrower must pay closing costs, which are estimated to be 3% of the outstanding balance, approximately $5,500 - $6,000 in this example.53
- The borrower lowers the monthly payment by $384 ($1,264 - $880 = $384).

Example created by author.

Because refinancing helps borrowers who are current, it is unlikely to have a major effect on the housing market but may prevent some foreclosures that would occur in the absence of a refinance by lowering payments. However, refinancing has the potential to have a larger effect on the economy by stimulating consumer spending and improving household balance sheets. A mortgage refinance lowers a borrower's monthly payment, freeing up more income for non-housing related spending. Some of the additional spending of borrowers may come at the cost of the financial sector. In a refinance, the previous owner of the mortgage is repaid earlier than expected and now faces reinvesting in a lower interest rate environment. Though some investors (including banks) may lose from refinancing, other banks and mortgage originators benefit from the increased business associated with refinancing. Similarly, mass refinancing might cause Fannie Mae and Freddie Mac to lose investment income but gain from the reduced likelihood of default, though it is unclear which effect is larger.

Current refinancing policy discussions center on two approaches: (1) develop a new program to refinance non-GSE loans into government-insured loans; and (2) expand the existing Home Affordable Refinance Program (HARP) to help more homeowners refinance their GSE loans. In his State of the Union address and a subsequent fact sheet,[54] President Obama endorsed both approaches. He proposed allowing borrowers who are current on their non-GSE loans to refinance through a program run by the FHA. The program would be funded through a tax on large financial institutions.[55] President Obama also proposed streamlining HARP to allow even more borrowers with GSE guaranteed loans to refinance.

The recent mortgage settlement between five banks and 49 state attorneys general and the federal government is estimated to provide at least $3 billion to refinance underwater borrowers.[56] Several congressional proposals, such as S. 170, the Helping Responsible Homeowners Act (Senator Barbara Boxer et al.), and H.R. 363, the Housing Opportunity and Mortgage Equity Act of 2011 (Representative Dennis Cardoza et al.), would require Fannie Mae and Freddie Mac to expand refinancing of GSE loans.[57] The specifics of these proposals are discussed in "Presidential and Legislative Proposals for Refinancing" below.

Barriers to Refinance

A mortgage is a callable loan, meaning that borrowers can pay off the balance of the loan at any time, usually without penalty. When a borrower refinances, the borrower is exercising this right to prepay by taking out a new loan and using it to pay off the previous loan.[58] A borrower can refinance with the existing lender or with a new lender. Although the existing lender has control over its own underwriting standards (the determination about who it will lend to), it does not have control over its competitors' underwriting standards. The existing lender faces the risk that a borrower will prepay the loan using a different lender and has little control over it. The value of a mortgage that a lender holds reflects this prepayment risk.

Mortgage interest rates are one of the major factors that influence a borrower's decision to refinance.[59] When interest rates fall, refinances typically increase, causing prepayment risk to rise. Although rates are at historic lows, mortgage refinances have not been as high as some would predict. *Figure 7* tracks the interest rate from the Primary Mortgage Market Survey (PMMS) compiled by Freddie Mac and the Mortgage Bankers Association (MBA) Refinance Index, a measure of refinancing activity. Although interest rates have fallen significantly and the government is encouraging refinancing, the MBA Refinancing Index has not reached the peak reached in 2003 when interest rates also fell substantially.

Insufficient home equity is a significant barrier to refinancing. Traditionally, lenders' underwriting standards require borrowers to have at least 20% positive equity in their home to refinance.[60] If a borrower's home is valued at $200,000 and the borrower owes $160,000 or less on the mortgage (LTV below 80%), then the borrower is potentially eligible to refinance at a bank, credit union, or other traditional avenue. A financial institution that is refinancing a mortgage wants a borrower to have positive equity in the home to protect the value of the collateral in the event house prices fall. If a borrower has little or no equity in the home and house prices fall, then should the borrower default, the financial institution could not recover the full value of its loan by selling the house.

In addition to insufficient equity, closing costs are a potential barrier to refinance for some borrowers. Borrowers will not refinance every time interest rates fall because there are fixed costs to refinancing. A borrower may save a little each month from having a lower interest rate, but it is only worthwhile to refinance if the amount saved is greater than the cost of refinancing. A typical estimate is that interest rates have to fall by 1 to 2 percentage points below a borrower's existing rate for it to be in the borrower's best interest to refinance.[61]

Large-scale refinancing proposals generally target those excluded from traditional refinancing efforts either due to insufficient equity or to high closing costs.

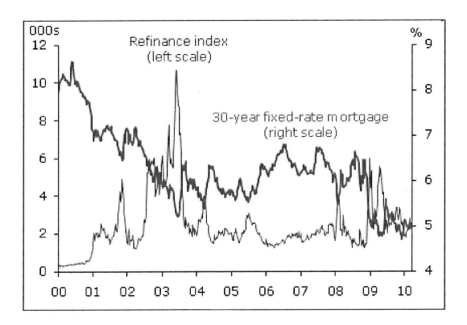

Source: William Hedberg and John Krainer, Mortgage Prepayments and Changing Underwriting Standards, Federal Reserve Bank of San Francisco, July 2010, at http://www.frbsf.org/publications/economics/letter/2010/el2010-22.html.

Figure 7. Refinancing Index.

Potential Impact of Large-Scale Refinancing

Housing Market

Mass refinancing proposals for underwater borrowers generally target borrowers who are current on their mortgages and are therefore not necessarily borrowers in imminent danger of default. A refinancing program would impact the housing market by preventing foreclosures that would have otherwise occurred had the program not been in place by lowering borrowers' monthly payments.

Any potential impact on house prices is likely to be through averted foreclosures. However, because refinancing programs target borrowers who are current, the number of averted foreclosures is likely to be limited. An analysis of a stylized large-scale refinancing program for GSE loans conducted by the Congressional Budget Office (CBO) estimated that 3.8% of homeowners that receive a refinance would have been foreclosed on in the absence of a refinance.[62]

Similarly, a study by Glenn Hubbard, Chris Mayer, and Alan Boyce (Hubbard et al.) of a refinancing program for GSE loans estimates that 5% of homeowners would lose their home without a refinance.[63] However, these studies focused on refinancing for GSE loans, which tend to be of a higher credit quality than non-GSE loans. Proposals that allow non-GSE loans to refinance may have a larger impact on avoided foreclosures.

Consumer Spending

Some argue that by targeting refinancing proposals to only current borrowers, the primary motivation for mass refinancing is economic stimulus.[64] In his testimony before the Senate Committee on Banking, Housing, and Urban Affairs, Mark Zandi, the chief economist and cofounder of Moody's Analytics, estimated that refinancing would save the average borrower approximately $2,500 a year.[65] The magnitude of the potential stimulus depends on the number of borrowers that participate. Zandi calculated that 6.8 million borrowers would refinance under the President's proposals, increasing growth of gross domestic product (GDP) by 0.1 percentage points this year. CBO's analysis of a stylized refinancing program predicted fewer refinances, 2.9 million borrowers, whereas Hubbard et al. estimated 14 million refinances. The estimates of refinances vary due to the eligibility criteria of the analyzed programs and the assumptions about borrower participation.

Although a refinancing increases the amount of disposable income for a borrower, it reduces the potential income for the investor holding the mortgage. Borrowers are more likely to refinance when it is in their best interest, such as when interest rates fall. When a borrower refinances, the remaining amount of principal that is owed is returned to the mortgage holder, requiring the mortgage holder to reinvest at a time when rates are low. Similar to what happens in a principal reduction, the gains to borrowers and the losses to investors in mass refinancing are not necessarily zero-sum.[66] If borrowers spend more domestically of an additional dollar than investors would have spent of the same dollar, then refinancing would increase aggregate spending and support the economic recovery.[67] In addition, a significant percentage of mortgage-backed securities (MBS) are held by foreign investors and the federal government.

Reducing the investment income to those holders of MBS is unlikely to have a large negative impact on consumer spending in the United States. See *Figure 8* for a breakdown of the major investors in agency MBS by type of investor. Agency MBS include securities guaranteed by Fannie Mae, Freddie Mac, and Ginnie Mae.[68] The Federal Reserve Bank of New York estimates that every dollar that a borrower's monthly payment is reduced by a refinancing would generate nearly 50 cents of additional spending.[69]

Some argue that it is unfair to target economic stimulus through a relatively small number of homeowners who happen to meet certain eligibility criteria.[70] They suggest that if there is going to be fiscal stimulus, it should be broader based and discussed more openly and directly, not necessarily within the framework of housing policy.

Financial Sector

Even if the benefits to borrowers of large-scale refinancing are greater than the losses to the mortgage holders, mortgage holders are still taking a loss. As *Figure 8* shows, a large-scale refinancing of agency MBS would not only impact large institutional investors, but would also impact mutual funds and individuals' savings in public and private pension funds, which hold approximately 18.6% of agency MBS.

The Investment Company Institute (ICI), the national association of U.S. investment companies, estimates that 64% of mutual fund-owning households had annual incomes of less than $100,000 in 2010.[71]

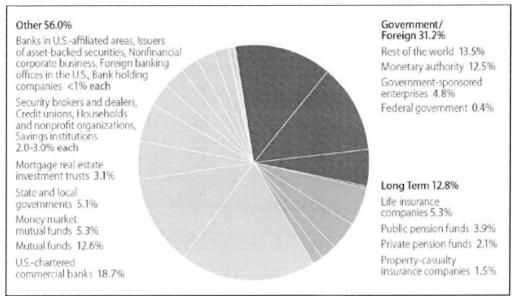

Other 56.0%

Banks in U.S.-affiliated areas, Issuers
of asset-backed securities, Nonfinancial
corporate business, Foreign banking
offices in the U.S., Bank holding
companies <1% each

Security brokers and dealers,
Credit unions, Households
and nonprofit organizations,
Savings institutions
2.0-3.0% each

Mortgage real estate
investment trusts 3.1%

State and local
governments 5.1%

Money market
mutual funds 5.3%

Mutual funds 12.6%

U.S.-chartered
commercial banks 18.7%

Government/
Foreign 31.2%

Rest of the world 13.5%

Monetary authority 12.5%

Government-sponsored
enterprises 4.8%

Federal government 0.4%

Long Term 12.8%

Life insurance
companies 5.3%

Public pension funds 3.9%

Private pension funds 2.1%

Property-casualty
insurance companies 1.5%

Source: Data from the Federal Reserve System, Flow of Funds Accounts of the United States, Fourth
2011, Table L. 210, at http://www.federalreserve.gov/releases/z1/ Current/z1.pdf. Chart modeled
off of Joseph Tracy and Joshua Wright, Why Mortgage Refinancing Is Not a Zero-Sum Game,
Federal Reserve Bank of New York, January 11, 2012, at http://libertystreeteconomics.
newyorkfed.org/ 2012/01/why-mortgage-refinancing-is-not-a-zero-sum-game.html.

Note: Percentages have been rounded.

Figure 8. Investors in Agency MBS. (as of Fourth Quarter of 2011)

However, as mentioned earlier, the value of the MBS held by investors already factors in prepayment risk.

A mass refinancing proposal would only impose a cost on investors if refinances were greater than anticipated. In addition, some banks and other institutions may benefit from the increased business associated with refinancing.

The Home Affordable Refinance Program

To help borrowers with GSE loans refinance even if they have little or no equity, the Obama Administration created HARP as part of its Making Home Affordable program.[72] To be eligible a borrower must

- have a mortgage owned or guaranteed by Fannie Mae or Freddie Mac;
- have a mortgage on a single-family home;
- owe more than 80% of the value of the home on the mortgage;
- be current on mortgage payments with no late payment in the past six months and no more than one late payment in the past 12 months;
- have the ability to make the new payments; and
- have had the mortgage sold to Fannie Mae or Freddie Mac by May 2009.[73]

Fannie Mae and Freddie Mac do not make loans themselves but buy loans from lenders. Through HARP, the GSEs agree to purchase a new loan from the originator if the borrower meets the eligibility criteria. The GSEs only refinance a borrower through HARP if the borrower's loan is already guaranteed by the GSEs. A refinance, therefore, does not add additional credit risk to the GSEs because they already own the credit risk of the borrower.[74] If a refinance lowers a borrower's monthly payments and makes it less likely that the borrower will default, then a refinance could lower the GSEs' credit risk.

The Administration originally estimated that HARP would aid between 4 million and 5 million borrowers, but the program has refinanced approximately 998,000 mortgages as of November 2011.[75] Most of the beneficiaries of HARP are those with some positive equity or only moderate negative equity, not those who are deeply underwater. Of those who refinanced through HARP, 91% had LTV ratios between 80% and 105%. Fewer than 9% had LTV ratios over 105%.

Experts have identified multiple factors that may be limiting the reach of HARP.[76] The GSEs charge additional fees, called loan level price adjustments, to some borrowers to compensate for the additional risk that they might pose based on their credit characteristics.[77] Loan level price adjustments, as well as other closing costs associated with getting a mortgage, such as an appraisal, may require more upfront expenses than a borrower can afford. In addition, HARP allows for more streamlined refinancing if performed through a borrower's existing servicer rather than a different servicer. This could potentially reduce competition and increase rates faced by borrowers. There are also questions about the capacity of originators to handle the increased refinance applications.[78] Also, HARP is a voluntary program; an eligible borrower needs to find a lender willing to offer them a new loan.

To address some of these concerns, FHFA announced changes to HARP in October 2011.[79] Previously, HARP eligibility was restricted to borrowers with LTV ratios below 125%, but the cap has been removed under HARP 2.0.[80] The GSEs have also agreed to eliminate or reduce some of the loan level price adjustments that were charged to borrowers. They will also attempt to reduce closing costs through greater use of automated valuation models in place of property appraisals. Fannie and Freddie are incentivizing lenders to refinance homeowners by waiving certain representations and warranties made on the original loans. Representations and warranties are assurances that lenders make to Fannie and Freddie about the quality of a loan when they are selling the loan to the GSEs. If it is later determined that the loan does not meet the criteria that the lender claimed the loan met, then the lender may be required to repurchase the loan.[81] By waiving the representations and warranties against the original loan, Fannie and Freddie are allowing the lender to re-underwrite the loan to ensure that it meets the agreed upon standards.[82]

Presidential and Legislative Proposals for Refinancing

In his 2012 State of the Union Address, President Obama proposed allowing some non-GSE borrowers to refinance through a new program to be run by the FHA and to streamline HARP to allow more borrowers with GSE loans to refinance. In a subsequent fact sheet,[83] the Administration outlined the proposed eligibility criteria for non-GSE borrowers. Any borrower with a mortgage not guaranteed by the GSEs would be eligible if the borrower

- has been current on the mortgage for the past six months and has not missed more than one payment in the previous six months;
- has a current FICO score greater than 580;
- has a mortgage no larger than the current FHA loan limit in his or her area;[84]
- is refinancing the loan on the borrower's owner-occupied, single-family primary residence;
- is employed or can otherwise prove that he or she can afford the new mortgage; and
- meets certain loan-to-value limits on the new mortgage.

The application process would be streamlined by eliminating the need for a new appraisal or a tax return to prove primary residency. The $5 billion-$10 billion cost of the program would be paid for through a fee on large financial institutions. A separate fund, independent of FHA's existing Mutual Mortgage Insurance (MMI) Fund, would be created for the new refinancing program. The Administration proposal would require enactment of legislation.

The GSE component of the Administration's plan would further streamline HARP beyond the changes made in October 2011. The Administration proposes reducing closing costs by eliminating manual appraisals entirely. The GSEs would be required to use automated valuation models or other appraisal alternatives if they are unable to use automated valuation models due to lack of recent comparable sales. The Administration proposal would also allow lenders who do not currently service a borrower's mortgage to have access to the same streamlined underwriting that the current service is allowed to use. This could increase competition and potentially lower costs to borrowers. The plan would make the streamlined refinancing available to all GSE borrowers, even those with significant equity in their home. Currently, borrowers with sufficient equity can more easily refinance through traditional channels, but they cannot take advantage of the lower costs and streamlined process associated with HARP.

Underwater borrowers who participate in either the FHA refinancing program or HARP would have the option to apply their savings from refinancing to either lower their monthly payments or keep their monthly payments at the same level but build equity more quickly in their home by shortening the term of the loan. Those who choose to build equity more quickly would have their closing costs covered by the GSEs or FHA.[85]

As mentioned previously, refinancing GSE loans does not add additional credit risk to the GSEs because they already own the credit risk of the borrower defaulting. However, the FHA refinancing program would require the government to assume additional risk. The loans that are eligible for the FHA program would not be guaranteed by the government prior to the refinancing but would be insured after the refinance.

Multiple proposals have been introduced in the 112th Congress to mandate greater refinancing of GSE loans. S. 170, the Helping Responsible Homeowners Act (Senator Barbara Boxer et al.), and H.R. 363, the Housing Opportunity and Mortgage Equity Act of 2011 (Representative Dennis Cardoza et al.), require Fannie Mae and Freddie Mac to establish refinancing programs for qualified mortgages that they own or guarantee. For both bills, a qualified mortgage is a first mortgage on a one – to – four family dwelling that is the principal residence of the borrower and is owned or guaranteed by Fannie Mae or Freddie Mac. Both also put certain restrictions on the GSEs' ability to charge additional fees besides the standard guarantee fees and place a cap on the interest rate that a borrower can be charged. Under both proposals, the refinancing program would expire one year after the enactment of the bills; S. 170 gives FHFA the option to extend the program.

S. 170 and H.R. 363 also differ in several ways. S. 170 requires borrowers to be current on their mortgages to participate, whereas H.R. 363 does not have such a restriction. H.R. 363 prohibits the mortgage servicer that is refinancing the loan from charging the borrower any fee for refinancing, but it instructs the GSEs to pay the servicer up to $1,000 for each qualified mortgage that it refinances. S. 170 does not put limits on the fees that the servicer may charge and does not pay the servicer for the refinancing. S. 170 and H.R. 363 are similar to HARP in that they target GSE loans for refinancing, but both bills put greater emphasis on reducing the costs associated with refinancing.

RENTING FORECLOSED HOMES

Federal Reserve Chairman Ben Bernanke and other policy experts state that the housing market is experiencing serious imbalances. Overbuilding leading up to the bursting of the housing bubble, the subsequent increase in foreclosures, and the fall in household formation[86] have led to an excess supply of homes in the market. Economic theory predicts that prices will continue to fall until the market clears. Falling house prices can contribute to a negative spiral in which falling prices lead to more foreclosures and prices falling even further.

The foreclosed homes that financial institutions assume control over are called real estate-owned (REO) properties. As of December 2011, single-family REOs valued at $11.6 billion, an estimated 79,000 units, are held by FDIC-insured institutions.[87] In addition, Fannie Mae and Freddie Mac held 179,063 REO properties at the end of 2011,[88] and FHA held 31,046 properties as of January 31, 2012.[89] According to some estimates, a third of REO inventory is from private-label securities.[90]

Because of the uncertainty surrounding the foreclosure process in the wake of investigations into the robo-signing allegations,[91] many large banks slowed down the rate at which they initiated foreclosure proceedings. With the recent mortgage settlement involving five of the banks that engaged in robo-signing, some expect the rate of foreclosures to increase as the backlog of foreclosures reaches the market.[92] *Figure 9* shows the shadow inventory, the approximately 1.5 million borrowers who are seriously delinquent and in danger of having their home become part of the REO inventory. In a January 2012 speech, William Dudley, the president and chief executive officer of the Federal Reserve Bank of New York, estimated that the flow of properties into REO could be as high as 1.8 million per year in 2012 and 2013, up from 1.1 million in 2011 and 600,000 in 2010.[93]

To address the imbalances in the housing market, some propose temporarily allowing financial institutions to rent the foreclosed homes or to sell the homes to investors who agree to rent the vacant units. Historically banks and the GSEs have been encouraged by their regulators to sell their REO property quickly and have not performed extensive property management services, though they are allowed to rent REOs for some limited periods.[94] Some proposals focus on renting properties as a way to help foreclosed homeowners through lease back or right-to-rent. Others do not address the foreclosed homeowners but focus on rentals as a way to stabilize neighborhoods and home prices. Given the imbalances in the owner-occupied housing market, supporters of a rental program believe expanding the amount of time that REOs can be rented is justified. Critics worry that if house prices do not increase while the homes are being temporarily rented, then the policy may serve to delay recovery by flooding a weak market with additional homes a few years in the future. Critics would rather allow the market to bottom out now rather than risk prolonging the housing slump.

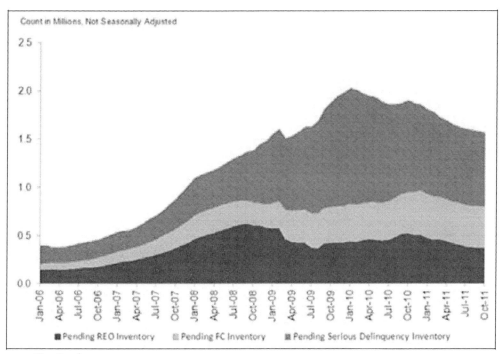

Source: CoreLogic.

Figure 9. Shadow Inventory.

Barriers to Renting

In a housing white paper prepared for Congress, the Federal Reserve outlined three obstacles to implementing an REO-to-rental program as well as possible policy solutions. First, as mentioned previously, regulators have discouraged financial institutions from holding REO properties.[95] Institutions are currently allowed to temporarily rent REO if doing so maximizes the potential return of the asset. On April 5, 2012, the Federal Reserve issued guidance to financial institutions that it regulates to "clarify supervisory expectations regarding rental of residential REO properties by such organizations while such circumstances continue."[96] The guidance explains to regulated REO holders how they may rent the properties within "the existing statutory and regulatory holding-period limits."[97]

Second, if the REO program involves sales to investors, then investors would need to purchase a large number of properties in close geographic proximity to each other to be profitable on a large scale. Many of the components of property management, such as processing payments, advertising for renters, and developing relationships with local contractors, benefit from economies of scale—the more houses a landlord has in a given area the more profitable it is. But if an investor must assemble a critical mass of properties one property at a time, then the investor must bear carrying costs, such as maintenance and taxes, without receiving any revenues.

To facilitate bulk transactions, the Federal Reserve notes that REO holders could auction their existing inventory in a given area to an investor as well as the future stream of REOs in an area. However, the Federal Reserve paper states that bulk sales can yield lower recoveries than individual sales in some cases because each property cannot be allocated to the highest individual bidder when sold in bulk.

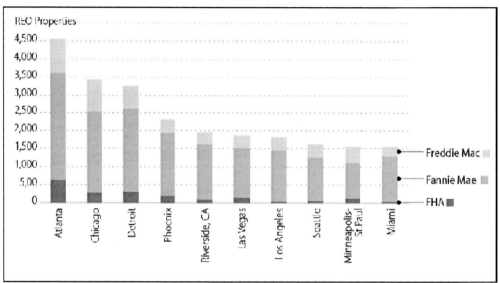

Source: Created by CRS from FHFA data.

Figure 10. Top 10 Metropolitan Statistical Areas for Freddie Mac, Fannie Mae, and FHA REO. (as of December 26, 2011)

But it may take longer to sell properties individually, during which the properties deteriorate.[98] Others predict that bulk investors will pay a premium for the opportunity to buy a large quantity at once rather than pay the expense of individually collecting properties.[99]

Third, to amass a sufficient number of properties, investors may need to obtain financing. However, financing for purchases of bulk pools of REO properties is not something that lenders traditionally offer. For example, Freddie Mac only allows investors to finance up to 4 homes and Fannie Mae sets the limit at 10 homes.[100] Without more accessible credit, there may be a limited number of investors able to participate.

In addition, not all communities are suited for a REO-to-rental program. The program may be most effective by targeting communities in which the number of REO properties is high, but the current demand among investors for one-at-a-time purchases is weak. *Figure 10* shows the communities with the most GSE and FHA REO properties.

Potential Impact of Rental Program

Housing Market

A REO-to-rental program would prevent foreclosed homes from flooding the "for-sale" market and instead temporarily shift them to the "rental" market. Foreclosed homes negatively impact house prices in several ways. First, foreclosed homes and other forms of distressed sales (such as a short sale) typically sell at a discount compared with non-distressed sales,101 potentially lowering the appraisal value for neighboring homes. Second, foreclosures increase the supply of homes that are on the market, which typically drives down home prices. Lower home prices may benefit those who are looking to purchase a home, but it hurts those who currently own their home. A Goldman Sachs research paper estimated that if 475,000 vacant REOs were converted to rentals, then house prices would rise by an additional 0.5% in the first year of the program and by 1% in the second year.102 If the program increases house prices in the for-sale market, then prices are expected to fall in the rental market. The Federal Reserve white paper on housing notes that the current movement in relative prices—prices that are falling or flat in the for-sale market but rising in the rental market—provides evidence that it may be appropriate to transition REO properties to rentals in some areas.103 Figure 11 shows the trend in prices for rent compared with sales.

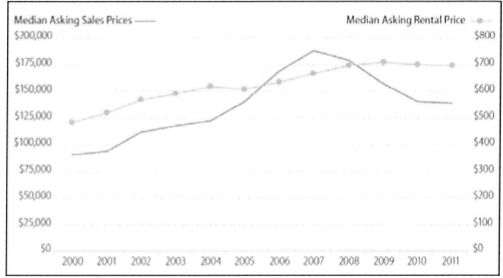

Source: U.S. Census Bureau, at http://www.census.gov/hhes/www/housing /hvs/ historic/index.html.

Figure 11. Rent-Versus-Own Prices.

Financial Sector

The major REO-to-rental policy proposals, discussed in "Legislative Proposals for Renting REO" below, have two variations: (1) allow banks, GSEs, and other institutions to rent properties directly themselves or (2) sell the properties in bulk to investors who will rent them. In both options, REO is rented, but how and when the assets are eventually sold will impact the balance sheet of the institutions.

If the REO properties are immediately sold in bulk to investors, then the institutions can have a relatively good idea of what price the properties can be sold given current trends, though some factors on the margin may influence the final price, such as whether auction methods are used or if financing is provided to facilitate the sale. However, if the institutions rent the properties for several years prior to eventually selling, then the direction of future house prices will significantly impact the price for which the properties are eventually sold. Supporters of policies that encourage institutions to rent for several years before selling are likely expecting future house prices to increase so that eventual sales occur in a more stable market. However, future asset prices are inherently unpredictable. If future house prices fall, then institutions would lose by postponing the sale of REO properties.

Consumer Spending

Unlike principal reductions and mass refinancing, renting foreclosed homes does not reduce existing homeowners' payments or increase their disposal income. Any impact on consumer spending is likely to be indirect through stabilizing house prices and preserving nearby homeowners' equity and net worth.

FHFA Pilot Program

In August 2011, FHFA, in consultation with the Treasury Department and the Department of Housing and Urban Development (HUD), submitted a request for information on ideas for asset disposition.[104] After receiving more than 4,000 responses, FHFA announced the first property sales under its Real Estate-Owned (REO) Initiative on February 27, 2012.[105] Under the REO Initiative, Fannie Mae and Freddie Mac REO properties in the hardest-hit metropolitan areas are to be sold to qualified investors who agree to rent the properties for a specified number of years. *Table 6* summarizes the Fannie Mae REO in the first transaction.

Table 6. Summary of Fannie Mae REO Assets

Sub-Portfolio	Term Lease Unit Count	Month-to-Month Lease Unit Count	Vacant Unit Count	Total Units	% by Total Units
Atlanta, GA	426	121	58	605	21.2
Chicago, IL	75	11	34	120	4.2
Florida-Central and Northeast	133	50	14	197	6.9
Florida-Southeast	166	222	52	440	15.4
Florida-West Coast	118	44	37	199	7.0
Las Vegas, NV	176	33	36	24.5	8.6
Los Angeles/ Riverside, CA	349	164	150	663	23.2
Phoenix, AZ	248	89	48	385	13.5
Total	1,691	734	429	2,854	100.0

Source: http://www.fhfa.gov/webfiles/23402/FNMASFRREO2012-1Summary of Assets.pdf.

Most of the properties in the first transaction (91.2%) are single-family homes or condominiums. However, most of the single-family homes and condominiums are already rented with fewer than 10% vacant. Because of their desire to see vacant homes rented out, some commentators expressed disappointment that a larger percentage of the homes were not vacant.[106] Others argue that by starting with properties with existing tenants, FHFA can attract more investors for the first sale; by having existing renters, investors are ensured of a future stream of income and may therefore face less uncertainty in attempting to price this new asset class.[107]

It is unclear if FHFA will allow Fannie Mae (and possibly Freddie Mac in potential future sales) to retain an ownership stake in the properties or if they will be true sales. It is also unclear if the GSEs will provide financing to investors and how the properties will be sold, whether to a single investor, multiple investors by metropolitan area, or some other method.[108]

Legislative Proposals for Renting REO

Multiple proposals have been introduced in the 112th Congress to establish REO rental programs. Some proposals focus on renting foreclosed properties to any renter, while others focus on allowing delinquent homeowners to stay in their home but pay rent. H.R. 2636, the Neighborhood Preservation Act of 2011 (Representative Gary Miller et al.), and S. 2080, the Keeping Families in their Home Act of 2012 (Senator Dean Heller), temporarily authorize depository institutions, depository institution holding companies,[109] Fannie Mae, and Freddie Mac to lease foreclosed property held by those institutions for up to five years. Section 2 of H.R. 2636 makes clear that one of the goals of the proposed REO program is to increase the options available to financial institutions to maximize the value of their assets. By temporarily renting a home before selling it, the institution could eventually sell the property into a more stable market and receive a higher return.

H.R. 1548, the Right to Rent Act of 2011 (Representative Raúl Grijalva et al.), gives eligible borrowers who are delinquent on their mortgage and subject to foreclosure proceedings the option to rent their home at a fair market rent for up to five years. To be eligible, a delinquent borrower must have a mortgage originated by July 1, 2007, on a single-family property that has been used as the borrower's principal residence for at least two years prior to the foreclosure filing. In addition, the borrower's home must have had a purchase price less than the median purchase price for residences in the metropolitan statistical area (or state if not in an MSA) at the time of the purchase for the borrower to be eligible. The fair market rent will be determined by the court and adjusted annually in line with the consumer price index.

End Notes

[1] For more on the current economic recovery, see CRS Report R41332, *Economic Recovery: Sustaining U.S. Economic Growth in a Post-Crisis Economy*, by Craig K. Elwell.

[2] Testimony of Ms. Laurie F. Goodman, a senior managing director at Amherst Securities Group, in U.S. Congress, Senate Committee on Banking, Housing, and Urban Affairs, Subcommittee on Housing, Transportation and Community Development, *New Ideas to Address the Glut of Foreclosed Properties*, hearing, 112th Cong., 1st sess., September 20, 2011, available at http://banking.senate.gov.

[3] The "reasonable" and "lower bound" default rates are estimated default rates based on Goodman's projections about how the different categories of mortgages will perform. The "lower bound" estimate is a more conservative estimate that assumes fewer defaults in the future.

[4] Using data from CoreLogic, William Dudley of the Federal Reserve Bank of New York estimated 11 million underwater borrowers in a January 2012 speech. See http://www. newyorkfed.org/newsevents/speeches/2012/dud120106.html. In his February 2012 congressional testimony, Mark Zandi estimated 14.6 million underwater borrowers using data from Equifax. See http://banking.senate.gov/public/index.cfm?FuseAction =Files. View& FileStore_id=65e8490f-7a21-43f8-a24b-7f7a856ece38.

[5] See Testimony of Mark Zandi, chief economist at Moody's Analytics, in U.S. Congress, Senate Committee on Banking, Housing, and Urban Affairs, *New Ideas for Refinancing and Restructuring Mortgage Loans*, 112th Cong., 1st sess., September 14, 2011. However, other experts find minimal relationship between negative equity and homeowner mobility; see Sam Schulhofer-Wohl, "Negative Equity Does Not Reduce Homeowners' Mobility," Federal Reserve Bank of Minneapolis Working Paper Series, December 2010.

[6] One study of borrowers in Massachusetts with negative equity in the 1990s found that more than 90% retained their homes, suggesting that opportunistic default may be overstated in some cases; see Christopher L. Foote, Kristopher Gerardi, and Paul S. Willen, "Negative Equity and Foreclosure: Theory and Evidence," Federal Reserve Bank of Boston, Working Paper No. 08-3, available at http://www.bos.frb.org/economic/ppdp/ 2008/ppdp0803.htm. The current housing downturn has seen steeper declines in house prices, potentially making the implications of negative equity more severe than the period studied by Foote et al.

[7] In this example, a borrower may attempt to arrange a short sale, but that option may not always be available. A short sale is a sale in which the mortgage holder allows the borrower to sell the house for an amount that is less than the amount owed and does not require the borrower to pay the difference.

[8] RealtyTrac, a publisher of one of the largest databases of foreclosures, estimates that the average price of a foreclosure-related sale is approximately 29% less than a non-foreclosure sale. See http://www.realtytrac. com/content/ foreclosure-market-report/q4-and-year-end-2011-us-foreclosure-sales-report-7060. There may also be additional costs associated with foreclosure, such as maintaining the property, that reduce the returns on a foreclosure.

[9] The following analysis of the principal reduction decision is based on Manuel Adelino, Kristopher Gerardi, and Paul S. Willen, *Why Don't Lenders Renegotiate More Home Mortgages? Redefaults, Self-Cures, and Securitization*, Federal Reserve Bank of Boston, Public Policy Discussion Paper No. 09-4, July 2009.

[10] The Type 4 borrower is a borrower that is determined to be net present value negative and therefore not considered a good candidate for a modification. A borrower that is net present value negative is one in which the servicer determines that the expected gains from no modification are likely to be greater than the gains associated with a modification. See https://www.hmpadmin.com/portal/programs/docs/ hamp_servicer/ npvmodeldocumentationv403.pdf.

[11] Strategic default behavior is characterized by Fannie Mae as "borrowers who walk-away and had the capacity to pay or did not complete a workout alternative in good faith." See http://www.fanniemae.com/portal/about-us/media/ corporate-news/2010/5071.html.

[12] Moral hazard refers to the phenomenon in which actors take on more risk because they do not bear the full consequences.

[13] For more on house lock, see the Council of Economic Advisers, *Economic Report of the President*, February 2012, at http://www.whitehouse.gov/sites/default/files/ microsites/ ERP_2012_Complete.pdf.

[14] A situation that is zero-sum is one in which the gains to one party are exactly offset by losses to another.

[15] The argument related to principal reduction potentially increasing consumer spending is modeled off of similar analysis for mortgage refinances; see Joseph Tracy and Joshua Wright, *Why Mortgage Refinancing Is Not a Zero-Sum Game*, Federal Reserve Bank of New York, January 11, 2012, at http://libertystreeteconomics. newyorkfed.org/2012/01/ why-mortgage-refinancing-is-not-a-zero-sum-game. html.

[16] Approximately 31.2% of all Fannie Mae, Freddie Mac, and Ginnie Mae mortgage-backed securities are held by the U.S. Treasury, the Federal Reserve System, foreign investors, and Fannie Mae and Freddie Mac. See the Federal Reserve System, *Flow of Funds Accounts of the United States*, Fourth 2011, Table L. 210, http://www.federalreserve.gov/releases/z1/ Current/z1.pdf.

[17] The Federal Reserve Bank of New York analysis also discusses the impact that foreclosures have on credit history and the prolonged drag this could be on the economy.

[18] For more on the household wealth effect, see Dean M. Maki and Michael G. Palumbo, *Disentangling the Wealth Effect: A Cohort Analysis of Household Saving in the 1990s*, The Federal Reserve System, April 2001, at http://www.federalreserve.gov/pubs/feds/2001/ 200121/200121pap.pdf.

[19] See CRS Report RL30354, *Monetary Policy and the Federal Reserve: Current Policy and Conditions*, by Marc Labonte.

[20] The owner of a mortgage loan or mortgage-backed security typically hires a mortgage servicer to act on its behalf. When loans are current, a mortgage servicer collects payments from borrowers and forwards them to the mortgage holders. If the borrower becomes delinquent, a servicer may offer the borrower an option that could allow the borrower to stay in his or her home, or the servicer may pursue foreclosure.

[21] See CRS Report R42041, *National Mortgage Servicing Standards: Legislation in the 112th Congress*, by Sean M. Hoskins. For examples of shortcomings in servicers' operational infrastructure, such as determining the return

of a short sale versus a foreclosure sale, see Kate Berry, "Banks Face Tough Choices Unloading REO Properties," *American Banker*, February 23, 2012.

[22] For more on coordination problems related to bankruptcy and distressed assets, see David Smith and Per Stromberg, "Maximizing the Value of Distressed Assets: Bankruptcy Law and the Efficient Reorganization of Firms," in *Systemic Financial Crises*, eds. Patrick Honohan and Luc Laeven (Cambridge: Cambridge University Press, 2005). Note that the article focuses on firms rather than individuals.

[23] See Senator Bob Corker, "Obama Administration's Principal Write-down Proposal for Underwater Home Mortgages is 'Terrible Public Policy,' Forces Tennesseans to Pay for Reckless Housing Practices in Other States," press release, January 30, 2012, at http://www.corker.senate.gov.

[24] See CRS Report RL34386, *Could Securitization Obstruct Voluntary Loan Modifications and Payment Freezes?*, by Edward V. Murphy.

[25] Using data from the Federal Reserve System on mortgage debt outstanding, non-GSE and non-government insured mortgages account for approximately 43% of mortgage debt outstanding at the end of September 2011. See http://www.federalreserve.gov/econresdata/ releases/mortoutstand/current.htm.

[26] There are other government programs involving principal reduction besides HAMP, such as the FHA Short Refinance, but HAMP is the largest program and is the focus of the next section. For more on federal government programs to reduce mortgage principal, see CRS Report R40210, *Preserving Homeownership: Foreclosure Prevention Initiatives*, by Katie Jones.

[27] See Making Home Affordable website, at http://www.makinghomeaffordable.gov.

[28] This section was prepared using material from CRS Report R40210, *Preserving Homeownership: Foreclosure Prevention Initiatives*, by Katie Jones.

[29] "The NPV Model compares the expected discounted cash flows associated with the modification of a loan – considering probabilities of default – under two scenarios: the loan is modified according to HAMP terms and the loan is not modified... A loan that is NPV 'positive' – where the value of the probability-weighted mod cash flows exceed the value of the probability-weighted no-mod cash flows – is considered to be a good candidate for modification." See Steve Holden, Therese Scharlemann, and Austin Kelly et al., *The HAMP NPV Model: Development and Early Performance*, Federal Housing Finance Agency, Working Paper 11-1, July 2011, p. 3, at http://www.fhfa.gov/webfiles/ 21680/REE_HAMP_ 07-22-11_FINAL.pdf.

[30] Detailed guidelines on the Principal Reduction Alternative were released in Supplemental Directive 10-05 on June 3, 2010. These guidelines are available at https://www.hmpadmin. com/portal/docs/hamp_servicer/ sd1005.pdf.

[31] U.S. Department of the Treasury, Making Home Affordable Program Servicer Performance Report Through January 2012, at http://www.treasury.gov/initiatives/financial-stability/results/MHA-Reports/Documents/Jan% 202012%20MHA%20Report_WITH_ SER VICER_ASSESSMENTS_FINAL.PDF.

[32] See http://www.treasury.gov/connect/blog/Pages/Expanding-our-efforts-to-help-more-home owners-and-strengthenhard-hit-communities.aspx.

[33] The five banks are Ally/GMAC, Bank of America, Citi, JPMorgan Chase, and Wells Fargo. For more information, see http://www.nationalmortgagesettlement.com/.

[34] For an overview of the settlement see http://www.atg.wa.gov/uploadedFiles/Home/ About_ the_Office/Cases/ National_Mortgage_Settlement/National_ Settlement_Executive_ Summary.pdf.

[35] The remaining funds are allocated among programs to refinance borrowers, other forms of homeowner assistance (such as facilitating short sales), to compensate individuals who were improperly foreclosed on, and the participating states' foreclosure relief and housing programs.

[36] See The Federal Reserve System, *Flow of Funds Accounts of the United States*, Fourth Quarter 2011, Table L. 218, at http://www.federalreserve.gov/releases/z1/Current/z1.pdf.

[37] In private-label securities and mortgages held in banks' portfolios, the investor who holds the mortgage (or its agent, the mortgage servicer) ultimately makes determinations about loan modifications. For GSE loans, Fannie Mae and Freddie Mac, which set guidance for the servicers because Fannie and Freddie are the ones who bear the credit risk, not the investors, make the determination about loan modifications. Loan modifications attempt to reduce the risk of default and are therefore made by those who bear the default risk.

[38] Since entering into conservatorship, Fannie Mae and Freddie Mac have performed approximately 1.8 million home retention actions, which include repayment plans, forbearance, and other approaches. See Federal Housing Finance Agency, *Foreclosure Prevention and Refinance Report November 2011*, at http://www.fhfa.gov/webfiles/23123/ Nov_2011_Foreclosure_Prev_Rpt.pdf.

[39] See http://www.fhfa.gov/webfiles/23056/PrincipalForgivenessltr12312.pdf. This CRS report does not attempt to interpret FHFA's mandate or comment on whether FHFA is interpreting it correctly or incorrectly.

[40] See http://www.fhfa.gov/webfiles/23056/PrincipalForgivenessltr12312.pdf.

[41] Fannie Mae and Freddie Mac also allow for other foreclosure prevention activities, such as short sales and deeds-inlieu. See Federal Housing Finance Agency, *Foreclosure Prevention and Refinance Report November 2011*, at http://www.fhfa.gov/webfiles/23123/Nov_2011_Foreclosure_Prev_Rpt.pdf.

[42] Ibid.

[43] See http://www.fhfa.gov/webfiles/23056/PrincipalForgivenessltr12312.pdf.

[44] See http://www.fhfa.gov/webfiles/23110/FHFAStmtHampChanges12712F.pdf. Acting Director DeMarco presented preliminary results of FHFA's analysis incorporating the HAMP incentive payments in a speech on April 10, 2012. The text is available at http:// www.fhfa.gov/webfiles/23876/Brookings_ Institution_ Principal_Forgiveness.pdf.

[45] See Office of the Comptroller of the Currency, *OCC Mortgage Metrics Report*, December 2011, at http://www.occ.treas.gov/publications/publications-by-type/other-publications-reports/mortgage-metrics-2011/mortgage-metrics-q3-2011.pdf.

[46] See http://www.fhfa.gov/webfiles/23056/PrincipalForgivenessltr12312.pdf.

[47] It is unclear why FHFA believes the price at which an institution purchases a mortgage should influence what future action maximizes the return on that mortgage. Economic theory states that sunk costs should not influence future action. However, there may be accounting issues as well as issues related to the timing of losses that FHFA does not describe that could explain its position.

[48] More information on the HAMP NPV Model is available at HMPAdmin.com.

[49] See http://www.makinghomeaffordable.gov/programs/lower-payments/Pages/hamp.aspx.

[50] The FHFA analysis does not explain the potential relationship between NPV positive borrowers and delinquent borrowers.

[51] Testimony of Laurie S. Goodman, a senior managing director at Amherst Securities Group, in U.S. Congress, Senate Committee on Banking, Housing, and Urban Affairs, Subcommittee on Housing, Transportation and Community Development, *Strengthening the Housing Market and Minimizing Losses to Taxpayers*, hearing, 112th Cong., 2nd sess., March 15, 2012, available at http://banking.senate.gov/.

[52] For an analysis of the legal issues surrounding cramdown and of previous cramdown legislation, see CRS Report RL34301, *The Primary Residence Exception: Legislative Proposals in the 111th Congress to Amend the Bankruptcy Code to Allow the Strip Down of Certain Home Mortgages*, by David H. Carpenter.

[53] For more on closing costs, see The Federal Reserve Board, *A Consumer's Guide to Mortgage Refinancings*, at http://www.federalreserve.gov/pubs/refinancings/default.htm#cost.

[54] See http://www.whitehouse.gov/the-press-office/2012/02/01/fact-sheet-president-obama-s-plan-help-responsible-homeowners-and-heal-h.

[55] The cost of the plan would be offset by using a portion of the proposed Financial Crisis Responsibility Fee.

[56] The five banks are Ally/GMAC, Bank of America, Citi, JPMorgan Chase, and Wells Fargo. For more information, see http://www.nationalmortgagesettlement.com/.

[57] Similarly, H.R. 3733, the Affordable Mortgage for Homeowners Act of 2011 (Representative Alcee Hastings et al.) requires Fannie Mae and Freddie Mac to lower the interest rates on GSE loans but does not do so through a refinance.

[58] A refinance involves taking out a new loan to pay off the existing loan. A modification, by contrast, changes the terms of the existing loan.

[59] See Sumit Agarwal, John C. Driscoll, and David Laibson, "Optimal Mortgage Refinancing: A Closed Form Solution," NBER Working Paper Series, October 2007.

[60] If a borrower has private mortgage insurance, the borrower may be able to refinance if the LTV is above 80%.

[61] See Sumit Agarwal, John C. Driscoll, and David Laibson, "Optimal Mortgage Refinancing: A Closed Form Solution," NBER Working Paper Series, October 2007.

[62] Mitchell Remy, Deborah Lucas, and Damien Moore, *An Evaluation of Large-Scale Mortgage Refinancing Programs*, Congressional Budget Office, Working Paper 2011-4, September 2011, at http://www.cbo.gov/sites/default/files/ cbofiles/attachments/09-07-2011-Large-Scale_Refinancing_ Program. pdf.

[63] Alan Boyce, Glenn Hubbard, and Chris Mayer et al., *Streamlined Refinancings for up to 14 Million Borrowers*, January 18, 2012, http://www4.gsb.columbia.edu/null/download? &exclusive=filemgr. download&file_id = 739308.

[64] See Testimony of the Honorable Phillip L. Swagel, in U.S. Congress, Senate Committee on Banking, Housing, and Urban Affairs, *State of the Housing Market: Removing Barriers to Economic Recovery*, hearing, 112th Cong., 2nd sess., February 9, 2012.

[65] See Testimony of Dr. Mark Zandi, chief economist of Moody's Analytics, in U.S. Congress, Senate Committee on Banking, Housing, and Urban Affairs, *State of the Housing Market: Removing Barriers to Economic Recover*, hearing, 112th Cong., 2nd sess., February 9, 2012.

[66] See Joseph Tracy and Joshua Wright, *Why Mortgage Refinancing Is Not a Zero-Sum Game*, Federal Reserve Bank of New York, January 11, 2012, at http://libertystreeteconomics. newyorkfed.org/2012/01/why-mortgage-refinancing-isnot-a-zero-sum-game.html.

[67] For more on the spending decisions across income levels, see Karen E. Dynan, Jonathan Skinner, and Stephen P. Zeldes, *Do the Rich Save More?*, Federal Reserve Board, November 2000, at http://www.federalreserve.gov /pubs/feds/2000/200052/200052pap.pdf.

[68] Ginnie Mae guarantees mortgage-backed securities backed by federally insured or guaranteed loans. See http://www.ginniemae.gov/about/about.asp?Section=About.

[69] See Joseph Tracy and Joshua Wright, *Why Mortgage Refinancing Is Not a Zero-Sum Game*, Federal Reserve Bank of New York, January 11, 2012, at http://libertystreeteconomics. newyorkfed.org/2012/01/why-mortgage-refinancing-isnot-a-zero-sum-game.html.

[70] See Testimony of the Honorable Phillip L. Swagel, in U.S. Congress, Senate Committee on Banking, Housing, and Urban Affairs, *State of the Housing Market: Removing Barriers to Economic Recovery*, hearing, 112th Cong., 2nd sess., February 9, 2012.

[71] See Investment Company Institute, *Profile of Mutual Fund Shareholders, 2010*, February 2011, p. 105, at http://www.ici.org/pdf/rpt_11_profiles.pdf.

[72] For more on HARP, see CRS Report R40210, *Preserving Homeownership: Foreclosure Prevention Initiatives*, by Katie Jones. HARP is not the only government refinance program. FHA also established the FHA Streamline Refinance Program. However, HARP is the largest of the refinance programs and the subject of several proposals. Therefore it is the focus of this section.

[73] See http://www.makinghomeaffordable.gov/programs/lower-rates/Pages/harp.aspx.

[74] HARP is limited to GSE borrowers to prevent the GSEs from assuming additional credit risk.

[75] See Federal Housing Finance Agency, *Foreclosure Prevention and Refinance Report November 2011*, at http://www.fhfa.gov/webfiles/23123/Nov_2011_Foreclosure_Prev_Rpt.pdf.

[76] The list of barriers to refinancing is not exhaustive but highlights what some experts have identified as major factors in HARP performing below what was expected by the Administration.

[77] For more on loan level price adjustments, see https://www.efanniemae.com/sf/ refmaterials/ llpa/pdf/ llpamatrixrefi.pdf.

[78] See Kate Berry, "Bank of America Says It Can't Process All Refinance Applications," *American Banker*, February 8, 2012, at http://www.americanbanker. com/issues/ 177_27/ bank-of-america-harp-refinance-applications-1046498-1.html.

[79] See http://www.fhfa.gov/webfiles/22721/HARP_release_102411_Final.pdf.

[80] However, as mentioned previously, most HARP participants had an LTV below 105 and would therefore be unaffected by eliminating the cap.

[81] FHFA has filed lawsuits against at least 17 lenders in cases related to put-back claims, which are lawsuits related to potential violations of representations and warranties or other underwriting violations. See http://www.fhfa.gov/ Default.aspx?Page=110.

[82] The waiving of certain representations and warranties applies only to refinances through the same servicer and not through different servicers. See Amherst Securities Group LP, *HARP: Program Changes and Their Implications*, October 24, 2011.

[83] The President's plan also includes other components such as a Homeowner Bill of Rights and expanding forbearance for the unemployed, but this analysis focuses on the refinancing proposals. See http://www.whitehouse.gov/the-pressoffice/2012/02/01/fact-sheet-president-obama-s-plan-help-responsible-homeowners-and-heal-h.

[84] To find the FHA Mortgage Limits in a particular area, see https://entp.hud.gov/ idapp/html/ hicostlook.cfm.

[85] To encourage borrowers to refinance into shorter-term mortgages, FHFA eliminated certain risk-based fees for borrowers who chose that option under HARP 2.0. See http://www.fhfa.gov/webfiles/22721/ HARP_release_102411_Final.pdf.

[86] For more on household formation, see Robert Denk and David Crowe, "Pent-Up Housing Demand: The Household Formation That Didn't Happen - Yet," February 2, 2011, at http://www.nahb.org/generic.aspx? genericContentID= 152243&channelID=311.

[87] The Federal Deposit Insurance Corporation (FDIC) reports the dollar value of REO and not the number of properties. See http://www2.fdic.gov/qbp/index.asp, and Lewis S. Ranieri, Kenneth T. Rosen, and Andrea Lepico et al., *Options for REO: The Private Sector Solution to the Foreclosure Problem*, Rosen Consulting Group and Ranieri Partners Management LLC, February 2012.

[88] See Fannie's Form 10-K at http://fanniemae.com/resources/file/ir/pdf/quarterly-annual-results/2011/10k_2011.pdf and Freddie's Form 10-K at http://www.freddiemac. com/investors/er/pdf/10k_030912.pdf.

[89] See Office of Risk Analysis and Regulatory Affairs, Federal Housing Administration, Department of Housing and Urban Development, *Monthly Report to the FHA Commissioner on FHA Business Activity*, January 2012, at http://portal.hud.gov/ hudportal/documents/huddoc?id=12jan.pdf.

[90] See Lewis S. Ranieri, Kenneth T. Rosen, and Andrea Lepico et al., *Options for REO: The Private Sector Solution to the Foreclosure Problem*, Rosen Consulting Group and Ranieri Partners Management LLC, February 2012.

[91] See CRS Report R41491, *"Robo-Signing" and Other Alleged Documentation Problems in Judicial and Nonjudicial Foreclosure Processes*, by David H. Carpenter.

[92] See Prashant Gopal and John Gittelsohn, "Foreclosure Deal to Spur New Wave of U.S. Home Seizures, Help Heal Market," *Bloomberg*, February 10, 2012, at http://www.bloomberg. com/news/2012-02-09/foreclosure-deal-to-spurnew-wave-of-u-s-home-seizures-help-heal-market.html.

[93] William C. Dudley, *Housing and the Economic Recovery*, Federal Reserve Bank of New York, January 6, 2012, at http://www.newyorkfed.org/newsevents/ speeches/2012/ dud120106. html.

[94] The Federal Reserve Board of Governors, *The U.S. Housing Market: Current Conditions and Policy Considerations*, white paper, January 4, 2012, at http://federalreserve.gov/ publications/other-reports/files /housing-white-paper20120104.pdf.

[95] For FDIC guidance to financial institutions on their handling of REO, see http://www. fdic.gov/news/news/ financial/ 2008/fil08062a.html. Also, see 12 U.S.C. § 29.

[96] The Federal Reserve Board of Governors, *The U.S. Housing Market: Current Conditions and Policy Considerations*, white paper, at January 4, 2012, http://federalreserve.gov /publications/other-reports/files/ housing-white-paper20120104.pdf.

[97] See http://www.federalreserve.gov/newsevents/press/bcreg/bcreg20120405a1.pdf.

[98] For more on REO disposition issues, see Testimony of Laurie S. Goodman, a senior managing director at Amherst Securities Group, in U.S. Congress, Senate Committee on Banking, Housing, and Urban Affairs, Subcommittee on Housing, Transportation and Community Development, *Strengthening the Housing Market and Minimizing Losses to Taxpayers*, hearing, 112th Cong., 2nd sess., March 15, 2012. Available at http://banking.senate.gov/.

[99] Testimony of Laurie S. Goodman, a senior managing director at Amherst Securities Group, in U.S. Congress, Senate Committee on Banking, Housing, and Urban Affairs, Subcommittee on Housing, Transportation and Community Development, *Strengthening the Housing Market and Minimizing Losses to Taxpayers*, hearing, 112th Cong., 2nd sess., March 15, 2012, available at http://banking.senate.gov/.

[100] Testimony of Ms. Laurie F. Goodman, a senior managing director at Amherst Securities Group, in U.S. Congress, Senate Committee on Banking, Housing, and Urban Affairs, Subcommittee on Housing, Transportation and Community Development, *New Ideas to Address the Glut of Foreclosed Properties*, hearing, 112th Cong., 1st sess., September 20, 2011, available at http://banking.senate.gov.

[101] RealtyTrac estimates that the average price of a foreclosure-related sale is approximately 29% less than a non-foreclosure sale. See http://www.realtytrac.com/content/foreclosure-market-report/q4-and-year-end-2011-us-foreclosure-sales-report-7060.

[102] Alex Phillips and Hui Shan, *US Daily: Thoughts on a Federal REO-to-Rental Program*, Goldman Sachs Research, January 5, 2012.

[103] The Federal Reserve Board of Governors, *The U.S. Housing Market: Current Conditions and Policy Considerations*, white paper, January 4, 2012, p. 9,at http:// federalreserve.gov/ publications/other-reports/files/housingwhite-paper-20120104.pdf.

[104] See http://www.fhfa.gov/webfiles/22366/RFIFinal081011.pdf.

[105] See http://www.fhfa.gov/webfiles/23403/REOPR22712F.pdf.

[106] Kerri Panchuk, "Bulk REO pilot plan disappoints: Capital Economics," *HousingWire,* at http://www.housingwire.com/article/bulk-reo-pilot-plan-disappoints-capital-economics.

[107] Suzy Khimm, "Can we fix housing by turning foreclosures into rentals?," *The Washington Post*, at http://www.washingtonpost.com/blogs/ezra-klein/post/can-we-fix-housing-by-turning-foreclosures-into-rentals/2012/ 02/28/gIQAENTsgR_blog.html.

[108] HUD was also part of the initial Request for Information (RFI) on REO sales in August 2011. It is unclear if HUD will convert FHA REO properties into rentals in a manner similar to FHFA.

[109] For more on depository institutions and their holding companies, see CRS Report R41339, *The Dodd-Frank Wall Street Reform and Consumer Protection Act: Titles III and VI, Regulation of Depository Institutions and Depository Institution Holding Companies*, by M. Maureen Murphy.

In: Melissa O. Murray and Willie T. Cole
Editors: Melissa O. Murray and Willie T. Cole

ISBN: 978-1-62257-294-6
© 2012 Nova Science Publishers, Inc.

Chapter 2

THE U.S. HOUSING MARKET: CURRENT CONDITIONS AND POLICY CONSIDERATIONS[*]

Board of Governors of the Federal Reserve System

The Honorable Tim Johnson Chairman
Committee on Banking,
Housing,and Urban Affairs
United States Senate

The Honorable Richard Shelby Ranking Member
Committee on Banking,
Housing, and Urban Affairs
United States Senate

Dear Mr. Chairman and Ranking Member:

Restoring the health of the housing market is a necessary part of a broader strategy for economic recovery. There has been much discussion about the pathway forward, and the Federal Reserve has received questions and requests for our input and assistance. We have been looking at these issues and in the interest of continuing a dialogue, my staff has written a white paper, entitled "The US Housing Market: Current Conditions and Policy Considerations."

In this report, we do not attempt to address every problem faced by the housing market; rather, it is our intention to provide a framework for thinking about certain issues and tradeoffs that policymakers might consider.

---

[*] This is an edited, reformatted and augmented version of a Board of Governors of the Federal Reserve System publication, dated January 4, 2012.

I have enclosed a copy of the white paper for your review. I and my staff would be happy to discuss these ideas more fully. I hope that you will not hesitate to contact me if we can be of assistance.

Sincerely,

Enclosure

INTRODUCTION

The ongoing problems in the US housing market continue to impede the economic recovery. House prices have fallen an average of about 33 percent from their 2006 peak, resulting in about $7 trillion in household wealth losses and an associated ratcheting down of aggregate consumption. At the same time, an unprecedented number of households have lost, or are on the verge of losing, their homes. The extraordinary problems plaguing the housing market reflect in part the effect of weak demand due to high unemployment and heightened uncertainty. But the problems also reflect three key forces originating from within the housing market itself: a persistent excess supply of vacant homes on the market, many of which stem from foreclosures; a marked and potentially long-term downshift in the supply of mortgage credit; and the costs that an often unwieldy and inefficient foreclosure process imposes on homeowners, lenders, and communities.

Looking forward, continued weakness in the housing market poses a significant barrier to a more vigorous economic recovery. Of course, some of the weakness is related to poor labor market conditions, which will take time to be resolved. At the same time, there is scope for policymakers to take action along three dimensions that could ease some of the pressures afflicting the housing market. In particular, policies could be considered that would help moderate the inflow of properties into the large inventory of unsold homes, remove some of the obstacles preventing creditworthy borrowers from accessing mortgage credit, and limit the number of homeowners who find themselves pushed into an inefficient and overburdened foreclosure pipeline. Some steps already being taken or proposed in these areas will be discussed below.

Taking these issues in turn, the large inventory of foreclosed or surrendered properties is contributing to excess supply in the for-sale market, placing downward pressure on house prices and exacerbating the loss in aggregate housing wealth. At the same time, rental markets are strengthening in some areas of the country, reflecting in part a decline in the homeownership rate. Reducing some of the barriers to converting foreclosed properties to rental units will help redeploy the existing stock of houses in a more efficient way. Such conversions might also increase lenders' eventual recoveries on foreclosed and surrendered properties.

Obstacles limiting access to mortgage credit even among creditworthy borrowers contribute to weakness in housing demand, and barriers to refinancing blunt the transmission of monetary policy to the household sector. Further attention to easing some of these obstacles could contribute to the gradual recovery in housing markets and thus help speed the overall economic recovery.

Finally, foreclosures inflict economic damage beyond the personal suffering and dislocation that accompany them.[1]

In particular, foreclosures can be a costly and inefficient way to resolve the inability of households to meet their mortgage payment obligations because they can result in "deadweight losses," or costs that do not benefit anyone, including the neglect and deterioration of properties that often sit vacant for months (or even years) and the associated negative effects on neighborhoods.'

These deadweight losses compound the losses that households and creditors already bear and can result in further downward pressure on house prices. Some of these foreclosures can be avoided if lenders pursue appropriate loan modifications aggressively and if servicers are provided greater incentives to pursue alternatives to foreclosure.

And in cases where modifications cannot create a credible and sustainable resolution to a delinquent mortgage, more-expedient exits from homeownership, such as deeds-in-lieu of foreclosure or short sales, can help reduce transaction costs and minimize negative effects on communities.

Intertwined in these issues is the unresolved role of the government-sponsored enterprises (GSEs) Fannie Mae and Freddie Mac, in both the near term and long term.[3] The GSEs hold or guarantee significant shares of delinquent mortgages and foreclosed properties.

Because of their outsized market presence, the GSEs' actions affect not only their own portfolios, but also the housing market overall. However, since September 2008, the GSEs have operated in conservatorship under the direction of the Federal Housing Finance Agency (FHFA), with specific mandates to minimize losses for taxpayers and to support a stable and liquid mortgage market.

In many of the policy areas discussed in this paper--such as loan modifications, mortgage refinancing, and the disposition of foreclosed properties--there is bound to be some tension between minimizing the GSEs' near-term losses and risk exposure and taking actions that might promote a faster recovery in the housing market. Nonetheless, some actions that cause greater losses to be sustained by the GSEs in the near term might be in the interest of taxpayers to pursue if those actions result in a quicker and more vigorous economic recovery.

In this report, we provide a framework for thinking about directions policymakers might take to help the housing market.

Our goal is not to provide a detailed blueprint, but rather to outline issues and tradeoffs that policymakers might consider. We caution, however, that although policy action in these areas could facilitate the recovery of the housing market, economic losses will remain, and these losses must ultimately be allocated among homeowners, lenders, guarantors, investors, and taxpayers.

We begin with some background regarding housing market conditions. We then discuss proposals aimed at foreclosed properties that are owned by financial institutions such as the GSEs or banks. After that, we examine proposals aimed at homeowners at risk of default or foreclosure.

Finally, we discuss ideas for improving mortgage servicing practices.

HOUSING MARKET CONDITIONS

House Prices and Implications for Household Wealth

House prices for the nation as a whole (figure 1) declined sharply from 2007 to 2009 and remain about 33 percent below their early 2006 peak, according to data from CoreLogic. For the United States as a whole, declines on this scale are unprecedented since the Great Depression. In the aggregate, more than $7 trillion in home equity (the difference between aggregate home values and mortgage debt owed by homeowners)--more than half of the aggregate home equity that existed in early 2006--has been lost. Further, the ratio of home equity to disposable personal income has declined to 55 percent (figure 2), far below levels seen since this data series began in 1950.[4]

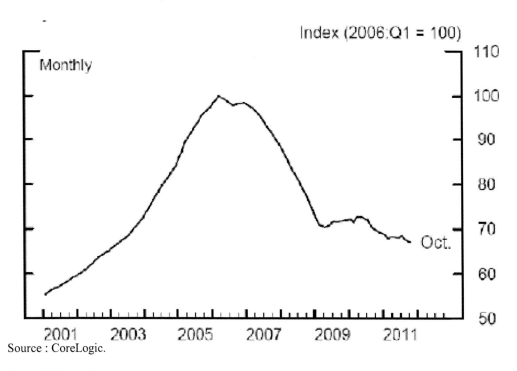

Source : CoreLogic.

Figure 1. House Prices.

This substantial blow to household wealth has significantly weakened household spending and consumer confidence. Middle-income households, as a group, have been particularly hard hit because home equity is a larger share of their wealth in the aggregate than it is for low-income households (who are less likely to be homeowners) or upper-income households (who own other forms of wealth such as financial assets and businesses). According to data from the Federal Reserve's Survey of Consumer Finances, the decline in average home equity for middle-income homeowners from 2007 through 2009 was about 66 percent of the average income in 2007 for these homeowners. In contrast, the decline in average home equity for the highest-income homeowners was only about 36 percent of average income for these homeowners.[5]

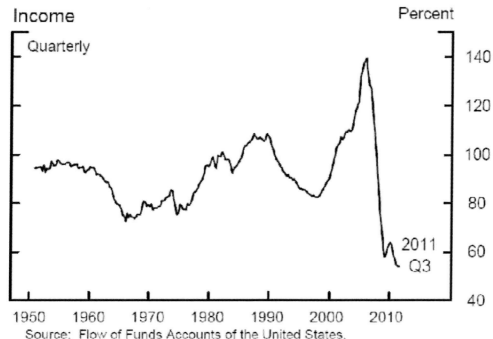

Source: Flow of Funds Account of the United States.

Figure 2. Ratio of Home Equity to Disposable Personal.

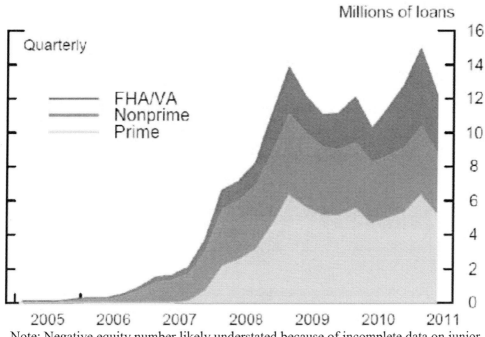

Note: Negative equity number likely understated because of incomplete data on junior liens.Nonprime category includes alt-A and subprime loans.

Figure 3. Mortgages with Negative Equity.

For many homeowners, the steep drop in house prices was more than enough to push their mortgages underwater--that is, to reduce the values of their homes below their mortgage balances (a situation also referred to as negative equity). This situation is widespread among borrowers who purchased homes in the years leading up to the house price peak, as well as those who extracted equity through cash-out refinancing. Currently, about 12 million homeowners are underwater on their mortgages (figure 3)--more than one out of five homes with a mortgage! In states experiencing the largest overall house price declines--such as Nevada, Arizona, and Florida--roughly half of all mortgage borrowers are underwater on their loans.

Negative equity is a problem because it constrains a homeowner's ability to remedy financial difficulties. When house prices were rising, borrowers facing payment difficulties could avoid default by selling their homes or refinancing into new mortgages. However, when house prices started falling and net equity started turning negative, many borrowers lost the ability to refinance their mortgages or sell their homes. Nonprime mortgages were most sensitive to house price declines, as many of these mortgages required little or no down payment and hence provided a limited buffer against falling house prices. But as house price declines deepened, even many prime borrowers who had made sizable down payments fell underwater, limiting their ability to absorb financial shocks such as job loss or reduced income.[7]

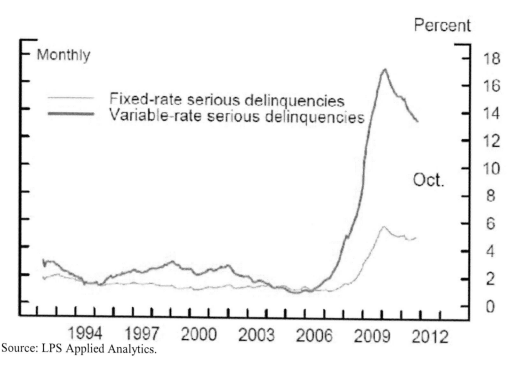

Source: LPS Applied Analytics.

Figure 4. Prime Mortgage Delinquency Rates.

The resulting surge of delinquencies (figure 4) has overwhelmed the housing finance system. Mortgage servicers were unprepared for the large number of delinquent borrowers and failed to invest the resources necessary to handle them properly, resulting in severely flawed and, in some cases, negligent servicing practices. Exacerbating the problem, some of the incentives built into servicing contracts encouraged foreclosures rather than loan modifications.

Mortgage Credit Conditions

As a result of these developments, mortgage credit conditions have tightened dramatically from their pre-recession levels. Mortgage lending standards were lax, at best, in the years before the house price peak, and some tightening relative to pre-crisis practices was necessary and appropriate. Nonetheless, the extraordinarily tight standards that currently prevail reflect, in part, obstacles that limit or prevent lending to creditworthy borrowers. Tight standards can take many forms, including stricter underwriting, higher fees and interest rates, more-stringent documentation requirements, larger required down payments, stricter appraisal standards, and fewer available mortgage products. Bank responses to the quarterly Senior Loan Officer Opinion Survey on Bank Lending Practices indicate persistent net tightening in lending standards for mortgages to purchase homes from 2007 through 2009, and surveys since then have yet to show any unwinding of that move, even for prime mortgages eligible for GSE or Federal Housing Administration (FHA) guarantees, for which lenders do not bear the credit risk.[9]

Other data show, for instance, that less than half of lenders are currently offering mortgages to borrowers with a FICO score of 620 and a down payment of 10 percent (figure 5)--even though these loans are within the GSE purchase parameters.[10] This hesitancy on the part of lenders is due in part to concerns about the high cost of servicing in the event of loan delinquency and fear that the GSEs could force the lender to repurchase the loan if the borrower defaults in the future.[11] Concerns about the high cost of servicing reflect recent experience, in which servicers were badly underprepared to deal with the volume of troubled loans, along with ongoing uncertainty about the cost of compliance with mortgage servicing-related regulatory requirements going forward; prospective capital treatment of mortgage servicing rights under Basel III may also be affecting the perceived costs and benefits of servicing operations. Lenders' reaction to the possibility of forced repurchases highlights the tradeoff between the GSEs pursuing a policy of reducing their near-term losses and risk exposure versus adopting policies to support the broader housing market. Aggressively putting back delinquent loans to lenders helps the GSEs maximize their profits on old business and thus limits their draws on the US Treasury, but at the same time, it discourages lenders from originating new mortgages. Meanwhile, for loans that are ineligible for GSE purchase, only high-credit-score borrowers generally have access to financing, and lenders often keep these loans in portfolio, leading them to be selective about the volume of such loans they originate.

Reduced mortgage lending is also notable among potential first-time homebuyers, who are typically an important source of incremental housing demand. These households often have relatively new credit profiles and lower-than-average credit scores, as they tend to be younger and have fewer economic resources to make a large down payment. Consumer credit record data show that the share of 29- to 34-year-olds getting a first-time mortgage was significantly lower in the past 2 years than it was 10 years earlier.12 The same data show that the drop-off was more pronounced among individuals with less-than-excellent credit scores, even in parts of the country where unemployment rates are better than the national average.13 These data suggest a large decline in mortgage borrowing by potential first-time homebuyers due to not only weaker housing demand, but also the effect of tighter credit conditions on all but the highest-creditquality borrowers.

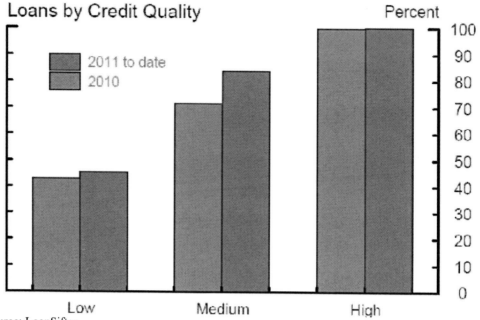

Source: LoanSifter.

Note: Hypothetical owner-occupied 30-year conventional fully documented mortgage. Low: FICO 620, LTV 90; Medium: FICO 680, LTV 90; High: FICO 720, LTV 80.

Figure 5. Percent of Lenders Offering GSE-Eligible.

At the same time, a host of factors have been weighing on housing demand. High unemployment and weak income growth have made it difficult for many households to purchase homes despite the large declines in house prices and mortgage rates. Uncertainty about the future prospects for the economy and labor market has also likely made some households reluctant to buy homes. The combination of weak demand to purchase homes and the restricted supply of mortgages has put considerable downward pressure on house prices in many areas.

Addressing Foreclosed Properties: REO to Rental

Background

At the same time that housing demand has weakened, the number of homes for sale is elevated relative to historical norms, due in large part to the swollen inventory of homes held by banks, guarantors, and servicers after completion of foreclosure proceedings. These properties are often called real estate owned, or REO, properties. While the total stock of REO properties is difficult to measure precisely, perhaps one-fourth of the 2 million vacant homes for sale in the second quarter of 2011 were REO properties. The combination of weak demand and elevated supply has put substantial downward pressure on house prices, and the continued flow of new REO properties--perhaps as high as 1 million properties per year in

2012 and 2013--will continue to weigh on house prices for some time.[14] To the extent that REO holders discount properties in order to sell them quickly, the near-term pressure on home prices might be even greater.

In contrast to the market for owner-occupied houses, the market for rental housing across the nation has recently strengthened somewhat. Rents have turned up in the past year (figure 6), and the national vacancy rate on multifamily rental properties has dropped noticeably from its peak in late 2009.

These developments have been fairly widespread across metropolitan areas. The relative strength of the rental market reflects increased demand as families who are unable or unwilling to purchase homes are renting properties instead. Rental demand has also been supported by families who have lost their homes to foreclosure--the majority of whom move to rental housing, most commonly to single-family rentals.[15]

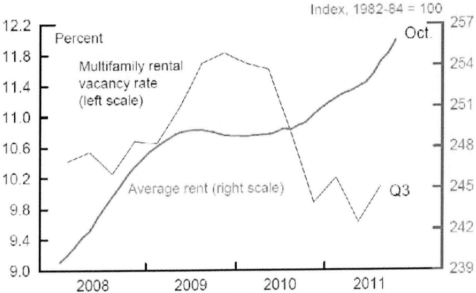

Source: For average rent. Bureau of Labor Statistics; for vacancy rate, Census Bureau.
Note: Rental vacancy rate is seasonally adjusted by Board staff.

Figure 6. Rent Index and Multifamily Rental Vacancy Rate.

The price signals in the owner-occupied and rental housing markets--that is, the decline in house prices and the rise in rents--suggest that it might be appropriate in some cases to redeploy foreclosed homes as rental properties. In addition, the forces behind the decline in the homeownership rate, such as tight credit conditions, are unlikely to unwind significantly in the immediate future, indicating a longer-term need for an expanded stock of rental housing. Although small investors are currently buying and converting foreclosed properties to rental units on a limited scale, larger-scale conversions have not occurred for at least three interrelated reasons. First, it can be difficult for an investor to assemble enough geographically proximate properties to achieve efficiencies of scale with regard to the fixed costs of a rental program.[16]

Second, attracting investors to bulk sales opportunities--whether for rental or resale--has typically required REO holders to offer significantly larger price concessions relative to direct sales to owner occupants through conventional realtor-listing channels, in part because it can be difficult for investors to obtain financing for such sales.

Third, the supervisory policy of GSE and banking organization regulators has generally encouraged sales of REO property as early as practicable. We discuss each of these issues in more detail later.[17]

Characteristics of REO Properties

Fannie Mae, Freddie Mac, and the FHA together hold about half of the outstanding REO inventory and so might be able to aggregate enough properties to facilitate a cost-effective rental program in many rental markets. As of early November 2011, about 60 metropolitan areas each had at least 250 REO properties currently for sale by the GSEs and FHA--a scale that could be large enough to realize efficiency gains." Atlanta has the largest number of REO properties for sale by these institutions with about 5,000 units. The next-largest inventories are in the metropolitan areas of Chicago; Detroit; Phoenix; Riverside, California; and Los Angeles, each of which have between 2,000 and 3,000 units.

Other financial institutions also hold or control substantial inventories of REO properties. More than one-fourth of REO properties are held by non-agency securitized pools, which are controlled by mortgage servicers under the terms of pooling and servicing agreements. Because these properties are more likely to have been financed by subprime and alt-A loans, they are concentrated in somewhat different metropolitan areas than the inventory held by the GSEs and FHA. About 50 metropolitan areas appear to have at least 250 REO properties held by securitized pools, with the largest inventories in Miami; Los Angeles; Riverside, California; Chicago; and Las Vegas.[19] The remaining REO inventory--a bit less than one-fourth--is held by commercial banks and thrifts. Roughly 50 metropolitan areas each have at least 250 properties held by these institutions, and the geographic distribution of these properties is similar to that of the inventory held by the GSEs.[20]

Not all of these REO properties are good candidates for rental properties, even in geographic markets with sufficient scale. As discussed in more detail later, some properties are badly damaged, in low-demand locations, or otherwise low value. Nonetheless, according to Federal Reserve staff calculations, many REO properties appear to be viable rental properties in terms of both physical adequacy and potential attractiveness to tenants. For example, most REO properties are in neighborhoods with median house values and incomes that are roughly similar to the medians for the metropolitan area overall.[21] Similarly, the vast majority of REO properties are in neighborhoods with an average commute time that is similar to the average for the entire metropolitan area, suggesting that the properties are not located unusually far from employment centers.[22]

Many REO properties also appear to be viable rental properties in terms of improving loss recoveries to the REO property holder. One method of gauging the profitability of renting a particular property is to calculate its capitalization rate, or cap rate--the expected annual cash flows from renting the property relative to the price at which the REO property holder could expect to sell it in the owner-occupied market.[23] Preliminary estimates suggest that about two-fifths of Fannie Mae's REO inventory would have a cap rate above 8 percent-- sufficiently high to indicate renting the property might deliver a better loss recovery than selling the property.[24] Estimated cap rates on the FHA's REO inventory are a bit higher-- about half of the current inventory has a cap rate above 8 percent--because FHA properties tend to have somewhat lower values relative to area rents. These cap rate calculations are illustrative examples subject to a number of assumptions, and do not control for the fact that holding on to properties and renting them may entail more risk than selling into the owner-occupied market. In particular, the REO holder receives cash in the event of a sale, but earns a potentially higher but more uncertain return from renting a property.

Finally, the number of properties currently in the foreclosure process is more than four times larger than the number of properties in REO inventory. The geographic distribution of these "pipeline" properties is similar to that of REO properties, although states that are experiencing significant foreclosure delays tend to have larger backlogs.[25] If recent trends continue, the share of REO inventory held by the GSEs and FHA should increase.

REO to Rental Program Design

The data cited earlier suggest that a government-facilitated REO-to-rental program has the potential to help the housing market and improve loss recoveries on REO portfolios. The FHFA released a request for information on August 10, 2011, to collect information from market participants on possible ways to accomplish this objective and received more than 4,000 responses. An interagency group in which the Federal Reserve is participating is considering issues related to the design of a program that would facilitate REO-to-rental conversions. As no such program currently exists, predicting its success or efficacy is difficult. Ongoing experimentation and analysis will be a crucial component of developing such a program.

A government-facilitated REO-to-rental program could take many forms. The REO holder could rent the properties directly, sell the properties to a third-party investor who would rent the properties, or enter into a joint venture with such an investor. In making this decision, policymakers should consider what program design will provide for the best loss recoveries and the best outcomes for communities.

To date, REO holders have avoided selling properties in bulk to third-party investors because the recoveries that REO holders receive on such sales are generally lower than the corresponding recoveries on sales to owner occupants. Investors considering such bulk-sale transactions tend to demand a higher risk premium than owner occupants and thus will purchase only at lower prices. Investors in such transactions also might have more difficulty obtaining debt financing than owner occupants. Although mortgage products are available for individual one- to four-family houses and for multifamily properties (albeit currently at tight terms), no mortgage products currently exist for a portfolio of single-family homes.[26] In addition, REO holders must absorb the costs of assembling inventory for bulk sale--that is, holding properties off the market until enough properties have been assembled to cover the fixed costs of a rental program. Until the inventory is assembled, the REO holder receives no revenue from the property but incurs direct financing costs; carrying costs such as taxes, utilities, and maintenance expenses; and the continued depreciation of the property.

An REO-to-rental program that relies on sales to third-party investors will be more viable if this cost-pricing differential can be narrowed. REO holders will likely get better pricing on these sales if the program is designed to be attractive to a wide variety of investors. Selling to third-party investors via competitive auction processes may also improve the loss recoveries.

Providing investors with debt financing will likely also affect the prices they offer on bulk pools of REO properties. As noted, such financing is largely unavailable now, thus limiting the number of potential investors. In the current tight mortgage lending environment, private lenders may not have the capacity to fund a large-scale rental program, and it may be appropriate for REO holders to fill the gap. However, whether such funding should be subsidized is an important question. Subsidized financing provided by the REO holder may increase the sales price of properties, but at the cost of reducing the REO holder's future income stream. If so, the costs of such financing need to be accounted for in the rental program.

In addition, a program that minimizes the amount of time that a vacant property lingers in REO inventory before being rented would reduce disposition costs to the REO holder. These costs might be reduced by including properties that are already rented, such as properties rented under the provisions of the Protecting Tenants at Foreclosure Act.[27] Another possibility is to auction to investors the rights to acquire, in a given neighborhood, a future stream of properties that meet certain standards instead of auctioning the rights to current REO holdings. A third possibility is to encourage deed-for-lease programs, which circumvent the REO process entirely by combining a deed-in-lieu of foreclosure--whereby the borrower returns the property to the lender--with a rent-back arrangement in which the borrower remains in the home and pays market rent to the lender.

If, after addressing these obstacles, selling to third-party investors still provides lower loss recoveries than selling to owner occupants, policymakers might want to consider the merits of allowing or facilitating the rental of properties by REO holders themselves. Alternatively, policymakers may judge that the broader positive effects on the economy from redirecting properties to the rental market justify a moderate decline in loss recoveries. Finally, even if the cost differential is large at this point, the calculation may change if the foreclosure process accelerates in some states and REO holders experience significant increases in their inventories.

An REO-to-rental program should also consider the effects that poorly managed or maintained properties have on communities and, in particular, ensure that communities are not damaged by rental practices. For example, investors might be allowed to bid on properties only after demonstrating some experience with property management and commitment to rehabilitation of properties. Experienced nonprofit organizations with established ties to the community could also play a natural role as rental managers. In the case of for-profit companies or joint ventures, investors might be given an incentive to provide appropriate property management by deferring some of their compensation. Investors might receive some proportion of their payment only after several years of renting properties in a manner consistent with "good landlord" practices and compliance with pertinent landlord-tenant and fair-housing requirements.

A final consideration is the length of time REO properties are rented before they are placed on the for-sale market. Given the depressed state of the housing market, properties may remain rental properties for an extended period. Rent-to-own provisions, which would give existing tenants the option to purchase their properties during their tenancies, might facilitate the transition of some renters back to the owner-occupied market. Such provisions may also reduce costs by encouraging renters to maintain their properties to a greater extent.

The Role of Banks

The GSEs, of course, do not hold all of the residential REO exposure. As of September 2011, US commercial banks had $10 billion in residential REO properties on their balance sheets, while savings and loans had an additional $1.4 billion.[28] Generally, banking organizations are not permitted to engage in real estate ownership or property management, and supervisory policy typically encourages banking organizations to dispose of REO property as early as practicable. However, current law clearly contemplates some scope for REO ownership to last beyond the fastest-possible disposition. In particular, federal laws dealing with bank holding companies and national banks and state laws dealing with state-chartered banks typically allow banking institutions to hold REO properties for a time (such as up to five years), and often include a possibility of extending the permissible holding period, if approved by the appropriate regulator. During this holding period, banking organizations are permitted to rent the REO properties on their balance sheets, as well as manage the properties directly or through a third-party vendor, and take steps necessary to keep up the properties' condition and value. Regulators generally expect that such rentals would be done with the goal of improving the ultimate recovery to the banking organizations. Regulators also expect that banking organizations engaged in rental of REO properties demonstrate ongoing good faith efforts to sell the properties within the statutory and regulatory time periods and as appropriate under prevailing market conditions.

In light of the current unusually difficult circumstances in many housing markets across the nation, the Federal Reserve is contemplating issuing guidance to banking organizations and examiners to clarify supervisory expectations regarding rental of residential REO properties by such organizations while such circumstances continue (and within relevant federal and statutory and regulatory limits). If finalized and adopted, such guidance would explain how rental of a residential REO property within applicable holding-period time limits could meet the supervisory expectation for ongoing good faith efforts to sell that property. Relatedly, if a successful model is developed for the GSEs to transition REO properties to the rental market, banks may wish to participate in such a program or adopt some of its features.

Land Banks: An Option for Low-Value Properties

Some REO properties are low value and less likely to be viable for an REO-to-rental program. About 5 percent of properties in the REO inventory of the GSEs and FHA are appraised at less than $20,000. In some markets, the share is significantly higher; for example, in Detroit and Cleveland, more than half of the REO inventory of these institutions is appraised below this value. In these markets, low-value properties are less suitable for disposition through sales in the owner-occupied market or through rental market strategies, and alternative disposition strategies may be needed.

Currently, a small number of these properties are disposed of through land banks, which are typically public or nonprofit entities created to manage properties that are not dealt with adequately through the private market. Land banks are government entities that have the ability to purchase and sell real estate, clear titles, and accept donated properties. Properties may be rehabilitated as rental or owner-occupied housing, or demolished, as market conditions dictate.

While the number of land banks has increased significantly over the past few years, capacity nationwide remains quite limited, in terms of both institutional infrastructure and funding. Only a handful of states have passed legislation to establish land banks, and, as a result, many areas lack land banks altogether. Only about half of the GSE and FHA inventory of low-value REO properties (properties with a value of $20,000 or less) is in metropolitan areas with an existing land bank. In addition, the land banks that have been created have only limited resources--the largest land bank can handle about 100 properties per month, but most handle just a few each month. This capacity pales in comparison with the number of low-value REO properties in current inventory. One potential strategy would be to consider increasing funding (at the federal, state, or local level) and technical assistance to land banks in existence, encourage the creation of more land banks on the local or regional level, or create a national land bank program, in order to scale up capacity to match current low-value inventories. Such initiatives would need appropriate controls to promote value to the communities affected and maximize efficiency whenever possible.

Credit Access and Pricing

As noted earlier, mortgage credit conditions have tightened dramatically from their pre-recession levels. Lax mortgage lending standards in the years before the house price peak contributed to problems in the housing market, so some tightening relative to pre-crisis practices was necessary and appropriate. The important question is whether the degree of tightness evident today accurately reflects sustainable lending and appropriate consumer protection.

Financial regulators have been in consultation with the GSEs and originators about the sources of the apparent tightness in lending standards. Continued efforts are needed to find an appropriate balance between prudent lending and appropriate consumer protection, on the one hand, and not unduly restricting mortgage credit, on the other hand. In particular, policymakers should recognize that steps that promote healthier housing and mortgage markets are good for safety and soundness as well.

Addressing Homeowners at Risk of Default or Foreclosure

Obstacles to Refinancing

Many homeowners have been unable to take advantage of historically low mortgage rates because of low or negative home equity, slightly blemished credit, or tighter credit standards. Perhaps only about half of homeowners who could profitably refinance have the equity and creditworthiness needed to qualify for traditional refinancing.

In response to some of these obstacles, the FHFA introduced the Home Affordable Refinance Program (HARP) in 2009. HARP allows qualifying borrowers who are current on their payments, and whose mortgages are owned or guaranteed by Fannie Mae or Freddie Mac, to refinance even if they have insufficient equity to qualify for a traditional refinance.[29] Participation in the program to date has been relatively modest, with only about 925,000 mortgages refinanced through HARP.[30]

The low participation rate has been attributed, in part, to lender worries about GSE putback risks. When a lender refinances a loan originated by a competitor, the new lender in effect takes on some of the original lender's putback risk. Because lenders are reluctant to take on this added risk, they tend to refinance only their own loans and do not aggressively market the program to borrowers.

GSE fees known as loan-level pricing adjustments (LLPAs) are another possible reason for low rates of refinancing. Under normal circumstances, LLPAs are used to provide higher compensation to the GSEs for the risk that they undertake when new loans are extended to borrowers with high loan-to-value (LTV) ratios or low credit scores. In a HARP refinancing, however, the GSEs already carry the credit risk on the original mortgage, and refinancing to a lower rate could even lower the credit risk of some such loans; thus, it is difficult to justify imposing a higher LLPA when refinancing in this circumstance.

To reduce these and other obstacles to refinancing, the FHFA announced changes to HARP in October 2011.[31] LLPAs for HARP loans were eliminated for borrowers shortening the term of their loans to 20 years or less and reduced for longer-term loans, certain representation and warranty requirements were waived, loans with LTVs greater than 125 percent were made eligible for the program, the appraisal process was largely automated, servicers were given greater flexibility to notify borrowers of their eligibility for refinancing through HARP, and private mortgage insurers agreed to facilitate the transfer of mortgage insurance. Some estimates suggest that another million or so homeowners could refinance their mortgages with these changes in effect.

Nonetheless, more might be done--for example, reducing even further or perhaps eliminating remaining LLPAs for HARP refinances (again, on the rationale that the GSEs already carry the credit risk on such loans); more comprehensively reducing putback risk; or further streamlining the refinancing process for borrowers with LTVs below 80 percent, a potentially large group of borrowers who face some (though not all) of the same obstacles confronting high-LTV borrowers. Fannie Mae has reduced putback risk for all loans (including those below 80 percent LTV as well as those above 80 percent LTV), while Freddie Mac has reduced putback risk for loans above 80 percent LTV but not those below 80 percent LTV. Harmonizing traditional refinancing programs for borrowers with LTVs less than 80 percent, so that these programs become operationally consistent with HARP, could facilitate more refinancing among this group of borrowers.

An important group of borrowers who are not able to take advantage of the HARP program is homeowners with high LTVs but whose mortgages are not guaranteed by the GSEs. For the most part, these borrowers are not able to refinance through any public or private program. One possible policy option might be to expand HARP--or introduce a new program--to allow the GSEs to refinance non-GSE, non-FHA loans that would be otherwise HARP eligible. Unlike HARP refinances, however, these refinances would introduce new credit risk to the GSEs because the GSEs do not currently guarantee the loans, even if the loans were offered only to borrowers who are current on their payments and would meet underwriting standards (for example, debt-to-income ratio and credit score), if not for their high loan-to-value ratios. Perhaps 1 million to 2-1/2 million borrowers meet the standards to refinance through HARP except for the fact that their mortgages are not GSE-guaranteed.[32]

To be sure, this change would introduce a host of risk-management issues, and the GSEs would likely require new underwriting and fees for insuring these loans. Moreover, legislative changes to GSE governing statutes would likely be needed because the GSEs are prohibited from purchasing or guaranteeing mortgages with LTV ratios exceeding 80 percent unless the mortgages have credit enhancement such as mortgage insurance. This policy, because it requires a potentially large expansion of the GSE balance sheet, would also have to be balanced against the other policy goals of winding down the GSEs over time and returning private capital to the mortgage market.

The structure of the HARP program highlights the tension between minimizing the GSEs' exposure to potential losses and stabilizing the housing market. Although the GSEs would take on added credit risk from expanding HARP to non-GSE loans, the broader benefits from an expanded program might offset some of these costs. In particular, some homeowners who are unable to refinance because of negative equity, slightly blemished credit, or tighter underwriting standards could reduce their monthly payments significantly, potentially reducing pressures on the housing market. A stronger housing market would in turn likely imply an earlier stabilization of house prices and reduced rates of mortgage delinquency, helping both borrowers and lenders. Neighborhoods would benefit from reduced rates of foreclosure and fewer vacant homes, while localities would experience gains, or less pronounced reductions, in property tax receipts. The reduction in aggregate mortgage payments could also provide some boost to consumer spending, although the net effect would likely be relatively small, in part because the gains to homeowners may be partially offset by corresponding reductions in the incomes of investors in mortgage-backed securities.

However, many GSE and non-GSE mortgages are not eligible for traditional or HARP refinancing because they are already delinquent or have been sufficiently delinquent in the past. These mortgages might be best addressed through loan modification programs--the topic of the next section.

Loan Modifications and the HAMP Program

Loan modifications help homeowners stay in their homes, avoiding the personal and economic costs associated with foreclosures. Modifying an existing mortgage--by extending the term, reducing the interest rate, or reducing principal--can be a mechanism for distributing some of a homeowner's loss (for example, from falling house prices or reduced income) to lenders, guarantors, investors, and, in some cases, taxpayers. Nonetheless, because foreclosures are so costly, some loan modifications can benefit all parties concerned, even if the borrower is making reduced payments.

About 880,000 permanent modifications have been made through the voluntary Home Affordable Modification Program (HAMP), which is part of the Making Home Affordable (MI-1A) program. HAMP pays incentives to lenders, servicers, and borrowers to facilitate modifications. Among its key program terms, HAMP reduces monthly payments for qualifying borrowers to 31 percent of income. For borrowers who have received HAMP modifications, the help is often substantial. For example, the median monthly payment after a permanent HAMP modification is about $831, compared with about $1,423 before the modification.[33] Millions of additional mortgages have been modified by lenders, guarantors, and the FHA.

As is the case with all loan modifications, some mortgages that have been modified under HAMP have ended up defaulting after modification. For example, among HAMP modifications made permanent in the first quarter of 2010, 16 percent of mortgages were more than 90 days late a year after modification, and 22 percent were 90 days late after 18 months.[34] These re-default rates are lower than those for non-HAMP modifications, according to Office of the Comptroller of the Currency (OCC) statistics.[35] Such defaults after modification highlight the difficulty that some homeowners have had in sustaining even substantially reduced mortgage payments over time. In some cases, this difficulty likely owes to the burden from other expenses, such as medical or elder care, or other debt, such as a second mortgage or consumer debt, which may make a 31-percent-of-income first mortgage payment unaffordable.

On the other hand, the 31 percent payment-to-income target has also precluded the participation of borrowers who might benefit from a modification even though their first-lien payment is already less than 31 percent of income. One potential method of expanding the reach of HAMP that may be worth exploring would involve allowing payments to be reduced below 31 percent of income in certain cases.

This exploration might consider incorporating all of a borrower's mortgage payments on a property in the debt-to-income calculation, instead of just the first lien. Alternatively, taking the entirety of a borrower's balance sheet into account or making allowances for other unavoidable borrower expenses might be considered. Expanding the magnitude of potential payment reduction in this way would, though, raise difficult issues of fairness and implementation.

Another issue is the fact that many borrowers have gone delinquent or have defaulted because of income loss resulting from unemployment or other presumably temporary factors, which impairs their ability to meet previously affordable payment obligations. The basic HAMP modifications focus on longer-term payment reduction to a level that can be supported by the borrower's income at the time of modification. This approach is often ill-suited for those who have lost their jobs because the income of unemployed borrowers is generally quite low.

Instead of a longer-term modification, a payment deferral may be more helpful to temporarily unemployed borrowers whose income, it is hoped, will rise in the near future. MHA has introduced an unemployment forbearance program under which servicers grant 12 months' forbearance.

Resources from the Hardest Hit Fund, which was created by the Department of the Treasury (Treasury) under the Troubled Asset Relief Program, have been used to provide assistance to unemployed homeowners through a variety of programs run by state housing finance agencies.

Programs of this type may prove helpful in preventing costly foreclosures among homeowners suffering temporary income reductions. Nonetheless, a significant challenge involves targeting these initiatives to the borrowers most likely to be reemployed. In the current economy, fewer than 60 percent of unemployed workers find reemployment within a year of losing their jobs (figure 7).

Moreover, even after reemployment, a borrower's income from the new job may be lower than in the previous job, and his or her savings may be depleted, reducing the borrower's ability to keep up with mortgage payments. Further work in this area is warranted to better understand the tradeoffs in devising such programs.

Broadly speaking, HAMP emphasizes modifications in which the net present value to the lender of the modification exceeds the net present value of pursuing a foreclosure. It should be recognized that other types of loan modifications may be socially beneficial, even if not in the best interest of the lender, because of the costs that foreclosures place on communities, the housing market, and the broader economy. However, although policymakers might very well decide that the social costs--while obviously difficult to gauge--are great enough to justify additional loan modifications, lenders are unlikely to be willing to make such modifications on their own.

Moving further in this direction is thus likely to involve additional taxpayer funding, the overriding of private contract rights, or both, which raises difficult public policy issues and tradeoffs.

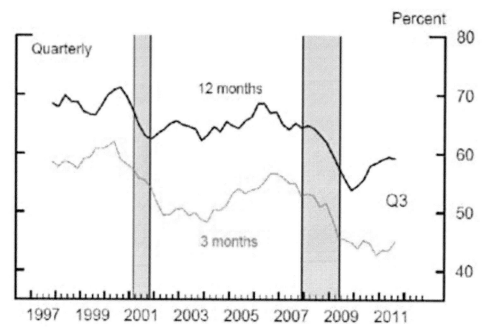

Note: Probability of being employed 3 and 12 months after losing job. Four-quarter moving average of
not seasonally adjusted data. Shaded areas indicate NEER-dated recessions.

Figure 7. Reemployment Probability Among Unemployed Workers.

Loan Modifications with Principal Reduction

Reducing monthly payments to a sustainable level for distressed borrowers who are
significantly underwater on their mortgages may require principal reductions--that is,
reductions in their mortgage balances--in addition to interest rate concessions and term
extensions. Consequently, HAMP allows principal reduction to be used as part of its standard
protocol when interest rate reduction and term extension are not sufficient to reduce a
borrower's debt-to-income ratio to 31 percent. In addition, the HAMP program introduced the
Principal Reduction Alternative (PRA), which allows the servicer to use principal reduction
as the first step in modifying the loan. In both cases, HAMP uses principal reduction
primarily as a means to improve the affordability of a borrower's mortgage, though with the
concomitant benefit of reducing negative equity.[36] The Hardest Hit Fund has also funded
principal reduction programs at the state level.

Negative equity is a problem, above and beyond affordability issues, because it constrains
the ability of borrowers to refinance their mortgages or sell their homes if they do not have
the means or willingness to bring potentially substantial personal funds to the transaction. An
inability to refinance, as discussed previously, blocks underwater borrowers from being able
to take advantage of the large decline in interest rates over the past years. An inability to sell
could force underwater borrowers into default if their mortgage payments become
unsustainable, and may hinder movement to pursue opportunities in other cities.

Principal reduction has been proposed and debated as one possible policy response to
negative equity, including for borrowers current on their mortgage payments. Principal
reduction has the potential to decrease the probability of default (and thus the deadweight

costs of foreclosure) and to improve migration between labor markets. Principal reduction may reduce the incidence of default both by improving a household's financial position, and thus increasing its resilience to economic shocks, and by reducing the incentive to engage in "strategic" default (that is, to default solely based on the household's underwater position rather than on the affordability of the payments).

These potential benefits, however, are hard to quantify. Based on the evidence to date, the effect of negative equity on migration between labor markets appears to be fairly small.[37] The effect of reducing negative equity on default is hard to estimate because borrowers with high LTV ratios tend to have other characteristics correlated with default.[38] For example, high-LTV homeowners often made small initial down payments--perhaps due to a lack of financial resources--and tend to live in areas with greater declines in house prices, where unemployment and other economic conditions also tend to be relatively worse. Hence, principal reduction is likely to lower delinquency rates by less than the simple correlation between LTV and default rates would suggest. Further research or policy experiments in this area would be useful.

At the same time, the costs of large-scale principal reduction would be quite substantial. Currently, 12 million mortgages are underwater, with aggregate negative equity of $700 billion. Of these mortgages, about 8.6 million, representing roughly $425 billion in negative equity, are current on their payments.[39] These costs might be reduced if it was possible to target borrowers who are likely to default without a principal reduction. However, identifying such borrowers among the many who are current on their payments is difficult. Moreover, targeting principal reduction efforts on those most likely to default raises fairness issues to the extent that it discriminates against those who were more conservative in their borrowing for home purchases or those who rent instead of own. Depending on the requirements for relief, such a program may also give some borrowers who otherwise would not have defaulted an incentive to do so.

An alternative to large-scale principal reduction for addressing the barriers that negative equity poses for mortgage refinancing and home sales could involve aggressively facilitating refinancing for underwater borrowers who are current on their loans, expanding loan modifications for borrowers who are struggling with their payments, and providing a streamlined exit from homeownership for borrowers who want to sell their homes, such as an expanded deedin-lieu-of-foreclosure program (described later). This approach focuses on reducing payments rather than reducing principal per se, and could be more effective at keeping committed borrowers in their homes if affordability is the prime consideration driving default.

Alternatives to Foreclosure

Despite the potential for loan modifications and targeted forbearance programs to prevent unnecessary foreclosures, many borrowers will not be able to keep their homes. In these cases, the most efficient solution may be to find an alternative to foreclosure such as a short sale or a deed-in-lieu-of-foreclosure (DIL).

In a short sale, the home is sold to a third-party buyer offering less than the amount owed by the homeowner. In a DIL, there is no sale, but the property is transferred directly to the lender or guarantor, rather than going through the formal foreclosure process. Both options are within the bounds of mortgage contracts and avoid some of the economic damage potentially caused by the foreclosure process. Short sales can be attractive because the property is transferred to a (presumably sustainable) new owner, keeping the property out of REO and reducing potential negative effects on communities from vacant properties. DILs can also be helpful because they can sometimes be easier to execute than a short sale and because they can fit into an REO-to-rental program to prevent a discounted sale that would otherwise occur. Both options may be particularly attractive to borrowers if lenders partially or fully waive borrower liability for deficiency balances. The MHA's Home Affordable Foreclosure Alternatives program provides incentive payments to facilitate both short sales and DILs.

Both short sales and DILs, however, face barriers in current markets. Short sales require a willing buyer, a price that is acceptable to all parties, and a timeline that allows the transaction to close before foreclosure (which is likely proceeding on a parallel path). DILs may not be actively pursued because of informational or logistical obstacles. Further, short sales and DILs often present additional obstacles to lenders, such as the disposition of second liens, the cost and uncertainty of loss recovery via mortgage insurance or deficiency judgments, and (in the case of DILs) accumulating additional REO properties.

For their part, borrowers may not know about DILs or short sales as an alternative to foreclosure and, in some cases, may see little reason to engage in a short sale or DIL rather than stay in their homes throughout the often drawn-out foreclosure process.

Given the scope of the economic losses associated with foreclosure, figuring out ways to surmount these obstacles is crucial.

Mortgage Servicing: Improving Accountability and Aligning Incentives

Mortgage servicers interact directly with borrowers and play an important role in the resolution of delinquent loans. They are the gatekeepers to loan modifications and other foreclosure alternatives and thus play a central role in how transactions are resolved, how losses are ultimately allocated, and whether deadweight losses are incurred.

Thus far in the foreclosure crisis, the mortgage servicing industry has demonstrated that it had not prepared for large numbers of delinquent loans. They lacked the systems and staffing needed to modify loans, engaged in unsound practices, and significantly failed to comply with regulations. One reason is that servicers had developed systems designed to efficiently process large numbers of routine payments from performing loans. Servicers did not build systems, however, that would prove sufficient to handle large numbers of delinquent borrowers, work that requires servicers to conduct labor-intensive, non-routine activities. As these systems became more strained, servicers exhibited severe backlogs and internal control failures, and, in some cases, violated consumers' rights. A 2010 interagency investigation of the foreclosure processes at servicers, collectively accounting for more than two-thirds of the nation's servicing activity, uncovered critical weaknesses at all institutions examined, resulting in unsafe and unsound practices and violations of federal and state laws.[40] Treasury has conducted compliance reviews since the inception of HAMP, and, beginning in June 2011, it released servicer compliance reports on major HAMP servicers. These reports have shown significant failures to comply with the requirements of the MHA program.[41] In several cases, Treasury has withheld MHA incentive payments until better compliance is demonstrated.

These practices have persisted for many reasons, but we focus here on four factors that, if addressed, might contribute to a more functional servicing system in the future. First, data are not readily available for investors, regulators, homeowners, or others to assess a servicer's performance. Second, even despite this limitation, if investors or regulators were able to determine that a servicer is performing poorly, transferring loans to another servicer is difficult. Third, the traditional servicing compensation structure can result in servicers having an incentive to prioritize foreclosures over loan modifications.[42] Fourth, the existing systems for registering liens are not as centralized or as efficient as they could be.

The lack of consistent metrics for assessing the quality of practices across servicers is a significant problem. Helpful metrics might include measures of borrowers' ability to contact representatives through call centers, results from third-party satisfaction surveys, or measures of investors' abilities to get data on loss-mitigation activities. Treasury has taken steps toward addressing this lack of consistent metrics in its monthly MHA reports, which include data on error rates, complaint response quality, and conversion rates (from trial to permanent modifications). These data could help inform the development of appropriate metrics for the industry.

The information provided by the metrics could be even more helpful if combined with lower costs when transferring servicing rights to a competing servicer. In a well-functioning servicing market, lower quality servicers would quickly lose business to competitors who are better able to reduce losses to investors, deliver a high quality of interaction with homeowners, and comply with regulations. However, because servicing systems are not interoperable or designed to easily import or export new records, transferring servicing responsibilities from one servicer to another is expensive, time consuming, and prone to error.

A third potential area for improvement in mortgage servicing is in the structure of compensation. Servicers usually earn income through three sources: "float" income earned on cash held temporarily before being remitted to others, such as borrowers' payments toward taxes and hazard insurance; ancillary fees such as late charges; and an annual servicing fee that is built into homeowners' monthly payments. For prime fixed-rate mortgages, the servicing fee is usually 25 basis points a year; for subprime or adjustable-rate mortgages, the fee is somewhat higher. From an accounting and risk-management perspective, the expected present value of this future income stream is treated as an asset by the servicer and accounted for accordingly.

The value of the servicing fee is important because it is expected to cover a variety of costs that are irregular and widely varying. On a performing loan, costs to servicers are small--especially for large servicers with highly automated systems. For these loans, 25 basis points and other revenue exceed the cost incurred. But for nonperforming loans, the costs associated with collections, advancing principal and interest to investors, loss mitigation, foreclosure, and the maintenance and disposition of REO properties might be substantial and unpredictable and might easily exceed the servicing fee.

The standard servicing compensation model assumes that the revenue streams are more than enough in low-default environments, allowing servicers to cross-subsidize for high-default scenarios. But most servicers do not appear to have invested in enough infrastructure, or reserved sufficient capital, for high-stress conditions. Thus, they were ill equipped to deal with the magnitude of the ongoing foreclosure wave. Also, the fee structure of the servicing industry helped create perverse incentives for servicers to, for example, reduce the costs associated with working out repayments and moving quickly to foreclosure, even when a loan modification might have been in the best interest of the homeowner and investor.

Possible changes to the compensation model might include aligning servicing fees more closely with expenses, such as smaller annual servicing fees for performing loans but higher compensation for servicing delinquent loans, with fees tied directly to expenses incurred and with incentives for loan performance.[43] A small part of the current servicing business, including niche institutions known as "special servicers," already operates under such a payment regime. In addition, servicers' contractual requirement to continue advancing payments of principal and interest to investors, even when a loan is delinquent, strengthens servicers' incentives to move quickly to foreclosure. One possibility might be to advance mortgage principal and interest only 60 days beyond the first missed payment. This change would affect payment streams to investors modestly, and the market could adjust pricing accordingly, but it could also help align the interests of servicers, borrowers, and investors in reaching final resolution of delinquent mortgages.

A final potential area for improvement in mortgage servicing would involve creating an online registry of liens. Among other problems, the current system for lien registration in many jurisdictions is antiquated, largely manual, and not reliably available in cross jurisdictional form. Jurisdictions do not record liens in a consistent manner, and moreover, not all lien holders are required to register their liens. This lack of organization has made it difficult for regulators and policymakers to assess and address the issues raised by junior lien holders when a senior mortgage is being considered for modification. Requiring all holders of loans backed by residential real estate to register with a national lien registry would mitigate this information gap and would allow regulators, policymakers, and market participants to construct a more comprehensive picture of housing debt.

The national lien registry could also record the name of the servicer. Currently, parties with a legitimate interest in contacting the servicer have little to go on from the land records because, among other reasons, many liens have been recorded only in the name of the trustee or of Mortgage Electronic Registration Systems (MERS).[44] Registering the servicer, and updating the information when servicing is transferred, could help local governments and nonprofits, for example, who might be working to resolve the status of vacant or abandoned properties. Implementing a modernized registry could build on systems that have been put in place locally in some jurisdictions and could be designed to retain a role for state and local governments as the default collectors of information, as long as the information is collected in an efficient and consistent manner.[45]

CONCLUSION

The challenges faced by the US housing market today reflect, in part, major changes taking place in housing finance; a persistent excess supply of homes on the market; and losses arising from an often costly and inefficient foreclosure process (and from problems in the current servicing model more generally). The significant tightening in household access to mortgage credit likely reflects not only a correction of the unsound underwriting practices that emerged over the past decade, but also a more substantial shift in lenders' and the GSEs' willingness to bear risk. Indeed, if the currently prevailing standards had been in place during the past few decades, a larger portion of the nation's housing stock probably would have been designed and built for rental, rather than owner occupancy. Thus, the challenge for policymakers is to find ways to help reconcile the existing size and mix of the housing stock and the current environment for housing finance. Fundamentally, such measures involve adapting the existing housing stock to the prevailing tight mortgage lending conditions--for example, devising policies that could help facilitate the conversion of foreclosed properties to rental properties--or supporting a housing finance regime that is less restrictive than today's, while steering clear of the lax standards that emerged during the last decade. Absent any policies to help bridge this gap, the adjustment process will take longer and incur more deadweight losses, pushing house prices lower and thereby prolonging the downward pressure on the wealth of current homeowners and the resultant drag on the economy at large.

In addition, reducing the deadweight losses from foreclosures, which compound the losses that households and creditors already bear and result in further downward pressure on house prices, would provide further support to the housing market as well as provide assistance to struggling homeowners. Policymakers might consider minimizing unnecessary foreclosures through the use of a broad menu of types of loan modifications, thereby allowing a better tailoring of modifications to the needs of individual borrowers; and servicers should have appropriate incentives to pursue alternatives to foreclosure. Policymakers also may want to consider supporting policies that facilitate deeds-in-lieu of foreclosure or short sales in order to reduce the costs associated with foreclosures and minimize the negative effects on communities.

Restoring the health of the housing market is a necessary part of a broader strategy for economic recovery. As this paper suggests, however, there is unfortunately no single solution for the problems the housing market faces. Instead, progress will come only through persistent and careful efforts to address a range of difficult and interdependent issues.

End Notes

[1]. This paper does not address the important issues surrounding whether lenders and servicers have appropriately carried out their roles in foreclosures. In April 2011, the Federal Reserve, along with the other federal banking agencies, announced formal enforcement actions requiring many large banking organizations to address a pattern of misconduct and negligence related to deficient practices in residential mortgage loan servicing and foreclosure processing. These deficiencies represented significant and pervasive compliance failures and unsafe and unsound practices at these institutions. For further information, see Board of Governors of the Federal Reserve System (2011), "Federal Reserve Issues Enforcement Actions Related to Deficient Practices in Residential Mortgage Loan Servicing and Foreclosure Processing," press release, April 13, www.federalreserve.govinewsevents/ press/enforcement/20110413a.htm, and Board of Governors of the Federal Reserve System (2011), "Federal Reserve Board Announces a Formal Enforcement Action against the Goldman Sachs Group, Inc., and Goldman Sachs Bank USA," press release, September 1, www. federalreserve.gov/newsevents/ press/ enforcement/2011090 lb . htm.

[2] See, for example, John Y. Campbell, Stefano S. Giglio, and Parag P Pathak (2011), "Forced Sales and House Prices," American Economic Review, vol. 101 (August), pp. 2108-31, www.aeaweb.org/atypon.php? return_to =/doi/pdfplus/10.1257/aer.101.5.2108; and Dan Immergluck and Geoff G. Smith (2006), "The External Costs of Foreclosure: The Impact of Single Family Mortgage Foreclosures on Property Values," Housing Policy Debate, vol. 17 (1), pp. 57-80 (Washington. Fannie Mae Foundation), http://content.knowledgeplex.org/ kp2/cache/documents/1860/186040.podf

[3]. This paper does not discuss alternatives for longer-term restructuring of the housing finance market, including the future form or role of the GSEs.

[4] Data are from the Federal Reserve Board's Flow of Funds Accounts.

[5] Middle-income households are defined as those in the 40th through 60th percentiles of the household income distribution. High-income households are defined as those with income exceeding the 90th percentile of the household income distribution. In 2007, the 40th percentile was around $40,000; the 60th percentile was around $65,000; and the 90th percentile was around $150,000.

[6] This calculation does not account fully for second liens. The share of underwater borrowers would likely be a bit higher if we had complete coverage of these liens. These estimates are derived from CoreLogic and LPS Applied Analytics data.

[7] For more discussion, see Christopher Mayer, Karen Pence, and Shane M. Sherlund (2009), "The Rise in Mortgage Defaults," Journal of Economic Perspectives, vol. 23 (Winter), pp. 27-50, www.aeaweb.orglatypon.php?return_to=idoi/pdfplus/10.1257/jep.23.1.27.

[8] With regard to appraisals, the Appraisal Foundation's Appraisal Practices Board has recently issued for public comment a draft of guidance that would address the special challenges of performing residential appraisals in declining-value markets, including the method by which appraisers assemble data on market conditions and the extent to which distressed transactions should affect the comparable-sales valuation of a property.

[9]. Results from the Senior Loan Officer Opinion Survey on Bank Lending Practices are available at www.federalreserve.gov/ boarddocs/snloan survey.

[10] Federal Reserve staff calculation based on data from LoanSifter.

[11] When the GSEs purchase mortgages from originators, the contracts specify that the originators make "representations and warranties" with respect to information related to the borrower, property, and so on. In the case of delinquency, if the GSEs believe these representations and warranties were violated (for example, information was false or inadequately verified), they can "put back" the loan to the originator, who is obligated to repurchase the mortgage at par value.

[12] In particular, 17 percent of individuals in this age group acquired a mortgage for the first time between mid-1999 and mid-2001, while only 9 percent did so between mid-2009 and mid-2011. These figures were calculated using data from the FRBNY/Equifax Consumer Credit Panel.

[13] For example, among individuals with credit scores between 620 and 740 and who lived in counties with unemployment rates less than 9 percent in 2010, the share obtaining first-time mortgages was 23 percent from 1999 through 2001 and only 14 percent from 2009 through 2011. In contrast, individuals with credit scores above 740 in the same counties experienced a decline of just 2 percentage points (26 percent to 24 percent). These figures were calculated using data from the FRBNY/Equifax Consumer Credit Panel.

[14] The timing of future REO flows is difficult to forecast because the foreclosure process has slowed considerably in many states since the October 2010 revelations of significant deficiencies in foreclosure processes at many servicers. Foreclosures in states with judicial foreclosure processes have been particularly affected.

[15] See Raven Molloy and Hui Shan (2011), "The Post-Foreclosure Experience of US Households," Finance and Economics Discussion Series 2011-32 (Washington: Board of Governors of the Federal Reserve System, May), www.federalreserve.gov/pubs/feds/ 2011/201132.

[16] Consider the most cost-effective form of rental housing: a large apartment building in which the costs of operating the building are spread over many units. By pooling nearby properties, a rental program can come closer to approximating the efficiencies of a large apartment building.

[17] As discussed later in this paper, under banking laws and regulations, banking organizations generally may not engage in property management as an ongoing business, although they are generally allowed to manage REO properties during the permitted REO holding periods. In contrast, those who make decisions regarding disposition of REO properties in securitized pools may be, or may feel, restrained from renting properties by provisions in the pooling and servicing agreements.

[18] Federal Reserve staff calculations from data on the Department of Housing and Urban Development's Real-Estate Owned Properties Portal, available at www.huduser.org/reo/reo. html. Recently, only around half of the properties in the REO inventories of the GSEs have been offered for sale at any given point. The other properties are leased to existing tenants under the provisions of the Protecting Tenants at Foreclosure Act, are located in states with a redemption period after foreclosure, or are under renovation or otherwise unavailable for sale.

[19] Federal Reserve staff calculation based on data from CoreLogic.

[20] Federal Reserve staff calculation based on data provided by McDash Analytics, LLC, a wholly owned subsidiary of Lender Processing Services, Inc.

[21] About three-fourths of REO properties are in neighborhoods where the median house values and incomes are greater than 80 percent of the medians for the metropolitan area.

[22] Data on median house values, income, and commute times are from the 2000 Census.

[23] For further discussion of cap rates in the real estate context more generally, see Board of Governors of the Federal Reserve System, Division of Banking Supervision and Regulation (2009), "Interagency Policy Statement on Prudent Commercial Real Estate Loan Workouts," Supervision and Regulation Letter, SR 09-07 (October 30), p. 31, www.federal reserve.gov/boarddocs/srletters/2009/sr0907al.pclf.

[24] The return from renting is the annual gross rental income less leasing costs, maintenance expenses, property taxes, management fees, and foregone rent when the property is vacant. This estimate assumes leasing costs are equal to one month's rent, management fees are 8 percent of monthly rent, maintenance expenses are 2 percent of the property's market value, and the property is vacant for one month per year. Data on rents are from Zillow and the 2010 American Community Survey, and data on property taxes are from the 2007-09 American Community Survey. The cap rate estimates are based on Fannie Mae's and the FHA's REO portfolios as of midsummer 2011.

[25] Of course, it is possible that properties will transition from foreclosure to REO at a faster rate in some locations than others, for instance due to state foreclosure laws, so the flow of incoming REO could be distributed somewhat differently than the current stock.

[26] It is unclear whether these mortgages have not existed because of a historical lack of demand (that is, under earlier housing market conditions, investors did not find operating large-scale rental programs of single-family homes attractive) or because lenders perceived such loans as not worth the risk.

[27] The Protecting Tenants at Foreclosure Act of 2009 protects tenants from immediate eviction by persons or entities that become owners of residential property though the foreclosure process. Title VII of the Helping Families Save Their Homes Act of 2009. Public Law 111-22, effective May 20, 2009 (www.gpo.gov/fdsys/pkg/PLAW111pub122/podf/ PLAW-111pub122.pdf).

[28] In aggregate, the serviced-for-others REO portfolios managed by banking organizations are significantly larger than their owned portfolios. These statistics are for the owned portfolios in depository institutions, as disclosed in bank and thrift regulatory reports.

[29] A traditional GSE refinance requires a loan-to-value (LTV) ratio of 80 percent or less unless the mortgage is enhanced with mortgage insurance provided by a third party. Initially, HARP allowed refinances of qualifying loans with LTVs up to 125 percent. To have qualified, loans must have been originated before May 31, 2009, and have been current with certain restrictions on late payments over the preceding year.

[30] Data from the FHFA's quarterly Foreclosure Prevention & Refinance Report. See Federal Housing Finance Agency (2011), "Foreclosure Prevention & Refinance Report: Third Quarter 2011," report (Washington: FHFA, October), www.fhfa.gov/webfiles/22827/ 3Q2011 ForePrevFull Report12611.podf.

[31] Federal Housing Financing Agency (2011), "Fannie Mae and Freddie Mac Announce HARP Changes to Reach More Borrowers," press release, October 24, www.fhfa.gov/webfiles/ 22721/HARPrelease_102411_Final pdf.

[32] Federal Reserve staff calculation based on data from CoreLogic and from McDash Analytics, LLC, a wholly owned subsidiary of Lender Processing Services, Inc.

[33] Data from the October 2011 Making Home Affordable program servicer performance report. See US Department of the Treasury (2011), October 2011 Making Home Affordable Report and Servicer Assessments for Third Quarter 2011, report (Washington: US Department of the Treasury, December), available at www.treasury.gov/initiatives/financial-stability/results/MHA-Reports/Pages/default. aspx.

[34] More recent modifications may have different default experiences due to different economic conditions during the life of the loan.

[35] For example, according to the OCC Mortgage Metrics Report for the third quarter of 2011 (table 32), some 17 percent of HAMP permanent modifications finalized in the second quarter of 2010 at a select group of national banks and thrifts had fallen 60 days delinquent within 12 months of the modification. In contrast, for this same group of financial institutions, some 31 percent of non-HAMP modifications made permanent in the second quarter of 2010 had become 60 or more days delinquent within the same interval. The lower rate of delinquency for HAMP permanent modifications has likely been influenced by differences in documentation standards, magnitudes of payment reduction, and requirements for a trial period. For the OCC report, see US Department of the Treasury, Office of the Comptroller of the Currency (2011), OCC Mortgage Metrics Report, Third Quarter 2011 (Washington: Department of the Treasury, December), www.occ.treas.gov/publications/publications-by-type/otherpublications-reports/mortgage-metrics-2011/mortgage-metrics-q3-2011.polf

[36] Reflecting the preference for capitalization and interest rate reduction that is built into the HAMP "waterfall," 98 percent of HAMP modifications reduced the interest rate and 31 percent reduced principal. Since its inception in October 2010, the PRA program has modified 32,000 loans.

[37] See Raven Molloy, Christopher Smith, and Abigail Wozniak (2011), "Internal Migration in the United States," Journal of Economic Perspectives, vol. 25 (Summer), pp. 173-96, www aeaweb org/article s.php?doi= 10 .1257/j ep. 25 .3 .173 .

[38] See Neil Bhutta, Jane Dokko, and Hui Shan (2010), "The Depth of Negative Equity and Mortgage Default Decisions," Finance and Economics Discussion Series 2010-35 (Washington: Board of Governors of the Federal Reserve System, June), www. federalre serve. gov/pub s/feds/2010/201035/201035pap. pclf.

[39] About 660,000 mortgages are 30 days past due, 310,000 are 60 days past due, 1 million are 90 days or more past due, and 1.4 million are in foreclosure.

[40] See Federal Reserve System, Office of the Comptroller of the Currency, and Office of Thrift Supervision (2011), Interagency Review of Foreclosure Policies and Practices, report (Washington: Board of Governors of the Federal Reserve System, April), www.federal reserve. gov/boarddocs/rptcongress/interagency_ review_ foreclosures_20110413.podf.

[41] The latest quarterly servicer assessment reports (through October) can be found in the Treasury's October 2011 Making Home Affordable Report (see note 33).

[42] See Larry Cordell, Karen Dynan, Andreas Lehnert, Nellie Liang, and Eileen Mauskopf (2008), "The Incentives of Mortgage Servicers: Myths and Realities," Finance and Economics Discussion Series 2008-46 (Washington: Board of Governors of the Federal Reserve System, November), www.federalreserve.gov/pubs/feds/ 2008/200846/revision/ index.html.

[43] The FHFA has proposed and sought comment on alternative servicer compensation structures. See Federal Housing Finance Agency (2011), "Alternative Mortgage Servicing Compensation Discussion Paper," white paper (Washington: FHFA, September), www.fhfa. gov/webfiles/22663/ ServicingCompDiscussionPaper Final092711.podf.

[44] MERS provides services related to tracking and registering residential mortgage ownership and servicing, acts as mortgagee of record on behalf of lenders and servicers, and initiates foreclosure actions. The April 2011 enforcement action included an action against MERS (see note 1).

[45] Although most of the information that would be registered is already in the public record, safeguards would be needed to protect privacy.

In: Melissa O. Murray and Willie T. Cole   ISBN: 978-1-62257-294-6
Editors: Melissa O. Murray and Willie T. Cole   © 2012 Nova Science Publishers, Inc.

Chapter 3

TESTIMONY OF MARK ZANDI, CHIEF ECONOMIST AND CO-FOUNDER OF MOODY'S ANALYTICS. HEARING ON "STATE OF THE HOUSING MARKET: REMOVING BARRIERS TO ECONOMIC RECOVERY"[*]

The six-year-old housing crash continues to threaten the US economic recovery. Home sales and housing construction remain weak, while house prices are still falling in many parts of the country. Millions of homeowners have lost their homes, and millions more are likely to follow them, given the unprecedented number of foreclosures.[1]

It is hard to be enthusiastic about the US economy's prospects as long as house prices are declining. A house is typically a family's most important asset. Many small-business owners also use their homes as collateral for business loans, and local governments rely on property tax revenues, which are tied to housing values, to fund schools and other important public services.

Most worrisome is the risk that housing will fall back into the vicious cycle that occurred at the depths of the last recession.

As prices fell, homeowners found they owed more than their homes could sell for; this led to more defaults, more distress sales, and still-lower prices. That cycle was broken only through unprecedented monetary and fiscal policy support.

The gloom in the housing and mortgage markets notwithstanding, there are reasons to be optimistic that housing's long slide will end soon. While a mountain of distressed property remains to be sold, investor demand appears strong. Prices have fallen enough to allow investors to profitably rent these homes until the market recovers. Rental vacancy rates have fallen meaningfully over the past two years, suggesting that new construction is slow enough to let builders work down the still-considerable number of vacant homes.

Nonetheless, risks remain uncomfortably high. Policymakers should thus consider taking additional modest steps to support housing temporarily. These should include facilitating more mortgage refinancing, supporting increased mortgage loan modifications, and aggressively pursuing efforts to convert distressed properties to rental use before they are sold and further depress prices.

---

[*] This is an edited, reformatted and augmented version of testimony presented February 9, 2011 before the Senate Committee on Banking, Housing & Urban Affairs.

These steps are consistent with the Obama administration's recent housing initiative and various policy steps proposed by the Federal Reserve in a recent white paper. Many of the proposals come at no cost to taxpayers; others have costs that are already accounted for in the budget.

While many of these policy steps will not be politically popular, the outcome may be much worse if policymakers stand by while a weak housing market continues to undermine the economy.

SIX LEAN YEARS

The housing crash is six years old and counting. Sales of existing homes—a gauge of demand—languish near an annual rate of 4.5 million, of which about a third are foreclosures and short sales.

Sales of new homes are even bleaker, running at a record low rate close to 300,000 units per year. In a well-functioning housing market, about a million more new and existing homes would change hands per year, and fewer than a tenth would be distress sales.[2]

Housing construction—the marker for supply—is also depressed. Single- and multifamily housing starts run close to 650,000 units annualized, and manufactured home placements barely reach 50,000 per year (see Chart 1). This is nearly the weakest pace for residential construction since World War II. A well-functioning housing market would produce closer to 1.75 million units annually.[3]

Chart 1. An Epic Housing Crash.

Nationwide, house prices remain fragile. The Fiserv Case-Shiller national house price index has dropped by a third since peaking in the first quarter of 2006, and prices are still falling in many parts of the country as a result of the pressure created by the large number of distressed property sales. In a well-functioning market, prices should rise around 3% per year.[4]

ECONOMIC FALLOUT

Although housing is no longer the drag it was during the worst of the Great Recession, it remains a significant weight on economic growth. This is particularly disappointing since housing is often a major source of growth early in an economic recovery (see Chart 2).

Falling house prices and the resulting hit to household wealth remain serious problems. Some $7.4 trillion in homeowners' equity was lost in the housing crash, with close to $500 billion of that occurring in 2011. Given the impact on consumer spending from lost housing wealth, this shaved about 0.2 percentage point from real GDP growth last year.[5]

The loss was particularly hard on middle-income households, who benefited less from rising stock prices than did their higher-income neighbors.

Shaky house prices also make it difficult for small-business owners to use their homes as collateral. Bank lending to small businesses picked up over the past year, but it is hard to see how credit will flow freely until house prices rise again. Since small businesses are a key part of job creation, this is a significant impediment to a stronger job market.

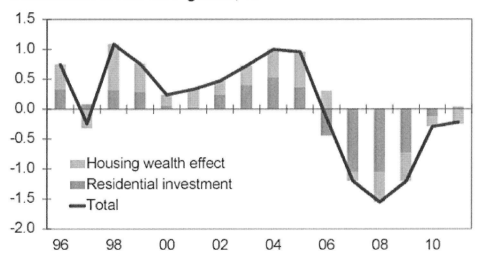

Source: Moody's Analytics.

Chart 2. Housing Weighs on the Economy.

Strapped local governments are also struggling with the impact of falling house prices on property tax revenues. Despite rising millage rates in many parts of the country, tax revenue is growing at nearly its slowest pace on record. Given the lag between market price changes and tax assessments, revenues are likely to slow even more in the coming year. Local governments will thus have little choice but to continue cutting budgets and laying off workers. Local government payrolls are off by more than 500,000 from their peak and shrinking by about 10,000 jobs per month.

Other effects of falling house prices are serious but harder to quantify, such as a reduction in labor mobility—an important way for the economy to adjust to shocks—and the erosion of retirement savings for low- and middle-income homeowners.

While the worst of the crash appears to be over, housing continues to grapple with big problems, including a glut of vacant homes and a mountain of properties in or approaching foreclosure. With so many home loans deeply under water, risks remain uncomfortably high that the vicious cycle of foreclosures and price declines that ravaged the economy during the Great Recession will be reignited. Aside from the European sovereign debt crisis, there is arguably no more serious threat to the current economic recovery than the troubled housing market.

EXCESS INVENTORY

The rampant overbuilding that occurred during the bubble years remains a significant impediment to a housing rebound. While builders have slashed construction and have made progress working down inventory, the market still struggles with excess vacant homes; we estimate just over 900,000 are either for sale, for rent, or being held off the market (see Chart 3). This is the difference between the 9.4 million vacant homes measured by the Census Bureau's Housing Vacancy Survey and the number of vacancies—around 8.5 million—that would be consistent with a well-functioning housing market. At current levels of supply and demand for new houses, it would take until mid-2013 to work off this excess inventory.

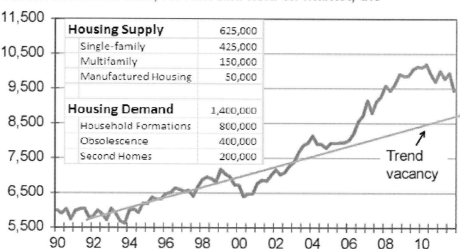

Vacant homes for sale, for rent and held off market, ths

Housing Supply	625,000
Single-family	425,000
Multifamily	150,000
Manufactured Housing	50,000
Housing Demand	1,400,000
Household Formations	800,000
Obsolescence	400,000
Second Homes	200,000

Sources: Census, Moody's Analytics.

Chart 3. Glut of Vacant Homes.

There is some evidence that the situation may not be quite as bad as these numbers suggest. It is unclear how well many vacant properties are being maintained, especially in heavily overbuilt markets such as Florida and California's Central Valley. Such houses may be unusable without significant renovation. Moreover, the excess-inventory problem is regionally concentrated. Atlanta, Florida, Nevada, Arizona, and the Central Valley are awash in vacancies; elsewhere the inventory problem is much less pronounced and will thus be resolved sooner.[6]

Demand and supply will not improve simultaneously, moreover. It is likely that demand for vacant homes will pick up more quickly than will new construction. The principal component of demand is household formation, which has been depressed recently because of the weak job market. With fewer job opportunities, young people have been staying in school; labor force participation has plunged among those between 16 and 29 years old. While the data here are sketchy, it appears that at its low point, household formation slowed to an annualized pace close to 300,000 in early 2010. It has picked up over the past year to closer to 750,000 per year; this has fueled a surge in rental absorption but is still well below the 1.25 million households expected to be formed each year in a well-functioning economy.

As the job market comes back to life and young people return go to work, household formation should accelerate. Many young people have stayed in their parents' homes longer than in normal times, suppressing household formation; this should be reversed in the next year or two. Formations in 2013 and 2014 could be well over the 1.25 million expected in a typical year.

Still, it will take a number of years for housing construction to really get going. Even as demand revives and the inventory of vacant homes is worked down, it will take time for builders to obtain construction and land development loans from banks, many of which are still processing the poor loans they made during the bubble. It also will take time for builders to ramp up new-home construction, a process that includes acquiring land, obtaining permits, and getting equipment on site. Multifamily construction will come back first—it already is reviving thanks to stronger absorption, falling vacancy rates, improving rents, and more ample credit—but even under the best of circumstances, single-family home construction will not be back to full strength until the middle of the decade.

FORECLOSURE CRISIS

A more serious threat is the huge number of first mortgage loans stuck in foreclosure or more than 90 days delinquent and thus headed for eventual foreclosure.

At the end of 2011, 3.6 million loans (out of 49.9 million loans outstanding) were in this predicament (see Chart 4).

Most will end up in foreclosure, short sale or distress sale over the next 12 to 24 months, pushing house prices lower.

The key to house prices in the current environment is the change in the share of home sales that involve distressed properties. Prices fall when the share rises, stabilize when the distressed share peaks, and rise when the share declines (see Chart 5).

It is important to note that house prices will rise if the share of distress sales declines, even if the share remains elevated, as it will for a number of years given the large number of troubled properties. The share of distress sales is likely to rise and house prices to fall further after the nation's largest mortgage servicers and state attorneys general resolve legal issues arising from the robo-signing scandal and other foreclosure process issues.

These issues have significantly slowed the pace of foreclosures and distress sales over the past year or so. Little progress has thus been made in reducing the number of troubled loans. Once the pending lawsuit is settled, which should be soon, the foreclosure process is likely to gear up again, resulting in more distress sales and more house price declines.

First mortgage loans, ths

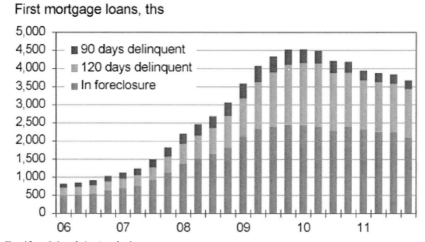

Sources: Equifax, Moody's Analytics.

Chart 4. A Mountain of Distressed Property.

NSA

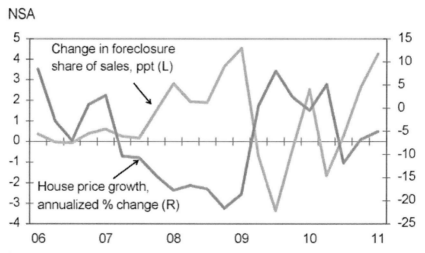

Sources: Fiserv, Zillow, Moody's Analytics.

Chart 5. Higher Distress Share...Lower House Prices.

House prices are expected to fall only modestly, no more than 5% from current levels. Sturdy investor demand for distressed properties will limit the declines, particularly in the hardest-hit markets. Prices have already fallen so sharply in Atlanta, much of Florida, Nevada, and Arizona that investors can purchase distressed properties and profitably rent them out. Many of these markets actually appear undervalued when current prices are compared with household incomes and effective rents. Unlike the house flippers who sought quick profits during the bubble, today's distressed-property investors seem willing to hold on. They include both individuals and institutions with investment horizons of more than a few years.

Prices for nondistressed homes are also holding up better than they did earlier in the foreclosure crisis, according to CoreLogic and FNC. Many distressed properties may be in less desirable areas and no longer in direct competition with nondistressed properties. This suggests that damage to homeowners' wealth will be less severe, with less economic fallout.

The flow of mortgage loans entering foreclosure should also begin to slow soon, since fewer troubled loans are in early stages of delinquency. The number of first mortgage loans between 30 and 90 days delinquent is falling quickly (see Chart 6).

This reflects a better job market and improvements in underwriting standards since the recession. Mortgage loans originated during the past three years are of excellent quality.

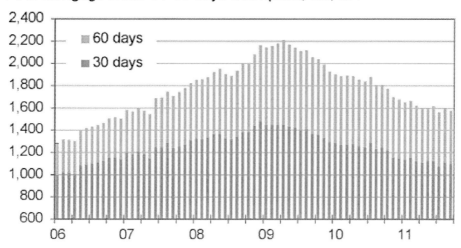

First mortgage loans 30-90 days delinquent, ths, SA

Sources: Equifax, Moody's Analytics

Chart 6. Early-Stage Mortgage Delinquency Is Falling Fast.

VICIOUS CYCLE

Notwithstanding our optimism that future house price declines will be modest, risks are too high that they will be more severe than anticipated. With so many underwater homeowners, it would not take much to reignite the vicious cycle that roiled the housing market and economy during the Great Recession: Falling prices pushed more homeowners under water, prompting more mortgage defaults and more distress sales and thus more price declines.

With an estimated 14.6 million homeowners under water, half by more than 30%, this is a real possibility (see Chart 7).[7] Adding to the concern, the average underwater homeowner's debt exceeds the market value of her home by nearly $50,000. It would not take much to induce many in this situation to mail their keys back to lenders; a leaky roof or broken air conditioner might be sufficient, particularly if rental housing is available nearby for less than the cost of the mortgage. Studies based on credit file data suggest the share of strategic defaults—involving homeowners who are current on other debt obligations—has risen and now accounts for approximately one-fourth of all defaults.

Decisions to default depend critically on expectations about future house prices. If homeowners think prices will rise, they are more likely to hold on; if they believe more price declines are coming, they are more likely to give up. This can quickly become a vicious cycle, as occurred during the depths of the recession.

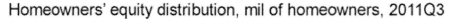

Homeowners' equity distribution, mil of homeowners, 2011Q3

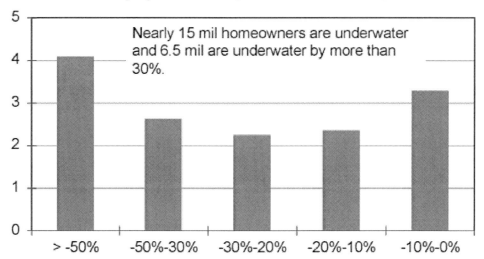

Sources: Equifax, Moody's Analytics.

Chart 7. Millions of Homeowners Sink Underwater.

Only a massive policy effort broke that vicious cycle. The federal government put Fannie Mae and Freddie Mac into conservatorship and the FHA aggressively expanded its lending. Today the federal government originates more than 90% of all new mortgages. In addition, conforming loan limits were increased and three rounds of housing tax credits were enacted as part of the federal fiscal stimulus. The Federal Reserve purchased $1.25 trillion in mortgage securities to bring mortgage rates down as part of its quantitative easing initiative. The government also took part in the mortgage-loan modification effort via the Home Affordable Mortgage Program and encouraged mortgage refinancing via the Home Affordable Refinancing Program.

Although various elements of this policy response may warrant criticism, it is important to remember that the effort was devised and implemented quickly, under extreme circumstances.

Moreover, in its totality, the policy response worked; the housing market stabilized beginning in 2009. Yet if housing were to begin another dark cycle, the policy response would not be nearly as aggressive.

There is little political appetite for another big-government intervention in the economy, particularly given Washington's precarious fiscal situation.

With housing and the economy still facing significant threats, and with policymakers unlikely to respond aggressively in another crisis, it is sensible to consider a number of modest additional steps now to make sure housing does not backtrack.

These should include facilitating more mortgage refinancing, supporting increased mortgage loan modifications, and aggressively pursuing efforts to convert more distressed properties to rental use before they are sold and further depress house prices.[8]

MORE MORTGAGE REFINANCING

Policymakers should move to substantially increase the amount of mortgage refinancing.[9] This is a particularly propitious time for homeowners to refinance, as mortgage rates have fallen to record lows. The 30-year fixed mortgage rate for prime borrowers is well below 4%, and likely to remain very low for some time given the Federal Reserve's stated resolve to keep interest rates low for the next several years.

Monetary authorities are also keeping open the possibility of more quantitative easing that would likely include purchasing more mortgage-backed securities.

Given record low borrowing costs, refinancing has been disappointingly slow. In 2003, when fixed mortgage rates were between 5.5% and 6%, home loans were being refinanced at an annualized rate above $4 trillion. The current level of activity is about one-fourth of that (see Chart 8). The 2003 boom was fueled by the large number of mortgages that had been originated when rates were much higher, making a sub-6% rate very attractive. Yet even today, some two-thirds of all outstanding mortgages carry coupons above 5%. Millions more US homeowners should be refinancing, significantly cutting their monthly payments.

This would be a boost both for individual household finances and for the ailing economic recovery.

The Obama administration has worked since the introduction of HARP in mid-2009 to encourage homeowners with little or negative equity, and whose loans are insured or owned by Fannie Mae and Freddie Mac, to refinance. Originally, the administration said HARP would allow between 4 million and 5 million homeowners to reduce their interest rates to market levels. But so far, only about 1 million homeowners have refinanced using HARP, and fewer than 100,000 underwater homeowners have refinanced.

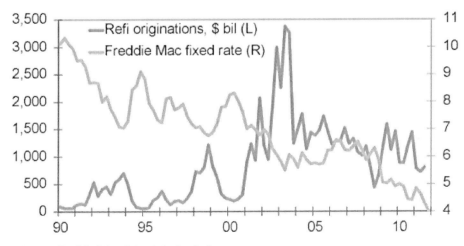

Sources: MBA, Freddie Mac, Moody's Analytics.

Chart 8. Rates Plunge, Refis Putter.

The disappointing results prompted the administration to unveil a number of important changes to the HARP program late last year. These included relaxed eligibility requirements, allowing borrowers with loan-to-value ratios (LTV) of above 80% to participate, streamlining the appraisal and underwriting process, getting most mortgage insurers to drop their recession rights, and requiring Fannie and Freddie to relax their reps and warranties. It has taken a few months for mortgage servicers and insurers to implement the new HARP rules, but the benefits of the new rules should become evident in coming months.[10] Servicers appear to be particularly enthusiastic about the possibility of reducing their put-back risk.[11]

As recently as early February, the administration proposed even more aggressive steps to support refinancing, affecting all mortgage loans including those insured by Fannie, Freddie, the FHA, and nongovernment lenders.[12] If implemented quickly, this proposal should boost refinancing, speeding the recovery in housing and beyond.

For Fannie and Freddie loans, the Obama administration proposes that the new HARP rules apply to all loans, not just those with LTVs over 80% as is now the case. For FHA/VA loans, the administration is proposing that the FHA drop refinanced loans from the "Compare Ratio" process by which the performance of lenders is assessed (analogous to Fannie and Freddie's reps and warranties). For nongovernment loans, the administration is proposing that the FHA refinance the mortgage. The administration is also proposing that taxpayers pay closing costs when homeowners agree to loans of 20 years or less, with monthly payments equal to those on their current loan. This would allow homeowners to build equity more quickly.

The administration's proposal substantially increases the pool of homeowners eligible to refinance and helps remove impediments to more refinancing. Significantly reducing the put-back risk faced by lenders on refinanced loans will encourage lenders to aggressively compete for refinancing business. Lowering borrowers' closing costs increases the incentive for them to participate as well.

Fully implemented, the administration's proposals would increase the number of homeowners eligible to refinance to nearly 28 million, covering more than half of all loans outstanding.[13] The plan would affect all mortgage loans on owner-occupied single-family homes for which the current mortgage rate is above 5%, and that have been current over the past six months. To qualify, borrowers would have to be no more than one month past due in the prior 12 months, be within the conforming loan limits, and have a credit score of more than 580 (see Chart 9).

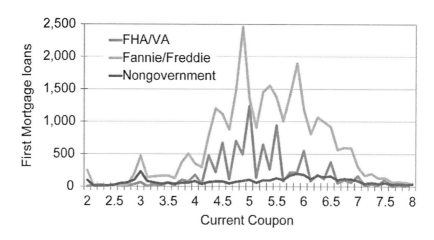

Sources: McDash, LPS.

Chart 9. Mortgage Loans Eligible for Refinancing.

There would be no restriction on when the loans were originated, unlike the current HARP, which is limited to loans originated before mid-2009.

For all this, many homeowners would still not refinance. Yet under reasonable assumptions—including mortgage rates remaining near their current 4%—we estimate that the administration's proposal would result in 6.8 million more refinancings by the end of 2013.[14] That number includes 3 million Fannie/Freddie borrowers, 2.5 million FHA/VA borrowers, and 1.3 million nongovernment borrowers.

There should be no cost to taxpayers for the additional Fannie, Freddie, and FHA/VA refinancings. As the FHA refinances loans of nongovernment borrowers it will take on added credit risk, the cost of which would be borne by the financial industry under the administration's plan. Since the industry will likely oppose this, jeopardizing the overall effort, Congress could instead use some of the remaining $20 billion in TARP money set aside to pay for policies targeted at addressing the housing crisis.

For the administration's efforts to be effective, the FHFA—Fannie and Freddie's regulator—will need to support the plan, and the FHA refinance plan for nongovernment borrowers will require legislation. The FHFA has been reluctant to engage in such efforts, ostensibly because it fears they will require more taxpayer support for the agencies.[15] This argument seems increasingly specious. While the agencies would lose some interest income on their $1.2 trillion in mortgage securities and whole mortgage loans, under reasonable assumptions the cost would be offset by lower default rates on loans that are refinanced. Borrowers are more likely to stay current if their monthly payments drop by $100 or $200. Indeed, under reasonable assumptions, Fannie and Freddie would break even if the probability of default on the loans and securities they own and insure falls by about 25 basis points.[16]

The benefit to borrowers is meaningful. Assuming the average homeowner can refinance into a 4% fixed-rate loan, the gross saving from lower mortgage payments would come close to $18 billion a year (6.8 million borrowers x $140,000 average mortgage balance x 1.8% average rate reduction). This would provide a quick cash boost for mostly middle-income homeowners. Some would be used to repay other debt, but the bulk would likely be spent on home improvements or other needs. Assuming about three-fourths of the extra cash is spent during the year, real GDP will see a small but meaningful boost, adding 0.1 percentage point to growth this year.[17] The fragile US recovery can clearly use all the help it can get.

More refinancing would also further the Federal Reserve's short-term goals. Monetary policymakers are considering a new round of quantitative easing—a process in which the Fed purchases long-term securities in an effort to bring down interest rates, including fixed mortgage rates. Indeed, the recent decline in mortgage rates is due in part to expectations that the Fed will resume quantitative easing. If it does, arguably the most significant benefit would involve increasing the pace of home-loan refinancing. Anything fiscal policymakers can do to support the Fed's efforts would be a plus.

While homeowners would clearly benefit from more refinancing and taxpayers would be largely unaffected, global investors in agency mortgage-backed securities would be hurt financially. As more loans are refinanced, higher-yielding MBS would be retired and replaced with lower-yielding MBS. To be precise, if a more effective HARP resulted in 6.8 million more refinancings, private investors would receive approximately $11 billion less in annual interest income.[18]

MBS investments are held by a wide array of institutions. Through its credit easing efforts last year, the Fed quickly became the largest owner of agency MBS, amassing $1.25 trillion or about a fourth of the total outstanding. The nation's central bank can easily absorb the lost interest income from increased prepayments, but this may put pressure on the Fed to be more aggressive in its quantitative easing efforts to forestall a counterproductive rise in mortgage rates. The interest rate spread between MBS and Treasury yields will increase regardless, but MBS yields need not rise if the Fed buys a sufficient amount of Treasury bonds.

While other private MBS investors will not be happy to get their money back when interest rates are low, they were aware of this prepayment risk when they purchased their securities. Indeed, investors are likely surprised that their securities have not been retired already, as they would have been in a more normally functioning mortgage market. The updated HARP can thus be seen as a way to correct a serious market failure. It is also important to note that MBS investors have been significant beneficiaries of the monetary and fiscal policy response to the financial panic and Great Recession. The Fed's massive purchases of agency MBS during a previous round of quantitative easing was a windfall. Myriad federal housing and foreclosure policies aiming to stem foreclosures have also significantly benefited investors through reduced prepayments.

Policymakers may be nervous that overseas investors, who constitute a sizable and growing source of capital for the US Treasury, will be annoyed by faster prepayments. Policymakers may also worry about implications for the financial health of the nation's depository institutions and pension funds, who also are big investors in agency MBS. While not unreasonable, these seem marginal concerns given the magnitude of the losses that will be widely distributed among investors.

Another potentially unwelcome side effect of boosting refinancing activity today could be less labor mobility in the future. Borrowers who lock in record low mortgage rates today will be less willing to move when rates start to climb. Given that homeowners tend to be more skilled than renters, this impediment to labor mobility could aggravate the US economy's current skills mismatch. However, it is difficult to know the scale of this consideration; it seems small against the sizable near-term benefits of a refinancing program. It is also worth noting that homeowners who switch from adjustable-rate to fixed-rate mortgages will be protected when interest rates ultimately rise.

PRINCIPAL REDUCTION MODIFICATIONS

A more dramatic and costly policy step, but one with the best odds of ending the housing crash more quickly and definitively, would be to encourage more mortgage modifications, particularly those involving substantial principal write-downs. Principal reduction has economic positives and negatives, but is a positive on net if it is well-designed. The main concerns are moral hazard and fairness. To deal with these, modifications must be well-targeted, with clearly articulated eligibility requirements. A long vesting period and some type of clawback provision for future capital gains to guard against potential fraud would also be helpful.

HAMP was reworked in late 2010 to promote principal reduction modifications, but the change has accomplished little so far. To date, there have been fewer than 1 million permanent HAMP modifications, and very few of these have involved principal reduction. When HAMP was unveiled in mid-2009, President Obama was hoping for between 2 million and 3 million HAMP modifications.[19] (see Chart 10)

Responding to this shortfall, the Obama administration proposes more changes to HAMP to increase eligibility and extend the program through 2013. More importantly, the new program will significantly increase incentives for mortgage servicers who modify mortgages by reducing principal. For every dollar that a servicer writes down a loan, the Treasury will pay the servicer up to 63 cents. The president proposes paying for this out of the remaining $20 billion in TARP money slated for housing.

This expansion of HAMP could be particularly effective given the impending settlement between state attorneys generals and mortgage servicers over robo-signing and other foreclosure process issues. This deal is reported to include a monetary settlement of up to $25 billion, a significant share of which will be allocated to modifications, including principal reduction, of loans on the servicers' balance sheets.

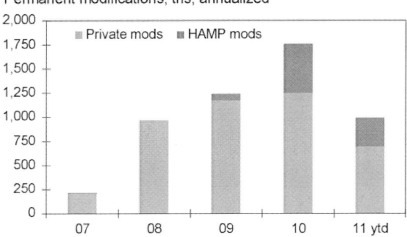

Sources: Hope Now, Moody's Analytics.

Chart 10. Modification Efforts Flag.

For scale, suppose a total of $20 billion is allocated to principal reduction modifications, including those done via the new HAMP and the mortgage settlement. If the average amount of principal reduction per homeowner is $30,000, more than 650,000 homeowners would benefit. This is approximately equal to the number who currently satisfy the following eligibility requirements:

- Homes are owner-occupied.
- Homes were bought before December 31, 2008.
- The homeowner took no cash out in past refinancings.
- First mortgages are below conforming loan limits.
- Loan principal is reduced by no more than $40,000.

Moreover, the modification would have to result in the following conditions:

- The loan could be no more than 10% above the home's market value (to limit the probability of redefault).
- The "front-end" debt-to-income ratio (counting only housing costs) could not exceed 31%, and the "back-end" DTI ratio (counting all obligations) could not exceed 50%.

Assuming a redefault rate of 25%, this would result in almost 500,000 sustainable modifications.[20] Along with those that would take place in any event, this is about the number needed to forestall anticipated house price declines. Without such a plan, the share of distress sales is expected to rise from more than a third to just under 40% by late 2012 (see Chart 11). House prices will decline as the share of distress sales rises. But if a modification program is implemented soon, the share of distress sales will level off and house prices will stabilize.

Share of home sales

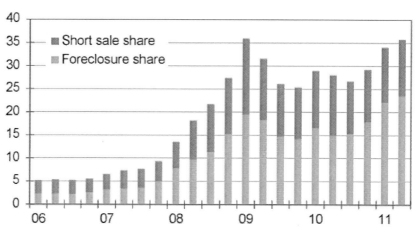

Sources: Zillow, Realtors, Moody's Analytics.

Chart 11. Distressed Share of Sales Are High and Rising.

REO TO RENTAL

Policymakers are also rightly focused on converting more distressed property to rentals. Reducing the number of distressed properties that go up for sale will reduce the share of such sales and thus support house prices. The number of properties classified by banks as "other real estate owned" or REO—the last stage of the foreclosure process before a distress sale— has declined over the past year, but only because the robo-signing scandals have slowed foreclosures (see Chart 12).

Once a settlement is reached between the state AGs and mortgage servicers, foreclosures and thus REO properties and the distressed share of home sales will pick up again. Converting more REO property rentals will mitigate this increase and thus slow further house price declines.

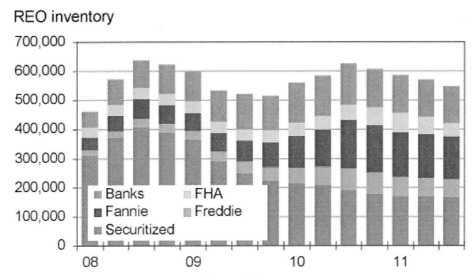

Sources: Fannie, Freddie, FHA, FDIC, Moody's Analytics.

Chart 12. REO Inventory Remains High.

A key to doing this is getting private investors and property managers involved. Investors show healthy interest in buying distressed property for rental, fueled by the fall in house prices alongside a sharp increase in rents.

Given strong rental absorption and very weak construction of rental space, rents are rising at a sturdy mid-single-digit pace and are at levels that can cover investors' costs while they wait for properties to appreciate.

Most investors are not flippers looking for quick profits—given the state of the housing market this would not be a winning strategy—but have investment horizons of three to seven years. Such investors would likely be willing to rent properties purchased from Fannie, Freddie and the FHA for at least several years, selling them after house prices begin to rise again.

It is important to note that many investors are local, living in the neighborhoods where they are buying. Many have also bought with cash, given the dearth of mortgage financing. Institutional investors are also participating, but at least so far have been cautious and selective in their purchases.

The Obama administration recognizes that converting REO properties to rentals is a potentially productive way to help the housing market. Last summer they asked various housing market participants how to design an REO-to-rental program. As part of the president's recent housing initiative, the FHFA announced it would pre-qualify investors to bid on Fannie and Freddie REO-to-rental transactions. Hopefully more initiatives will soon come to fruition.

It is also important for the FHFA to fully embrace this process. Fannie and Freddie have historically not engaged in bulk foreclosure sales to investors or entered into agreements with property managers. To successfully engage in these kinds of activities will require the blessing of the FHFA and significant investment. Even then, Fannie's and Freddie's lack of experience in this area is among the most significant impediments to success.

One way to significantly increase investor interest in purchasing REO properties is to allow buyers to expense their investments for tax purposes up front. This is the same benefit received last year by businesses for investments in equipment and software. Giving investors a small tax break should boost demand, supporting prices for distressed homes and the housing market in general. It would cost taxpayers little, since the tax liabilities of investors will be greater once they have exhausted their depreciation benefits.

CONCLUSION

The housing crash and foreclosure crisis are not over. Home sales and housing construction are stable but depressed, and house prices remain weak. With millions of foreclosures and short sales set to hit the housing market over the next two years, house prices are set to fall further.

While house prices are declining, the recovery will have difficulty gaining traction. For most Americans, the home is still the most important asset, and consumers will be reluctant to spend while their wealth erodes. Many small-business owners use their homes as collateral to grow, and local governments rely on property taxes tied to house prices.

There are some reasons to be optimistic that the crash is winding down. House prices have fallen far enough that single-family housing is affordable and increasingly attractive compared with renting. Investors are putting up cash to purchase distressed properties. Overbuilding remains a problem, but a decreasing one given a record-low pace of new construction and increased household formation.

But this optimism will be easily overwhelmed if house price declines reignite a vicious cycle, putting more homeowners under water, accelerating foreclosures and distress sales and driving prices even lower. Only an unprecedented monetary and fiscal policy response short-circuited that cycle during the recession.

Given the balance of risks, policymakers should thus consider providing additional temporary help to the housing and mortgage markets. Reinvigorating mortgage refinancing would provide a substantial boost with no meaningful cost to taxpayers. More refinancing will mean fewer borrower defaults and more money in the pockets of homeowners, supporting the recovery through a quick and sizable cash infusion.

Facilitating more well-targeted principal reduction loan modifications would be a much larger and costlier step but would bring the housing downturn to a quicker and more definite end. The number of modifications and the amount of principal reduction necessary to stabilize house prices can be reasonably financed with funds from the impending settlement between state attorneys general and mortgage servicers, and the president's proposals to expand HAMP.

Moving more property out of the foreclosure pipeline before it goes to a distress sale would also be a big plus, reducing the pressure on housing values. Given the sharp decline in house prices and the recent increase in effective rents, the returns to private investors participating in such efforts are increasingly attractive.

Each of these policy steps has their problems, but they are worth carefully considering given that the housing downturn remains among the most serious threats to the still-fragile economic recovery.

End Notes

[1] We estimate that nearly 6.5 million homeowners have lost homes through foreclosure, short sale, or deeds in lieu since the housing crash began in 2006. An additional 6 million homeowners are expected to lose homes before foreclosures return to levels consistent with a well-functioning housing market, expected in 2015.

[2] A well-functioning housing market is defined as one consistent with an economy operating at full employment and growing at its potential rate.

[3] The pace of new construction is supported by the annual formation of 1.25 million households, the obsolescence of 300,000 housing units, and the purchase of 200,000 vacation homes.

[4] House prices should increase at a pace between the annual rate of growth in household income (4%) and overall annual price inflation (2%). House prices are ultimately determined by replacement costs, which equal the cost of land plus the cost of construction. The cost of land is determined by its opportunity cost, or GDP per developable acre. The growth in GDP per acre is equal to the growth in household income (assuming that the profit share of GDP remains constant). Construction costs will grow at the rate of overall inflation in the long run, although material and labor costs can fluctuate substantially in the short run. Since the share of land costs in overall house prices varies considerably from place to place (very high in San Francisco, for example, much lower in Des Moines) growth in house prices will vary considerably among regions. For the past quarter century or so (the recent boom and bust aside), house prices have grown at a rate closer to household income. As financial and other incentives for homeownership increased, households spent as much on housing as their incomes would allow. These incentives have likely peaked and may well decline; therefore households will devote less of their income to housing, and prices are likely to increase at rates closer to inflation.

[5] There is a long literature with regard to the wealth effect. For a description of my estimates and how they are incorporated into the Moody's Analytics model of the US economy, see "The Wealth Effect," Mustafa Akcay. Regional Financial Review, November 26, 2008.

[6] The Housing Vacancy Survey may also overstate the problem. Recent data from the 2010 census suggest there are fewer rental vacancies than the survey implies. The Census Bureau's Housing Vacancy Survey is based on a sample that, given the 2010 census data, appears to be biased.

[7] CoreLogic estimates there are closer to 11 million underwater homeowners. The Moody's Analytics data are based on actual mortgage debt outstanding from Equifax credit files, while CoreLogic's estimate is based on debt outstanding at origination. The Moody's estimate of negative equity is nearly the same as CoreLogic's in California, much lower in Florida, and higher most everywhere else. CoreLogic may have some difficulty measuring debt outstanding in rural or exurban areas where homeowners generally have little equity even in good times (since house prices there do not rise much) and go into small negative-equity positions in difficult times. The Moody's estimate is much higher in Texas, for example. CoreLogic data are also unavailable for a half-dozen states.

[8] The Federal Reserve's recent white paper on housing advocates similar steps. See "The US Housing Market: Current Conditions and Policy Considerations," January 4, 2012. http://federalreserve.gov/publications/other-reports/files/housing-white-paper-20120104.pdf

[9] Calls for policymakers to enable mortgage refinancing have steadily increased since late 2010. See "Restringing HARP: The Case For More Refinancing Now," Mark Zandi and Cris DeRitis. Moody's Analytics Special Report, October 7, 2010. http://www.economy. com/mark-zandi/documents/HARP 100710.pdf

[10] See "Improved HARP Will Expand Refinancing and Boost Recovery," Mark Zandi and Cris DeRitis. Moody's Analytics Special Report, October 31, 2011. http://www.economy.com/ markzandi/documents/2011-10-26-Zandi-Improved-HARP-Will-Expand-Refinancing-Boost-Recovery.pdf

[11] Put-back risk is the chance that Fannie and Freddie will require the servicer to take back a loan that was improperly originated. There is also a risk that mortgage insurers will rescind insurance on a poorly underwritten loan. The cost to servicers of having loans put back has been considerable.

[12] A fact sheet describing the president's housing plan can be found at http://www. whitehouse.gov/thepress-office/2012/02/01/fact-sheet-president-obama-s-plan-help-responsible-homeowners-and-heal-h.

[13] This is based on an analysis conducted by LPS using the McDash servicing database and the LPS-AA HPI.

[14] This is a very conservative estimate of the number of homeowners who will refinance, excluding all eligible Fannie/Freddie/FHA/VA borrowers with LTVs of less than 100% and nongovernment borrowers with LTVs of less than 80%. The working assumption is that these borrowers have already had the opportunity to refinance and are thus unlikely to use the new programs.

[15] Taxpayers have already put more than $150 billion into Fannie Mae and Freddie Mac since they were put into conservatorship in September 2008.

[16] The break-even change in the default rate equals the lost interest income divided by the product of the mortgage debt owned and insured and the loss from default, which is assumed to be 50% of the mortgage balance.

[17] This assumes the proposed changes to HARP are implemented by early next year. The assumed spendout rate is consistent with that of the 2001 tax rebate and the refinancing wave early in the last decade. See Johnson, et. al. "Household Expenditure and the Income Tax Rebates of 2001," American Economic Review, vol. 96, no 5. pp. 1589-1610. The spendout would likely be greater given that homeowners will view lower mortgage payments as a more permanent increase in real incomes.

[18] This excludes the interest income that would be lost by Fannie, Freddie, and the Federal Reserve.

[19] There have been nearly 5 million total modifications, including those done under HAMP, by the FHA and in the private sector since the modification effort began in earnest in 2007. HAMP has arguably facilitated more private modifications by requiring private servicers to invest in their own modification efforts. Hope Now provides the most comprehensive accounting of the modification effort. See: http://www.hopenow.com/industry-data/2012-01-13-HOPENOW%20Data%20Report(November) %20DraftV3.pdf

[20] The redefault rate could be even lower given that this is comparable to the redefault rate on HAMP modifications.

In: Melissa O. Murray and Willie T. Cole
Editors: Melissa O. Murray and Willie T. Cole

ISBN: 978-1-62257-294-6
© 2012 Nova Science Publishers, Inc.

Chapter 4

Testimony of Philip L. Swagel, Professor of International Economic Policy, University of Maryland School of Public Policy. Hearing on "State of the Housing Market: Removing Barriers to Economic Recovery"[*]

Chairman Johnson, Ranking Member Shelby, and Members of the Committee, thank you for the opportunity to testify on housing policy and the state of the housing market. I am a professor at the University of Maryland's School of Public Policy and a faculty affiliate of the Center for Financial Policy at the Robert H. Smith School of Business at the University of Maryland. I am also a visiting scholar at the American Enterprise Institute and a senior fellow with the Milken Institute's Center for Financial Markets. I was previously Assistant Secretary for Economic Policy at the Treasury Department from December 2006 to January 2009.

The continued weak state of the housing market and the toll of millions of foreclosures already, millions more families still at risk of losing their home, and trillions of dollars of lost wealth all reflect the lingering impact of the collapse of the housing bubble and ensuing financial crisis. A range of policies have been undertaken over the past several years aimed at the housing market—a recent summary from the Department of Housing and Urban Development lists 10 separate policy actions.[1] These can be grouped into two broad categories. What might be seen as "backward-looking" policies seek to avoid foreclosures on past home purchases through actions such as incentives for mortgage modifications and refinancing. By avoiding foreclosures, these policies both assist individual families and help reduce the supply of homes for sale (and in the overhang of the so-called "shadow inventory") and thus reduce downward pressures on home prices that in turn affect household wealth and the broad economy. In contrast, "forward-looking" policies seek to boost demand for home purchases, such as with the first time homebuyer tax credit and the Federal Reserve's purchases of mortgage-backed securities (MBS).

The common feature of these housing policies is their limited effectiveness. To be sure, these policies have done something: MBS purchases resulted in lower interest rates for

---

[*] This is an edited, reformatted and augmented version of testimony presented February 9, 2011 before the Senate Committee on Banking, Housing & Urban Affairs.

families buying a home or refinancing a mortgage; some 930,000 homeowners have benefited from permanent mortgage modifications through the HAMP program; and so on. But relative to the scale of the weakness in home prices and housing market demand, and especially compared to the tragically huge number of foreclosures, the set of housing market policies to date appears to have underperformed compared to expectation set at each policy unveiling. Moreover, these programs have involved considerable costs for taxpayers, with the benefits accruing mainly to a relatively small group of recipients. And on top of the millions of foreclosures not prevented by the policies of the past several years, there is likely another huge wave of foreclosures set to take place in the next year or two, with many of these representing foreclosures that were delayed but not ultimately prevented by policies to date.

This experience is important to keep in mind as the Congress contemplates a range of new and expanded housing policy proposals from the administration, along with a white paper from the Federal Reserve that covers similar ground. Broadly speaking, the proposed actions look to provide homeowners with reduced monthly payments through government-assisted refinances; to lower principal mortgage balances; and to speed the pace at which vacant homes become rentals. The goal, as with all policies throughout the crisis, is to have fewer foreclosures and stronger consumer spending. These policies are well-intentioned.

Unfortunately, there is every reason to believe that the new policy proposals for streamlined refinancing and principal reduction are likely to have the same modest impact—and at an even worse tradeoff in terms of cost to taxpayers for each foreclosure avoided than for the policies to date. Simply put, we have learned that mortgage modification programs are difficult to implement and execute because of the intrinsically one-at-a-time nature of the transactions involved. And the expansions of some programs, such as considerably increased payments from the government to motivate reductions in mortgage principal, face less promising conditions now for being effective than was the case when many of these policies were launched in early 2009. Three years of a weak job market have forced many of the borrowers who might have been helped by reduced payments or a lower mortgage balance into foreclosure.

There are other approaches that can be taken to help heal the housing market and speed the recovery of home prices and construction while reducing the pain for American families. This testimony first provides a critical analysis of recent policy proposals and then discusses alternative steps that the Congress might consider. The goal of these policies is for the housing sector to once again contribute positively to the US economy and to American society—to have a housing system that works for families looking to buy homes, for investors with funds to lend, and for taxpayers who deserve a stable financial system and protection from another expensive bailout.

MASS REFINANCING PROPOSALS

It is useful to consider a specific example that raises the question of whether the latest policy proposals from the administration will perform differently than previous initiatives. The White House fact sheet for the administration's refinancing proposal for a single family, owner-occupied principal residence promises that there will be "no barriers and no excuses" (top of page 3) and no new appraisal or tax forms involved in enabling eligible homeowners to refinance their mortgages into an FHA-guaranteed loan with lower monthly payments. Without access to tax forms, however, it is not clear how lenders are meant to verify that a home is indeed owner-occupied—the natural mechanism would be to look at the address on the homeowner's 1040 tax form. Indeed, the lender could even just examine the address on the IRS form 4506 by which the borrower requests that a copy of the tax return be sent to the lender; this would be less intrusive than having the lender examine the 1040 itself but is again off-limits in the new proposal. A lesson of the past several years is that unverified mortgage applications (so called "no doc loans") are convenient but do not end well for either lender or borrower.

The alternative of having the lender send someone out to the home also runs counter to the stated policy proposal—there are to be no appraisals, and the need for possibly repeated site visits to confirm the owner-occupied status seems to be exactly the barriers and red tape that are not allowed (not to mention the intrusiveness of having someone peek through the windows to figure out who is living inside).

On the other hand, lenders clearly will not be willing to allow borrowers to simply attest that they are refinancing an owner-occupied property. After all, this was a common misrepresentation during the housing bubble and it would be outrageous for lenders not to check carefully for loans receiving a government-backed guarantee such as with the new refinancing proposal involving the Federal Housing Administration (FHA). Moreover, the administration has launched an investigation into possible abusive behavior in mortgage origination and servicing; presumably this investigation and the similar effort launched in 2009 will deter lenders from allowing potential fraud. But this leaves the problem of how to comply with the contradictions between the proposed policy and the rhetoric by which it has been introduced.

This is just one type of hurdle that implementation of the latest proposal for refinancing of non-GSE loans is likely to face—the desired ease of the refinancing is defeated by the conditions of the proposal itself. Perhaps there is some workaround in the offing for this and the other inevitable problems of implementation that have plagued past efforts, but it is now more than two weeks since the proposals were launched by the President in his State of the Union address and there is no legislative text to consider these important details. Similarly, the Fed's white paper on housing proposals includes a broad discussion of the possible beneficial impacts of widespread refinancing, but does not get into the operational details that are crucial to achieve actual policy outcomes.[2]

The lower monthly payments for homeowners that would result from the proposed FHA-based refinancing scheme for non-GSE loans and the expansion of the previous HARP (Home Affordable Refinance Program) for GSE loans announced in October 2011 are meant to both reduce foreclosures by improving affordability and to boost the economy through increased spending by families with greater free cash flow as a result of lower mortgage payments. That is, refinancing would be a sort of stimulus analogous to sending a monthly check to qualifying households. It is clear that mortgage credit was too easily available in the run-up to the crisis, and a good argument can be made that the pendulum has swing too far in the other direction now so that some credit-worthy borrowers do not have access to mortgages for home purchases or refinancing. An important lesson of the current situation, however, is to highlight the problem of having the government so intricately involved in setting mortgage standards. It would be preferable for private suppliers of capital to fund housing and to take on the risks and rewards of credit decisions. This provides an important motivation for moving forward with housing finance reform. With Fannie Mae and Freddie Mac in government control under conservatorship at present, it is inevitable that public officials will be involved in the choice of credit standards. The driving force for these decisions should be to find the appropriate balance between protection for taxpayers against overly risky loans while maintaining access to credit for homebuyers and rebuilding a responsible private mortgage market—and not to have these decisions motivated by a desire to implement a backdoor fiscal stimulus.

Indeed, stimulus is likely the best way to view the impact of the two mass refinancing proposals involving HARP 2.0 for GSE-backed mortgages and the FHA for non-GSE loans. Both refinancing proposals would benefit borrowers with high loan-to-value (LTV) mortgages, including underwater borrowers whose mortgage balances are greater than the value of their home and who thus have an incentive to walk away from their home and allow a foreclosure. The current proposals, however, are restricted to borrowers who have been in their homes since at least mid-2009 and have been nearly current on their payments for a year (six months with no late payments and no more than one 30-day late payment in the preceding six months). In other words, the refinancing assistance would go to borrowers who have shown that they want to stay in their home and have done so for several years in the face of declining home prices and a weak job market. To be sure, these borrowers will benefit from the lower mortgage payments. But the targeted population for the refinancing has already shown that they are resistant to foreclosure, meaning that the program will avoid relatively few incremental foreclosures per dollar of taxpayer expense. This leaves stimulus as the main motivator for mass refinancing.

As noted in the Fed's white paper and in recent analysis provided by the FHFA in a letter to Representative Elijah Cummings, both refinancing proposals involve costs to taxpayers because the US government is a beneficial owner of mortgages through MBS holdings of both the Federal Reserve and the GSEs. This is not to say that US government asset holdings should come before homeowners—not by any means. The point is that the costs of the refinancing proposal must be weighed against the benefits, keeping in mind that the principal benefit is through a relatively targeted fiscal stimulus going to particular homeowners (and not to renters, who tend to have lower incomes than homeowners). One could imagine policymakers calling for another round of taxpayer-funded fiscal stimulus such as through providing checks or other tax benefits, but this should be debated openly. It is hard to imagine that a new stimulus would involve the relatively narrow targeting of the population of homeowners with high LTV's who bought homes at a particular time period and who have been able to afford their monthly payments.

In a time of tight fiscal constraints, one could also imagine seeking to focus costly government programs on homeowners who could be seen as most in need of assistance and for whom refinancing programs might be most effective. The refinancing proposals are limited by the amount of the mortgage but one could further restrict this government assistance to people with desired income ranges. The White House has recently defined the middle class as households with the median income plus or minus 50 percent.[3] With median household income around $52,000, this would imply limiting the refinancing program to households with incomes of no more than around $78,000–the top of the White House definition of middle class. Alternately, one could use the approximately $64,000 median income of family households (that is, leaving out individuals, who tend to have lower incomes). This would give a maximum income for the middle class as defined by the White

House as $96,000—rounding up would then give $100,000 as the maximum income limit for eligibility for the administration's FHA refinancing proposal. One could imagine applying this income limit to all FHA programs in order to best focus the taxpayer-provided subsidy implicit in FHA activities to households most in need.

It should be noted as well that the February 2011 report to Congress on "Reforming America's Housing Finance Market" by the Treasury Department and HUD stated that the "FHA should return to its pre-crisis role as a targeted provider of mortgage credit access for low- and moderate-income Americans and first-time homebuyers."[4] The report notes that the FHA market share (around 30 percent in early 2011) is already substantially above what Treasury and HUD see as the historical norm of 10 to 15 percent. The administration's refinancing proposal thus represents a policy reversal that both goes in the wrong direction for housing finance reform and increases the taxpayer exposure to losses by the FHA when recent analyses indicate that the agency is likely to require a taxpayer bailout of $50 billion or more as a result of its existing obligations.[5]

The administration proposes to offset the costs of the FHA refinancing proposal with a tax on large banks. As Treasury Secretary Geithner noted at a press conference last week, "there are pockets where credit is tighter than it needs to be, including mortgage finance and small business." The bank tax would expand these pockets, with costs of the tax passed through to borrowers in the form of higher interest rates and reduced availability of credit.

It is the case, as noted in a recent analysis from the Federal Reserve Bank of New York, that foreigners have meaningful holdings of US mortgages in the form of mortgage-backed securities and would bear some of the cost of the refinancing proposals.[6] Given the US fiscal imbalance and ongoing current account deficit, it is likely that the United States will rely on inflows of foreign capital for the foreseeable future. Policies that are seen as unexpected or unfair to foreign investors might then result in reduced demand for Treasury securities and other dollar assets and thus higher financing costs for American borrowers including the United States government. This is not a reason to avoid a refinancing proposal, but the potential impact on future interest rates should be taken into account in evaluating the costs and benefits.

Similar considerations apply to domestic suppliers of capital for housing finance. Buyers of mortgages and mortgage-backed securities plainly take on refinancing risk—the compensation demanded for this risk accounts for part of the spread between yields on GSE-backed MBS and Treasury securities. Continued expansions of refinancing proposals, however, could give rise to the belief that mortgages going forward have embedded in them a new feature that gives borrowers easier access to a downward adjustment of interest rates than was believed to be the case in the past. This regime change would then translate into market demands for higher yields on mortgage-related securities and thus higher interest rates going forward. In other words, current homeowners would benefit from refinancing but future ones would pay more. This is akin to the impact of so-called "cramdown" proposals that would change the bankruptcy code to allow reductions in the principal balance of mortgages: current homeowners would benefit from having reduced debt but future homeowners would face higher interest rates and reduced availability of credit. Relatively risky future borrowers, who tend to have lower incomes, would be most adversely affected.

As noted above, there are reasons for concern about the impact and cost-benefit calculus of mass refinancing programs. Nonetheless, it is possible for the administration to move forward with some aspects without Congressional action. The expanded HARP refinancing is moving forward though financial firms' computer systems are reportedly not yet fully ready for the new program. Some FHA guidelines could be adjusted as well to streamline the appraisal process and include some additional mortgages (though the expansion to underwater loans would require Congressional action). In other words, there are steps that could be taken without waiting for the inevitable rejection of the proposed bank tax.

EXPANSION OF THE HOME AFFORDABLE MODIFICATION PROGRAM (HAMP)

The HAMP program involves government payments to incentive mortgage modifications that lower homeowner payments and thus seek to prevent foreclosures. Lenders (typically servicers acting on the behalf of the beneficial owners of mortgages) have an incentive to make such modifications to avoid the considerable costs involved with foreclosure, but many institutional features slowed the modification process—to widespread frustration, including at the Treasury Department when I served as Assistant Secretary. The difficulty with a modification is to find the right targeting, amount, and structure of the modification that balances effectiveness with cost. A lender will not want to modify a loan for a borrower who can afford their original payments or for a borrower who could not afford the lower payments resulting from a modification that has an economic value equal to the cost of foreclosure.

The presence of underwater borrowers is an important consideration, since an underwater borrower has an incentive to walk away from a home even if the payments are affordable and the lender will not recover the full value of the loan in a foreclosure. But a modification involving principal reduction is especially costly for the lender and gives rise to important concerns about strategic behavior and spillover effects such as having other homeowners seek unnecessary principal reductions.

A further complication is that the weak economy of the past several years has meant that some homeowners who could initially afford the lower payments of a modified loan might suffer an income decline such as from a job loss and then "redefault" on the modified loan (that is, default). It has been said that this combination of factors leaves a potentially narrow aperture through which to make a successful modification.

HAMP uses taxpayer dollars to tip the balance toward increased modifications. Under certain conditions, the Treasury puts in money to pay for part of the cost of the modification. The selection criteria are crucial to the outcome of the policy and involve profound challenges. It is natural to focus taxpayer dollars as tightly as possible on incentivizing incremental modifications rather than providing a windfall for ones that lenders would have done on their own and to avoid as much as possible providing an incentive for homeowners to stop paying their mortgages in order to qualify for assistance.

At the same time, implementing a tighter screening to focus on the right set of borrowers translates into fewer incremental modifications.[7] These considerations presumably went into the cost-benefit calculations that were done with the original HAMP program, which was initially predicted to lead to three to four million modifications by the end of 2012 but had chalked up somewhat less than one million permanent modifications through December 2011.

A key feature of the administration's recent HAMP proposal is to substantially increase the taxpayer-provided payments to lenders that reduce principal as part of a modification for underwater borrowers. This is a relatively costly way of reducing monthly mortgage payments compared to reducing a borrower's interest rate.

If the focus of modifications is on affordability, it would be more effective to extend the term of a loan and reduce interest payments rather than writing down principal. Still, one could justify a focus on principal reduction if the goal is to avoid foreclosures by homeowners who can pay their mortgage but choose not to because they are underwater. The key issue is whether this is a cost-effective approach.

A concern about the expanded HAMP incentives recently announced by the administration is that this is a policy that would have been much more cost-effective in terms of a lower cost to taxpayers for each foreclosure avoided in early 2009.

Three years later, underwater borrowers who are still in their homes have demonstrated their attachment to it. To be sure, a principal reduction will benefit homeowners. But the cost to taxpayers will be much larger with the expansion of HAMP payments, and the impact in terms of foreclosures avoided is likely to be much modest than in 2009 given that the target population has made it this far. This leaves a high cost-benefit ratio from the HAMP expansion—presumably a much higher cost-benefit ratio than was judged to be prudent when the program was designed in 2009.

A natural question then is to consider what is different today than in 2009 that results in the apparent imperative to reduce foreclosures in 2012 regardless of the cost effectiveness of the policy tools involved. This is a worrisome approach to policymaking and to the stewardship of taxpayer resources.

PILOT PROGRAM TO TRANSITION REAL ESTATE OWNED (REO) PROPERTY TO RENTAL HOUSING

The aftermath of the bubble has left the US economy with too many homes for sale or in the so-called "shadow inventory" of homes that will be for sale once prices firm. The announcement by the FHFA of a pilot program to transition REO properties to rentals is a welcome step to speed up the adjustment of the housing market to post-bubble conditions. Facilitating purchases of vacant homes by firms that can manage them as rentals will help speed up the market adjustment, at least modestly. This program will not be helpful in all parts of the country, but it will be most useful in areas in which foreclosures and vacant homes are especially acute. The inventory of REO properties held by Fannie Mae and Freddie Mac has been declining as properties are sold while inflows of new REO dwellings have slowed as the result of legal uncertainties surrounding the foreclosure process. But there is likely to be a wave of foreclosures in the pipeline and having this program ready will be useful. At the same time, it will be important to ensure that buyers of REO properties bring capital to the table rather than relying heavily on the GSEs for financing. With Fannie and Freddie under taxpayer control, this would constitute yet another government involvement in the housing sector. GSE financing of institutional buyers would increase the firms' balance sheets and thus taxpayer exposure to risk.

The importance of putting vacant homes to use can been seen in the combination of rising rental costs and declining prices for home sold under "distress" such as following a foreclosure.[8] Overall indices of home prices such as the S&P/Case-Shiller index declined to post-bubble lows in the most recent data for November 2011, while the FHFA purchase-only price index rose in November and has moved slightly above the low point of March 2011. Downward price pressures involved in distressed sales likely contribute to differences between these price indicators. This conclusion is bolstered by recent press reports citing RealtyTrac as calculating that bank-owned foreclosures and short sales sold at a discount of 34 percent to non-distressed properties in the third quarter of 2011.

As discussed in the Fed white paper, the use of short sales and deeds-in-lieu of foreclosure can reduce losses for lenders and provide a better financial outcome for borrowers (and with greater dignity than a foreclosure). Recent press reports indicate that use of these tools is growing, along with payments by lenders to homeowners willing to move out rather than go through the foreclosure process. With the foreclosure process taking 24 to 36 months in states with a judicial foreclosure process, quite large payments could be rational on the part of lenders.[9] The Treasury's Home Affordable Foreclosure Alternatives (HAFA) program similarly provides modest payments to market participants (servicers, homeowners, and investors) to choose short sales over foreclosure. Given the substantial private incentives for these short sales to take place it is not clear that the HAFA program is needed.

HOUSING MARKET ADJUSTMENT AND ALTERNATIVE POLICY APPROACHES

Housing markets naturally adjust slowly because the typical homebuyer must sell their existing home at the same time that they buy a new one, while the stock of homes evolves slowly given that homes tend to last for 50 years or more. The adjustment has been especially slow in the wake of the crisis and recession as the result of reduced household formation that has diminished the natural growth in demand for housing.

The goal of policy moving forward should be to facilitate the ongoing adjustment and quicken the recovery of both housing prices and construction. By definition, a recovery commences only after the market hits bottom. It is desirable to lift off the bottom quickly. Fostering a stronger overall economy is perhaps the most important element of this, since a stronger economy will boost housing demand, including through increased household formation. Other policies could be useful as well, notably actions that facilitate a more rapid market adjustment and that strengthen demand.

Rhetoric about not wanting the market to hit bottom is a combination of empty and factually incorrect—after all, a housing market recovery by definition will start only after the market hits bottom. What is desirable is for the recovery to start immediately—that is, for the bottom to have been reached already.

In considering housing policy going forward, it is important both to avoid policies that will prolong the housing downturn or lengthen the time at which the market rests on the bottom. This implies that it would be valuable to resolve legal and regulatory uncertainty facing mortgage servicers and originators as quickly as possible. To be sure, past wrongdoing should be punished, notably including inappropriate foreclosures on servicemen and servicewomen. On the other hand, a lengthy period of uncertainty will affect the willingness of banks to take on housing-related risks. This concern has practical relevance for the administration's recent proposals. Bank A, for example, will naturally hesitate to refinance a loan originally made by Bank B even with an FHA guarantee if there is a concern about the possibility of future litigation. The same applies to concerns about the ability of banks to foreclose on borrowers in default—if a mortgage is no longer a securely collateralized asset, then there would be widespread ramifications to the detriment of future homebuyers. Imagine the cost of financing a home purchase with an unsecured loan facility such as credit cards.

There are important institutional and legal overhangs slowing the housing recovery, including lawsuits and regulatory actions involving the MERS title system, settlement discussions related to so-called robosigning, putbacks of bad loans to originators by the GSE, and perhaps others. Again, there should be appropriate consequences for past wrongdoing and steps to avoid repetition. But there is also a value in a rapid resolution of these uncertainties so that the mortgage financing system can once again operate effectively to the benefit of US homebuyers and homeowners. A desire to punish the financial industry sits awkwardly with the desire for a housing recovery. It is important to keep in mind as well that some foreclosures are unavoidable—just as hundreds of thousands of foreclosures took place in years with a strong housing market before the recession. It is important to have a foreclosure process that is accurate and fair and that can move forward responsibly but without unnecessary delays. Foreclosures are difficult and tragic events for households. Yet some foreclosures are inevitable. A housing rebound ultimately requires that adjustments including unavoidable foreclosures take place.

Government policies could also play a positive role in improving industry weaknesses that have been highlighted in the various judicial actions. The MERS titling system, for example, arose in part to compensate for the varying information systems by which property title information is kept, generally at the county level. A useful initiative would be to develop standard formats for these data. This would preserve local control over intrinsically local decisions and information, but facilitate nation-wide transmittal and analysis of information. Similarly, better coordination of information regarding second liens would facilitate some additional modifications based on bargaining between owners of the primary mortgage and second lien. Finally, moving forward with housing finance reform remains vital for a sustained housing market recovery. It is now a year since the Treasury Department and HUD released a report on housing finance reform and concrete action is long overdue. Uncertainty about the future of the housing finance system, notably the role of the government, will make private providers of capital hesitate to fund mortgages. This leaves government officials to make crucial decisions regarding credit availability that are better left to market participants with incentives based on having their own capital at risk.

I have written at length elsewhere about steps for housing finance reform, including the future of Fannie Mae and Freddie Mac.[10] The steps involved in moving forward with reform involve a combination of several policy levers: bringing in private capital to takes losses ahead of taxpayers; reducing the scope of any guarantee; and increasing the price or reducing the quantity offered of the guarantee. Moving forward in these dimensions would help increase the role of the private sector in housing finance and reduce government involvement and taxpayer exposure. Importantly, these steps could be taken without a firm conclusion about whether there will be a government guarantee on housing at the end. Enough progress in utilizing these policy levers would eventually lead to a housing finance system that is entirely private, but the path to a private system would involve a mix of private capital and incentives backstopped by a secondary government guarantee. This means that starting with reform that involves a secondary government guarantee does not rule out ending up with a fully private housing finance system. The key is to move forward expeditiously in order to provide increased certainty about future market conditions and thereby bring private capital back into housing finance. A useful additional step would be to make transparent the budgetary impact of GSE activities. The use of the TARP to compensate the GSEs for costs related to the administration's housing proposals, for example, obscures the underlying reality that the financial consequences of activities of both the TARP and the GSEs show up on the public balance sheet. H.R. 3581, the Budget and Accounting Transparency Act that passed in the House of Representatives earlier this week, provides a step forward in ensuring desirable clarity in budget treatment.[11] It would useful as well for the GSEs to make available loan-level data that facilitates analysis of market conditions and helps private participants to enter the housing finance market. Recent news reports indicate that Freddie Mac is developing a pilot program under which private owners of capital would purchase a security that absorbs losses on a pool of loans ahead of Freddie Mac itself. This would have Freddie in a senior position and outside investors in a first-loss position. Such a structure would have the GSEs lay off housing risk on private market participants while obtaining a market-based indication of the return market participants require to take on housing credit risk. Such a pilot program would thus test the appetite of the private market for first-loss risk on housing assets in exchange (presumably) for higher returns, indicate the market's assessment of the value of the government guaranteed on mortgages, and illuminate the path leading to a reduced role of the government in housing finance. We have learned that it is difficult for the government to price its guarantee for taking on risk, making it extremely useful to have a market-based indication. One could imagine applying such a framework to FHA loans as well to reduce government exposure and protect taxpayers compared to the current model under which the FHA does not share risk.

CONCLUSION

A revitalized housing sector and an end to the sadly elevated number of foreclosures would mark salient progress in moving past the consequences of the housing bubble and financial crisis. Government policies can usefully contribute to the needed adjustment. But it is essential to be clear about the costs associated with proposals such as those from the administration that would expand efforts to use taxpayer funds to avoid foreclosures. It is far from clear that these efforts will be effective and even less apparent that they will have a positive impact commensurate with the taxpayer resources involved. It would be better instead for Congress to consider steps that would hasten the housing market adjustment, facilitate the return of private capital into housing finance, and bring the housing sector more quickly to the point at which home prices and construction activity lift off the bottom into recovery.

End Notes

[1] See the appendix of the January 2012 HUD-Treasury Housing Scorecard: http://portal.hud. gov/hudportal/ documents/huddoc?id =JanNat 2012_ Scorecard.pdf

[2] This is in some ways reminiscent of the 2008 Hope for Homeowners program that likewise had only modest impact in reducing foreclosures.

[3] See http://www.whitehouse.gov/sites/default/files/krueger_cap_speech_final_remarks.pdf

[4] See http://portal.hud.gov/hudportal/documents/huddoc?id=housingfinmarketreform.pdf.

[5] See Joseph Gyourko, "Is FHA the next housing bailout?" November 11, 2011. http://www.aei.org/papers/economics/financial-services/housing-finance/is-fha-the-next-housing-bailout/

[6] See Joseph Tracy and Joshua Wright, "Why Mortgage Refinancing Is Not a Zero-Sum Game," January 11, 2012. http://libertystreeteconomics.newyorkfed.org/2012/01/why-mortgage-refinancing-is-not-a-zero-sum-game.html

[7] For more discussion, see Phillip Swagel, April 2009, "The Financial Crisis: An Inside View," http://www.brookings.edu/economics/bpea/~/media/Files/Programs/ES/BPEA/2009_spring_bpea_papers/2009_spring_bpea_swagel.pdf

[8] For longer discussions from which this is drawn, see "The Housing Bottom is Here" on http://www.calculatedriskblog.com/2012/02/housing-bottom-is-here.html and Prashant Gopal, February 7, 2012, "Banks Paying Homeowners to Avoid Foreclosures," Bloomberg News. http://www.bloomberg.com /news/2012- 02-07/banks-paying-homeowners-a-bonus-to-avoid-foreclosures-mortgages.html.

[9] See Gopal, op cit. http://www.bloomberg.com/news/2012-02-07/banks-paying-homeowners-a-bonus-to-avoid-foreclosures-mortgages.html

[10] See Phillip Swagel, "The Future of Housing Finance Reform," October 2011 paper for the Boston Fed Annual Research conference, http://www.bos.frb.org/economic/ conf/LTE2011/ papers/Swagel.pdf, and Phillip Swagel, "Reform of the GSEs and Housing Finance," Milken Institute White Paper, July 2011. http://www.milkeninstitute.org/pdf/Housing FinanceReform.pdf

[11] For more discussion, see Chris Papagianis and Phillip Swagel, "Put Fannie and Freddie on Federal Books," Bloomberg View oped, January 22, 2012. http://www.bloomberg.com /news/2012-01-23/put- fannie-and-freddieon-federal-books-papagianis-and-swagel.html

In: Melissa O. Murray and Willie T. Cole
Editors: Melissa O. Murray and Willie T. Cole

ISBN: 978-1-62257-294-6
© 2012 Nova Science Publishers, Inc.

Chapter 5

PRESERVING HOMEOWNERSHIP: FORECLOSURE PREVENTION INITIATIVES[*]

Katie Jones

SUMMARY

The foreclosure rate in the United States began to rise rapidly beginning around the middle of 2006. Losing a home to foreclosure can hurt homeowners in many ways; for example, homeowners who have been through a foreclosure may have difficulty finding a new place to live or obtaining a loan in the future. Furthermore, concentrated foreclosures can drag down nearby home prices, and large numbers of abandoned properties can negatively affect communities. Finally, the increase in foreclosures may destabilize the housing market, which could in turn negatively impact the economy as a whole.

There is a broad consensus that there are many negative consequences associated with rising foreclosure rates. Both Congress and the Bush and Obama Administrations have initiated efforts aimed at preventing further increases in foreclosures and helping more families preserve homeownership. These efforts currently include the Making Home Affordable program, which includes both the Home Affordable Refinance Program (HARP) and the Home Affordable Modification Program (HAMP); the Hardest Hit Fund; the Federal Housing Administration (FHA) Short Refinance Program; and the National Foreclosure Mitigation Counseling Program (NFMCP), which provides funding for foreclosure mitigation counseling and is administered by NeighborWorks America. Two other initiatives, Hope for Homeowners and the Emergency Homeowners Loan Program (EHLP), expired at the end of FY2011. Several states and localities have also initiated their own foreclosure prevention efforts, as have private companies. A voluntary alliance of mortgage lenders, servicers, investors, and housing counselors has also formed the HOPE NOW Alliance to reach out to troubled borrowers.

In March 2011, the House of Representatives passed a series of bills that, if enacted, would terminate the Home Affordable Modification Program (H.R. 839), the FHA Short Refinance Program (H.R. 830), and the Emergency Homeowners Loan Program (H.R. 836), as well as the Neighborhood Stabilization Program (H.R. 861), which is not a foreclosure prevention program but is intended to address the effects of foreclosures on

---

[*] This is an edited, reformatted and augmented version of Congressional Research Service, Publication No. R40210, dated January 12, 2012.

communities. While many observers agree that slowing the pace of foreclosures is an important policy goal, there are several challenges associated with foreclosure prevention plans. These challenges include implementation issues, such as deciding who has the authority to make mortgage modifications, developing the capacity to complete widespread modifications, and assessing the possibility that homeowners with modified loans will default again in the future. Other challenges are related to the perception of unfairness, the problem of inadvertently providing incentives for borrowers to default, and the possibility of setting an unwanted precedent for future mortgage lending.

This report describes the consequences of foreclosure on homeowners; outlines recent foreclosure prevention initiatives, largely focusing on initiatives implemented by the federal government; and discusses the challenges associated with foreclosure prevention.

INTRODUCTION AND BACKGROUND

The foreclosure rate in the United States has been rising rapidly since around the middle of 2006. The large increase in home foreclosures since that time has negatively impacted individual households, local communities, and the economy as a whole. Consequently, an issue before Congress is whether to use federal resources and authority to help prevent further increases in home foreclosures and, if so, how to best accomplish this objective. This report details the impact of foreclosure on homeowners. It also describes recent attempts to preserve homeownership that have been implemented by the government and private lenders, and briefly outlines current proposals for further foreclosure prevention activities. It concludes with a discussion of some of the challenges inherent in designing foreclosure prevention initiatives. Foreclosure refers to formal legal proceedings initiated by a mortgage lender against a homeowner after the homeowner has missed a certain number of payments on his or her mortgage.[1] When a foreclosure is completed, the homeowner loses his or her home, which is either repossessed by the lender or sold at auction to repay the outstanding debt. In general, the term "foreclosure" can refer to the foreclosure process or the completion of a foreclosure. This report deals primarily with preventing foreclosure completions. In order for the foreclosure process to begin, two things must happen: a homeowner must fail to make a certain number of payments on his or her mortgage, and a lender must decide to initiate foreclosure proceedings rather than pursue other options (such as offering a repayment plan or a loan modification). A borrower that misses one or more payments is usually referred to as being delinquent on a loan; when a borrower has missed three or more payments, he or she is generally considered to be in default. Lenders can choose to begin foreclosure proceedings after a homeowner defaults on his or her mortgage, although lenders vary in how quickly they begin foreclosure proceedings after a borrower goes into default. Furthermore, the rules governing foreclosures, and the length of time the process takes, vary by state.

Recent Market Trends

Home prices rose rapidly throughout some regions of the United States beginning in 2001. Housing has traditionally been seen as a safe investment that can offer an opportunity for high returns, and rapidly rising home prices reinforced this view. During this housing "boom," many people decided to buy homes or take out second mortgages in order to access their increasing home equity. Furthermore, rising home prices and low interest rates contributed to a sharp increase in people refinancing their mortgages; for example, between 2000 and 2003, the number of refinanced mortgage loans jumped from 2.5 million to over 15 million.[2]

Around the same time, subprime lending, which generally refers to making mortgage loans to individuals with credit scores that are too low to qualify for prime rate mortgages, also began to increase, reaching a peak between 2004 and 2006. However, beginning in 2006 and 2007, home sales started to decline, home prices stopped rising and began to fall in many regions, and the rates of homeowners becoming delinquent on their mortgages or going into foreclosure began to increase.

The percentage of home loans in the foreclosure process in the U.S. began to rise rapidly beginning around the middle of 2006. Although not all homes in the foreclosure process will end in a foreclosure completion, an increase in the number of loans in the foreclosure process is generally accompanied by an increase in the number of homes on which a foreclosure is completed.

According to the Mortgage Bankers Association, an industry group, about 1% of all home loans were in the foreclosure process in the second quarter of 2006. By the fourth quarter of 2009, the rate had more than quadrupled to over 4.5%. In the third quarter of 2011, the rate of loans in the foreclosure process was about 4%

The foreclosure rate for subprime loans has always been higher than the foreclosure rate for prime loans. For example, in the second quarter of 2006, just over 3.5% of subprime loans were in the foreclosure process compared to less than 0.5% of prime loans.

However, both prime and subprime loans have seen increases in foreclosure rates over the past several years. Like the foreclosure rate for all loans combined, the foreclosure rates for prime and subprime loans both more than quadrupled since 2006, with the rate of subprime loans in the foreclosure process increasing to over 15.5% in the fourth quarter of 2009 and the rate of prime loans in the foreclosure process increasing to more than 3% over the same time period. As of the third quarter of 2011, the rate of prime loans in the foreclosure process was about 3%, while the rate of subprime loans in the foreclosure process was nearly 15%.

Figure 1 illustrates the trend in the rate of mortgages in the foreclosure process over the past several years. According to the Congressional Oversight Panel, many observers, including the Federal Reserve, expect high numbers of foreclosures to continue through at least 2012.[3]

In addition to mortgages that were in the foreclosure process, an additional 3.5% of mortgages were 90 or more days delinquent but not yet in foreclosure in the third quarter of 2011. These are mortgages that are in default and generally could be in the foreclosure process, but for one reason or another the mortgage servicer has not started the foreclosure process yet.

Such reasons could include the volume of delinquent loans that the servicer is dealing with, delays due to efforts to modify the mortgage before beginning foreclosure, or voluntary foreclosure moratoria put in place by the servicer. Considering mortgages that are 90 or more days delinquent, as well as mortgages that are actively in the foreclosure process, may give a more complete picture of the number of mortgages that are in danger of foreclosure.

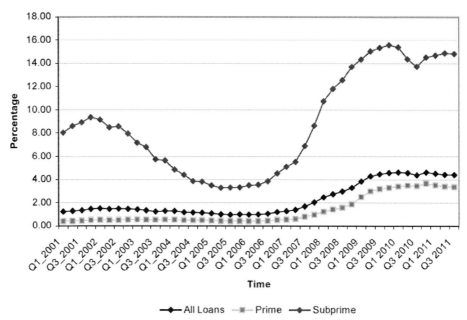

Source: Figure created by CRS using data from the Mortgage Bankers Association.
Notes: The Mortgage Bankers Association (MBA) is one of several organizations that reports
    delinquency and foreclosure data, but it does not represent all mortgages. MBA estimates that its
    data cover about 80% of outstanding first-lien mortgages on single-family properties.

Figure 1. Percentage of Loans in Foreclosure by Type of Loan; Q1 2001 – Q3 2011.

Impacts of Foreclosure

Losing a home to foreclosure can have a number of negative effects on a household. For
many families, losing a home can mean losing the household's largest store of wealth.
Furthermore, foreclosure can negatively impact a borrower's creditworthiness, making it
more difficult for him or her to buy a home in the future. Finally, losing a home to foreclosure
can also mean that a household loses many of the less tangible benefits of owning a home.
Research has shown that these benefits might include increased civic engagement that results
from having a stake in the community, and better health, school, and behavioral outcomes for
children.[4]

Some homeowners might have difficulty finding a place to live after losing their home to
foreclosure. Many will become renters. However, some landlords may be unwilling to rent to
families whose credit has been damaged by a foreclosure, limiting the options open to these
families. There can also be spillover effects from foreclosure on current renters. Renters
living in units facing foreclosure may be required to move, even if they are current on their
rent payments. As more homeowners become renters and as more current renters are
displaced when their landlords face foreclosure, pressure on local rental markets may
increase, and more families may have difficulty finding affordable rental housing. Some
observers have also raised the concern that a large increase in foreclosures could increase
homelessness, either because families who lost their homes have trouble finding new places

to live or because the increased demand for rental housing makes it more difficult for families to find adequate, affordable units.

If foreclosures are concentrated, they can also have negative impacts on communities. Many foreclosures in a single neighborhood may depress surrounding home values.[5] If foreclosed homes stand vacant for long periods of time, they can attract crime and blight, especially if they are not well-maintained. Concentrated foreclosures also place pressure on local governments, which can lose property tax revenue and may have to step in to maintain vacant foreclosed properties.

The Policy Problem

There is a broad bipartisan consensus that the recent rapid rise in foreclosures is having negative consequences on households and communities. For example, Representative Spencer Bachus, chairman of the House Committee on Financial Services, has said that "[i]t is in everyone's best interest as a general rule to prevent foreclosures. Foreclosures have a negative impact not only on families but also on their neighbors, their property value, and on the community and local government."[6] Former Senator Chris Dodd, during his tenure as chairman of the Senate Committee on Banking, Housing, and Urban Affairs, described an "overwhelming tide of foreclosures ravaging our neighborhoods and forcing thousands of American families from their homes."[7]

There is less agreement among policymakers about how much the federal government should do to prevent foreclosures. Proponents of enacting government policies and using government resources to prevent foreclosures argue that, in addition to being a compassionate response to the plight of individual homeowners, such action may prevent further damage to home values and communities that can be caused by concentrated foreclosures. Supporters also suggest that preventing foreclosures may help stabilize the economy as a whole. Opponents of government foreclosure prevention programs argue that foreclosure prevention should be worked out between lenders and borrowers without government interference. Opponents also express concern that people who do not really need help, or who are not perceived to deserve help, will unfairly take advantage of government foreclosure prevention programs. They argue that taxpayers' money should not be used to help people who can still afford their loans but want to get more favorable terms, people who may be seeking to pass their losses on to the lender or the taxpayer, or people who knowingly took on mortgages that they could not afford. Despite the concerns surrounding foreclosure prevention programs, and disagreement over the proper role of the government in preserving homeownership, Congress and the executive branch have both recently taken actions aimed at preventing foreclosures. Many private companies and state and local governments have also undertaken their own foreclosure prevention efforts. This report describes why so many households are currently at risk of foreclosure, outlines recent initiatives to help homeowners remain in their homes, and discusses some of the challenges inherent in designing successful foreclosure prevention plans.

Why Might a Household Find Itself Facing Foreclosure?

There are many reasons that a household might fall behind on its mortgage payments. Some borrowers may have simply taken out loans on homes that they could not afford. However, many homeowners who believed they were acting responsibly when they took out a mortgage nonetheless find themselves facing foreclosure. The reasons households might have difficulty making their mortgage payments include changes in personal circumstances, which can be exacerbated by macroeconomic conditions, and features of the mortgages themselves.

Changes in Household Circumstances

Changes in a household's circumstances can affect its ability to pay its mortgage. For example, a number of events can leave a household with a lower income than it anticipated when it bought its home. Such changes in circumstances can include a lost job, an illness, or a change in family structure due to divorce or death. Families that expected to maintain a certain level of income may struggle to make payments if a household member loses a job or faces a cut in pay, or if a two-earner household becomes a single-earner household. Unexpected medical bills or other unforeseen expenses can also make it difficult for a family to stay current on its mortgage.

Furthermore, sometimes a change in circumstances means that a home no longer meets a family's needs, and the household needs to sell the home. These changes can include having to relocate for a job or needing a bigger house to accommodate a new child or an aging parent. Traditionally, households that needed to move could usually sell their existing homes. However, the recent decline in home prices in many communities nationwide has left some homeowners "underwater," meaning that borrowers owe more on their homes than the houses are worth. This limits homeowners' ability to sell their homes if they have to move; many of these families are effectively trapped in their current homes and mortgages because they cannot afford to sell their homes at a loss.

The risks presented by changing personal circumstances have always existed for anyone who took out a loan, but deteriorating macroeconomic conditions, such as falling home prices and increasing unemployment, have made families especially vulnerable to losing their homes for such reasons. The fall in home values that has left some homeowners owing more than the value of their homes not only traps those people in their current homes; it also makes it difficult for homeowners to sell their homes in order to avoid a foreclosure, and it increases the incentive for homeowners to walk away from their homes if they can no longer afford their mortgage payments. Along with the fall in home values, another recent macroeconomic trend has been high unemployment. More households experiencing job loss and the resultant income loss have made it difficult for many families to keep up with their monthly mortgage payments.

Mortgage Features

Borrowers might also find themselves having difficulty staying current on their loan payments due in part to features of their mortgages. In previous years, there had been an increase in the use of alternative mortgage products whose terms differ significantly from the traditional 30-year, fixed interest rate mortgage model.[8] While borrowers with traditional mortgages are not immune to delinquency and foreclosure, many of these alternative mortgage features seem to have increased the risk that a homeowner will have trouble staying current on his or her mortgage. Many of these loans were structured to have low monthly payments in the early stages and then adjust to higher monthly payments depending on prevailing market interest rates and/or the length of time the borrower held the mortgage. Furthermore, many of these mortgage features made it more difficult for homeowners to quickly build equity in their homes. Some examples of the features of these alternative mortgage products are listed below.

Adjustable-Rate Mortgages

With an adjustable-rate mortgage (ARM), a borrower's interest rate can change at predetermined intervals, often based on changes in an index. The new interest rate can be higher or lower than the initial interest rate, and monthly payments can also be higher or lower based on both the new interest rate and any interest rate or payment caps.[9] Some ARMs also include an initial low interest rate known as a teaser rate. After the initial low-interest period ends and the new interest rate kicks in, the monthly payments that the borrower must make may increase, possibly by a significant amount.

Adjustable-rate mortgages make economic sense for some borrowers, especially if interest rates are expected to go down in the future. ARMs can help people own a home sooner than they may have been able to otherwise, or make sense for borrowers who cannot afford a high loan payment in the present but expect a significant increase in income in the future that would allow them to afford higher monthly payments. Furthermore, the interest rate on ARMs tends to follow short-term interest rates in the economy; if the gap between short-term and long-term rates gets very wide, it might make sense for borrowers to choose an ARM even if they expect interest rates to rise in the future. Finally, in markets with rising property values, borrowers with ARMs may be able to refinance their mortgages to avoid higher interest rates or large increases in monthly payments. However, if home prices fall, refinancing the mortgage or selling the home to pay off the debt may not be feasible, and homeowners can find themselves stuck with higher mortgage payments.

Zero-Downpayment or Low-Downpayment Loans

As the name suggests, zero-downpayment and low-downpayment loans require either no downpayment or a significantly lower downpayment than has traditionally been required. These types of loans make it easier for homebuyers who do not have a lot of cash up-front to purchase a home. This type of loan may be especially useful in areas where home prices are rising more rapidly than income, because it allows borrowers without enough cash for a large downpayment to enter markets they could not otherwise afford. However, a low- or no-downpayment loan also means that families have little or no equity in their homes in the early phases of the mortgage, making it difficult to sell the home or refinance the mortgage in response to a change in circumstances if home prices decline. Such loans may also mean that a homeowner takes out a larger mortgage than he or she would otherwise.

Interest-Only Loans and Negative Amortization Loans

With an interest-only loan, borrowers pay only the interest on a mortgage—but no part of the principal—for a set period of time. This option increases the homeowner's monthly payments in the future, after the interest-only period ends and the principal amortizes. These types of loans limit a household's ability to build equity in its home, making it difficult to sell or refinance the home in response to a change in circumstances if home prices are declining.

With a negative amortization loan, borrowers have the option to pay less than the full amount of the interest due for a set period of time. The loan "negatively amortizes" as the remaining interest is added to the outstanding loan balance. Like interest-only loans, this option increases future monthly mortgage payments when the principal and the balance of the interest amortizes. These types of loans can be useful in markets where property values are rising rapidly, because borrowers can enter the market and then use the equity gained from rising home prices to refinance into loans with better terms before payments increase. They can also make sense for borrowers who currently have low incomes but expect a significant increase in income in the future. However, when home prices stagnate or fall, interest-only loans and negative amortization loans can leave borrowers with negative equity, making it difficult to refinance or sell the home to pay the mortgage debt.

Alt-A Loans

Alt-A loans are mortgages that are similar to prime loans, but for one or more reasons do not qualify for prime interest rates. One example of an Alt-A loan is a low-documentation or no-documentation loan. These are loans to borrowers with good credit scores but little or no income or asset documentation. Although no-documentation loans allow for more fraudulent activity on the part of both borrowers and lenders, they may be useful for borrowers with income that is difficult to document, such as those who are self-employed or work on commission. Other examples of Alt-A loans are loans with high loan-to-value ratios or loans to borrowers with credit scores that are too low for a prime loan but high enough to avoid a subprime loan. In all of these cases, the borrower is charged a higher interest rate than he or she would be charged with a prime loan.

Many of these loan features may have played a role in the recent increase in foreclosure rates. Some homeowners were current on their mortgages before their monthly payments increased due to interest rate resets or the end of option periods. Some built up little equity in their homes because they were not paying down the principal balance of their loan or because they had not made a downpayment. Stagnant or falling home prices in many regions also hampered borrowers' ability to build equity in their homes. Borrowers without sufficient equity find it difficult to take advantage of options such as refinancing into a more traditional mortgage if monthly payments become too high or selling the home if their personal circumstances change.

Types of Loan Workouts

When a household falls behind on its mortgage, there are options that lenders or servicers[10] may be able to employ as an alternative to beginning foreclosure proceedings. Some of these options, such as a short sale and a deed-in-lieu of foreclosure,[11] allow a homeowner to avoid the foreclosure process but still result in a household losing its home. This section describes methods of avoiding foreclosure that allow homeowners to keep their homes; these options generally take the form of repayment plans or loan modifications.

Repayment Plans

A repayment plan allows a delinquent borrower to become up-to-date on his or her loan by paying back the payments he or she has missed, along with any accrued late fees. This is different from a loan modification, which changes one or more of the terms of the loan (such as the interest rate). Under a repayment plan, the missed payments and late fees may be paid back after the rest of the loan is paid off, or they may be added to the existing monthly payments. The first option increases the time that it will take for a borrower to pay back the loan, but his or her monthly payments will remain the same. The second option may result in an increase in monthly payments. Repayment plans may be a good option for homeowners who experienced a temporary loss of income but are now financially stable. However, since they do not generally make payments more affordable, repayment plans are unlikely to help homeowners with unaffordable loans avoid foreclosure in the long term.

Principal Forbearance

Principal forbearance means that a lender or servicer removes part of the principal from the portion of the loan balance that is subject to interest, thereby lowering borrowers' monthly payments by reducing the amount of interest owed. The portion of the principal that is subject to forbearance still needs to be repaid by the borrower in full, usually after the interest-bearing part of the loan is paid off or when the home is sold. Because principal forbearance does not actually change any of the loan terms, it resembles a repayment plan more than a loan modification.

Principal Write-Downs/Principal Forgiveness

A principal write-down is a type of mortgage modification that lowers borrowers' monthly payments by forgiving a portion of the loan's principal balance. The forgiven portion of the principal never needs to be repaid. Because the borrower now owes less, his or her monthly payment will be smaller. This option is costly for lenders but can help borrowers achieve affordable monthly payments, as well as increase the equity that borrowers have in their homes and therefore increase their desire to stay current on the mortgage and avoid foreclosure.[12]

Interest Rate Reductions

Another form of loan modification is when the lender voluntarily lowers the interest rate on a mortgage. This is different from a refinance, in which a borrower takes out a new mortgage with a lower interest rate and uses the proceeds from the new loan to pay off the old loan. Unlike refinancing, a borrower does not have to pay closing costs or qualify for a new loan to get an interest rate reduction, which can make interest rate reductions a good option for borrowers who owe more on their mortgages than their homes are worth. With an interest rate reduction, the interest rate can be reduced permanently, or it can be reduced for a period of time before increasing again to a certain fixed point. Lenders can also freeze interest rates at their current level in order to avoid impending interest rate resets on adjustable rate mortgages. Interest rate modifications are relatively costly to the lender, but they can be effective at reducing monthly payments to an affordable level.

Extended Loan Term/Extended Amortization

Another option for lowering monthly mortgage payments is extending the amount of time over which the loan is paid back. While extending the loan term increases the total cost of the mortgage for the borrower because more interest will accrue, it allows monthly payments to be smaller because they are paid over a longer period of time. Most mortgages in the U.S. have an initial loan term of 25 or 30 years; extending the loan term from 30 to 40 years, for example, could result in a lower monthly mortgage payment for the borrower.

CURRENT FORECLOSURE PREVENTION INITIATIVES

The federal government, state and local governments, and private companies have all implemented a variety of plans to attempt to slow the recent increase in foreclosures. This section describes a number of recent foreclosure prevention initiatives, focusing on those implemented by the federal government.

Home Affordable Refinance Program (HARP)

On February 18, 2009, President Obama announced the Making Home Affordable (MHA) program, aimed at helping homeowners who are having difficulty making their mortgage payments avoid foreclosure.[13] (The program details originally referred to the program as the Homeowner Affordability and Stability Plan, or HASP. Further program details released on March 4, 2009, began referring to the plan as Making Home Affordable.) Making Home Affordable is part of the Administration's broader economic recovery strategy, along with the Financial Stability Plan (an administrative initiative aimed at shoring up the financial system) and the American Recovery and Reinvestment Act of 2009 (enacted legislation (P.L. 111-5) aimed at stimulating the economy.[14]

Making Home Affordable includes three main parts. The first two parts of the plan allow certain homeowners to refinance or modify their mortgages, and each of those pieces are described below. The third part of the plan, which provided additional financial support to Fannie Mae and Freddie Mac, is not discussed in detail in this report.[15]

The refinancing piece of MHA is the Home Affordable Refinance Program (HARP). HARP allows homeowners with mortgages owned or guaranteed by Fannie Mae or Freddie Mac[16] to refinance into loans with more favorable terms even if they owe more than 80% of the value of their homes. Generally, borrowers who owe more than 80% of the value of their homes have difficulty refinancing and therefore cannot take advantage of lower interest rates. By allowing borrowers who owe more than 80% of the value of their homes to refinance their mortgages, the plan is meant to help qualified borrowers lower their monthly mortgage payments to a level that is more affordable. Originally, qualified borrowers were eligible to refinance under this program if they owed up to 105% of the value of their homes. On July 1, 2009, the Administration announced that it would expand the program to include borrowers who owe up to 125% of the value of their homes. In October 2011, the Federal Housing Finance Agency (FHFA), Fannie's and Freddie's conservator, announced that it would remove the loan-to-value ratio cap entirely.

In addition to having a mortgage owned or guaranteed by Fannie Mae or Freddie Mac,[17] a borrower must have a mortgage on a single-family home, live in the home as his or her primary residence, and be current on the mortgage payments in order to be eligible for this program. Rather than targeting homeowners who are behind on their mortgage payments, this piece of the MHA plan targets homeowners who have kept up with their payments but have lost equity in their homes due to falling home prices. HARP is scheduled to end on December 31, 2013.[18]

Changes to HARP Announced in October 2011

In October 2011, the Federal Housing Finance Agency (FHFA) announced a number of changes to HARP designed to allow more people to qualify for the program. [19] As discussed earlier, one of these changes removed the cap on the loan-to-value ratio, which had previously limited eligibility for the program to those with loan-to-value ratios up to 125%. Another change is that Fannie Mae and Freddie Mac have eliminated or reduced certain fees that are paid by borrowers who refinance through HARP. Fannie and Freddie will also waive certain representations and warranties made by lenders on the original loans, which may make lenders more likely to participate in HARP by releasing them from some responsibility for any defects in the original loan. The changes also encourage greater use of automated valuation models instead of property appraisals in order to streamline the refinancing process. Finally, as part of these HARP changes, FHFA extended the end date for the program to December 31, 2013.

Fannie Mae and Freddie Mac have each released their own guidance governing how the HARP changes will be implemented for loans that they own or guarantee.[20] Many of these changes became effective in December 2011 or January 2012; however, specific changes go into effect on different dates, and the effective dates can vary between Fannie Mae and Freddie Mac. Individual lenders might also vary in when they implement the program changes, or, since HARP is not mandatory, whether they adopt all of the changes allowed by FHFA.

HARP Results to Date

The Administration originally estimated that HARP could help up to between 4 million and 5 million homeowners. According to a recent report from the Federal Housing Finance Agency (FHFA), Fannie Mae and Freddie Mac had refinanced over 962,000 loans with loan-to-value ratios above 80% through October 2011.[21] The majority of these mortgages (over 879,000) had loan-to-value ratios between 80% and 105%, while nearly 83,000 mortgages had loan-to-value ratios above 105% up to 125%.

Home Affordable Modification Program (HAMP)

The mortgage modification piece of the Administration's Making Home Affordable program is the Home Affordable Modification Program (HAMP).[22] HAMP has been modified or updated a number of times since its original details were announced, including changes to the program's rules and the implementation of additional HAMP programs to attempt to assist certain groups, such as unemployed and underwater borrowers. These changes are described in the "Additional HAMP Components and Program Changes" section.[23]

Through HAMP, the government provides financial incentives to participating mortgage servicers that provide loan modifications to eligible troubled borrowers in order to reduce the borrowers' monthly mortgage payments to no more than 31% of their monthly income. In order to qualify, a borrower must have a mortgage on a single-family residence that was originated on or before January 1, 2009, must live in the home as his or her primary residence, and must have an unpaid principal balance on the mortgage that is no greater than the Fannie Mae/Freddie Mac conforming loan limit in high-cost areas ($729,750 for a one-unit property). Furthermore, the borrower must currently be paying more than 31% of his or her monthly gross income toward mortgage payments, and must be experiencing a financial hardship that makes it difficult to remain current on the mortgage. Borrowers need not already be delinquent on their mortgages in order to qualify.

Servicers participating in HAMP conduct a "net present value test" (NPV test) on eligible mortgages that compares the expected returns to investors from doing a loan modification to the expected returns from pursuing a foreclosure. If the expected returns from a loan modification are greater than those from foreclosure, servicers are required to reduce borrowers' payments to no more than 38% of monthly income. The government then shares half the cost of reducing borrowers' payments from 38% of monthly income to 31% of monthly income. Servicers reduce borrowers' payments by reducing the interest rate, extending the loan term, and forbearing principal, in that order, as necessary to reach the payment ratio. Servicers can reduce interest rates to as low as 2%. The new interest rate must remain in place for five years; after five years, if the interest rate is below the market rate at the time the modification agreement was completed, the interest rate can rise by one percentage point per year until it reaches that market rate. Borrowers must make modified payments on time during a three-month trial period before the modification is converted to permanent status.

The Home Affordable Modification Program is voluntary, but once a servicer signs an agreement to participate in the program, that servicer is bound by the rules of the program and is required to modify eligible mortgages according to the program guidelines. The government provides incentives to servicers, investors, and borrowers for participation. Servicers receive an upfront incentive payment for each successful permanent loan modification, an additional payment for modifications made for borrowers who are not yet delinquent, and a "pay-for-success" payment for up to three years if the borrower remains current after the modification. The borrower can also receive a "pay-for-success" incentive payment (in the form of principal reduction) for up to five years if he or she remains current after the modification is finalized. Investors receive the payment cost-share incentive (that is, the government's payment of half the cost of reducing the monthly mortgage payment from 38% to 31% of monthly income), and can receive incentive payments for loans modified before a borrower becomes delinquent. Companies that receive funding through Troubled Assets Relief Program (TARP) or Financial Stability Plan (FSP) programs announced after the announcement of Making Home Affordable are required to participate in HAMP. Modifications can be made through HAMP until December 31, 2012, unless the program is terminated before that date. On March 29, 2011, the House passed H.R. 839, which, if enacted, would terminate the program and rescind unobligated funds. Borrowers who are currently participating in the program would not be affected if this bill becomes law. CBO estimated that H.R. 839 would reduce direct federal spending by $1.4 billion over a 10-year period.[24]

HAMP Funding

The Administration originally estimated that HAMP would cost $75 billion. Of this amount, $50 billion was to come from TARP funds, and $25 billion was to come from Fannie Mae and Freddie Mac for the costs of modifying mortgages that those entities own or guarantee.[25] Treasury has since revised its estimate of the amount of TARP funds that will be used for HAMP, and has used some of the $50 billion originally allocated to HAMP to help pay for other foreclosure-related programs (the Hardest Hit Fund and the FHA Refinance program, both described in later sections of this report).Treasury has now committed $45.6 billion to its foreclosure prevention programs, rather than the initial $50 billion. Of this amount, nearly $30 billion is committed to HAMP and its related programs, $7.6 billion is committed to the Hardest Hit Fund, and up to just over $8 billion is committed to the FHA Short Refinance Program. As of January 10, 2012, $2.26 billion of the funding committed to HAMP has been disbursed.[26]

HAMP Results to Date

The Administration originally estimated that HAMP could eventually help up to between 3 million and 4 million homeowners. The Treasury Department releases monthly reports detailing the program's progress. These reports offer a variety of information, including the number of overall trial and permanent modifications made under HAMP and the number of each that are currently active, the number of trial and permanent modifications made by individual servicers, and the number of trial and permanent modifications underway in each state.[27] According to the November 2011 report, which includes data through the November 2011 HAMP reporting cycle, there are nearly 831,000 HAMP modifications that are currently active. Of these, about 80,000 are active trial modifications and nearly 751,000 are active permanent modifications.[28] Over 764,000 trial modifications and over 159,000 permanent modifications have been canceled since the program began.

Figure 2 illustrates the total number of active modifications, both trial and permanent, in each month since January 2010. Since mid-2010, the total number of active modifications has generally been increasing, driven by an increasing number of active permanent modifications. The total number of active trial modifications has generally been decreasing as trial modifications convert to permanent status or are canceled, and fewer new trial modifications have been started as the program has aged.

Figure 3 shows the number of new HAMP trial modifications and new HAMP permanent modifications in each month from the beginning of 2010 to the present. As the figure illustrates, the number of new trials declined sharply during the beginning of 2010. This was probably at least in part due to a program change that required servicers to verify a borrower's income information before approving a trial modification, rather than allowing servicers to verify borrower income during the trial period but before the modification became permanent. (See the "Additional Changes" section for more information on this program change.)

The number of new permanent modifications increased each month in the beginning of 2010, with a peak of over 68,000 new permanent modifications in April 2010, before decreasing and then leveling out. Since mid-2010, the number of new permanent modifications beginning each month has generally been between 25,000 to 35,000.

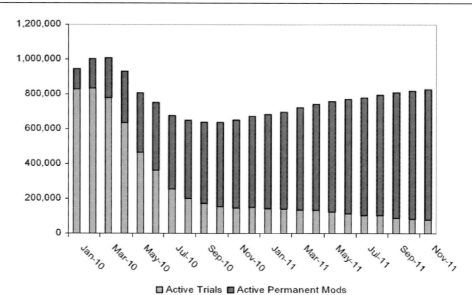

Source: Figure created by CRS based on data from Treasury's monthly Making Home Affordable Program Servicer Performance Reports.

Figure 2. Total Active HAMP Modifications by Month; January 2010–November 2011.

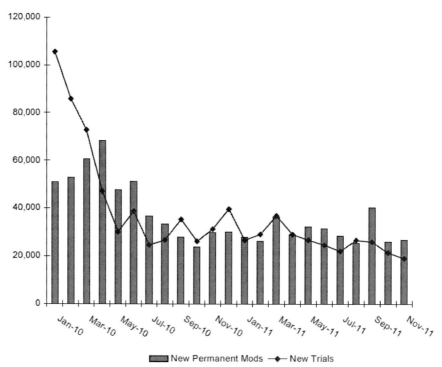

Source: Figure created by CRS based on data from Treasury's monthly Making Home Affordable Program Servicer Performance Reports.

Figure 3. New Trial and Permanent HAMP Modifications by Month; January 2010–November 2011.

Since around May 2010, the number of new trial modifications that have begun each month has fluctuated within a range of between about 20,000 and 40,000.

Conversion of Trial Modifications to Permanent Status

After HAMP had been in place for several months, many observers began to express concern at the high number of trial modifications that were being canceled rather than converting to permanent status and the length of time that it was taking for trial modifications to become permanent. In order for a modification to become permanent, a borrower must make all of the trial period payments on time, and must submit all necessary documentation (such as tax returns, proof of income, and a signed Modification Agreement) to the servicer. In response to these concerns, Treasury took a number of steps to attempt to facilitate the conversion of trial modifications to permanent modifications. These steps have included increased reporting requirements and monitoring of servicers, and outreach efforts to borrowers to help them understand and meet the program's documentation requirements.[29] Additionally, as noted earlier and described more fully in the "Additional Changes" section of this report, Treasury changed the program guidelines to require servicers to have documented income information from borrowers before offering a trial modification; previously, servicers were allowed to begin a trial modification based on stated income information, but had to verify this information in order for a modification to become permanent. This change was expected to result in more of trial modifications converting to permanent modifications going forward. As of November 2011, Treasury reported that 83% of trial modifications that had begun since June 1, 2010 had converted to permanent status.

Beginning with the April 2010 monthly report, Treasury began reporting conversion rates of trial modifications to permanent modifications for individual servicers, along with other metrics related to individual servicers' performance.

Servicer Performance

In the April 2011 monthly report, Treasury released comprehensive results of an examination of the performance of the ten largest servicers participating in HAMP, and indicated that it would continue to release the results of these servicer assessments on a quarterly basis. As a result of this examination, Treasury announced that it was going to withhold incentive payments to three of the largest participating servicers due to findings that the servicers' performance under the program was not meeting Treasury's standards. The servicers, Bank of America, JP Morgan Chase, and Wells Fargo, were all found to need "substantial" improvement in several areas. Treasury said that it would reinstate the incentive payments when the servicers' performance improved. A fourth servicer, Ocwen, was found to need substantial improvement as well, but Treasury did not withhold incentive payments from Ocwen at that time due to a finding that its performance was partially due to a loan portfolio that it had bought from another company. The remaining six of the ten largest servicers were found to need moderate improvement, but Treasury did not withhold incentive payments from those servicers at that time.[30]

In the July 2011 monthly report, Treasury continued to find that Bank of America and JP Morgan Chase needed substantial improvement. Five servicers, including Wells Fargo and Ocwen, were found to need moderate improvement, while three servicers (GMAC, Litton, and OneWest Bank) were found to need only minor improvement.[31] By the October monthly report, only one servicer, JP Morgan Chase, was found by Treasury to need substantial improvement. Seven servicers, including Bank of America, Wells Fargo, Ocwen, GMAC, and Litton, were found to need moderate improvement, and two servicers, OneWest Bank and Select Portfolio Servicing, were found to need only minor improvement.[32]

Additional HAMP Components and Program Changes

Since the program's announcement, Treasury has announced several changes to HAMP, as well as a number of additional components of the program. Some of the major changes and additional components include the following:

Second Lien Modification Program (2MP)[33]

Many borrowers have second mortgages on their homes. Second mortgages can cause problems for loan modification programs because (1) modifying the first lien may not reduce households' total monthly mortgage payments to an affordable level if the second mortgage remains unmodified, and (2) holders of primary mortgages are often hesitant to modify the mortgage if the second mortgage holder does not agree to re-subordinate the second mortgage to the first mortgage, or to modify the second mortgage as well. Under 2MP, if the servicer of the second lien is participating in 2MP, then that servicer must agree either to modify the second lien in accordance with program guidelines, or to extinguish the second lien entirely, when a borrower's first mortgage is modified under HAMP. (Servicers sign up to participate in 2MP separately from signing up to participate in HAMP.)

Under 2MP, if a servicer modifies a second lien, it can receive an upfront incentive payment of $500. Servicers can also receive "pay-for-success" payments of up to $250 per year for up to three years, if the monthly second mortgage payments are reduced by 6% or more and if the borrower remains current on both the HAMP modification and the 2MP modification. Borrowers can receive annual "pay-for-success" payments of up to $250 per year for up to five years (in the form of principal reduction) if the second mortgage payments have been reduced by 6% or more and if the borrowers remain current on both the HAMP and 2MP modifications.

Investors can receive compensation for modified second liens according to a cost-sharing formula. Servicers can also receive incentives for extinguishing second liens, and investors receive compensation for extinguished second liens according to a cost-sharing formula. Treasury reports that nearly 44,000 second-lien modifications are active under 2MP as of November 2011.[34]

Home Affordable Foreclosure Alternatives Program (HAFA)[35]

Through the Home Affordable Foreclosure Alternatives Program (HAFA), when a borrower meets the basic eligibility criteria for HAMP, but does not ultimately qualify for a modification, does not successfully complete the trial period, or defaults on a HAMP modification, participating servicers can receive incentive payments for completing a short sale or a deed-in-lieu of foreclosure as an alternative to foreclosure.[36] Servicers can receive incentive payments of $1,500 for each short sale or deed-in-lieu that is successfully executed, and borrowers can receive incentive payments of $3,000 to help with relocation expenses.[37] Investors can receive up to a maximum of $2,000 if they agree to share a portion of the proceeds of the short sale with any subordinate lienholders. (The subordinate lienholders, in turn, must release their liens on the property and waive all claims against the borrower for the unpaid balance of the subordinate mortgages.) In order to attempt to streamline the process of short sales and deeds-in-lieu of foreclosure under HAFA, Treasury provides standardized documentation and processes for participating servicers to use. HAFA became active on April 5, 2010, although servicers had the option to begin implementing the program before this date. Treasury reports that over 24,000 HAFA transactions have been completed as of November 2011.[38] Most of these transactions have been short sales rather than deeds-in-lieu of foreclosure.

Home Price Decline Protection

To encourage modifications even in markets where home prices are continuing to fall, lenders or investors are eligible for Home Price Decline Protection incentive payments for successful modifications in areas with declining home prices. The calculation of these incentive payments takes into account the recent rate of home price declines in the area where the home is located and the unpaid principal balance of the mortgage.

Home Affordable Unemployment Program (UP)

On March 26, 2010, the Administration announced the Home Affordable Unemployment Program (UP), which targets borrowers who are unemployed. Under UP, participating servicers are required to offer forbearance periods to unemployed borrowers who apply for HAMP and meet the UP eligibility criteria before evaluating those borrowers for HAMP. The forbearance period lasts for a minimum of twelve months, or until the borrower becomes re-employed.[39] Borrowers' mortgage payments are lowered to 31% or less of their monthly income through principal forbearance during this time period. After the forbearance period ends, it is expected that some borrowers will have regained employment and will not need further assistance. Other borrowers, such as those who are re-employed but at a lower salary, may be able to qualify for a regular HAMP modification. Still other borrowers may qualify for a foreclosure alternative such as a short sale or a deed-in-lieu of foreclosure, and some borrowers ultimately may not be able to avoid foreclosure. Participating servicers were required to begin offering forbearance plans to qualified unemployed borrowers by July 1, 2010, but could choose to implement the program earlier.[40] Treasury reports that nearly 17,000 UP forbearance plans have begun through November 2011.[41]

Principal Reduction Alternative (PRA)

Another change to HAMP announced on March 26, 2010, is the Principal Reduction Alternative (PRA), in which participating servicers are required to consider reducing principal balances as part of HAMP modifications for homeowners who owe at least 115% of the value of their home. Servicers will have to run two net present value tests for these borrowers: the first will be the standard NPV test, and the second will include principal reduction. If the net present value of the modification is higher under the test that includes principal reduction, servicers have the option to reduce principal. However, they are not required to do so. If the principal is reduced, the amount of the principal reduction will initially be treated as principal forbearance; the forborne amount will then be forgiven in three equal amounts over three years as long as the borrower remains current on his or her mortgage payments. The Administration will also offer incentives to servicers specifically for reducing principal. The PRA went into effect on October 1, 2010.[42] According to Treasury, over 52,000 PRA modifications were active as of November 2011. About 16,000 of these are active trial modifications, and about 36,000 are active permanent modifications.[43]

Additional Changes

A number of other changes to the HAMP guidelines have been implemented since the program began. Some notable changes include the following:

- When HAMP began, Treasury allowed servicers to approve borrowers for trial modifications on the basis of stated income information. Borrowers then had to submit documentation verifying their income information before the trial modification could convert to permanent status. In cases where the stated income information differed from the documented information, servicers often had to re-evaluate borrowers for the program (for example, by running a new NPV test), which sometimes resulted in borrowers who had been approved for a trial modification being denied for a permanent modification. Since June 1, 2010, Treasury requires all income information to be verified before a borrower can be approved for a trial period plan. [44] As described earlier in the "HAMP Results to Date" section, this change was expected to result in a greater proportion of trial modifications converting to permanent status.

- The original HAMP guidelines prohibited servicers from conducting a foreclosure sale while they were evaluating a borrower for HAMP, or while a borrower was in a HAMP trial period. Servicers also were not allowed to refer new loans to foreclosure during the 30-day window that borrowers had to submit documentation indicating that they intended to accept a trial modification offer. However, foreclosures in process were allowed to continue, as long as no foreclosure sale occurred, and loans could be referred to foreclosure at the same time that a borrower was being evaluated for HAMP. Since June 1, 2010, Treasury prohibits servicers from referring eligible borrowers to foreclosure until they have been evaluated for HAMP, or until reasonable outreach efforts have not been successful. Foreclosures that were already in process prior to this change are allowed to continue, although servicers must take any actions that they have the authority to undertake to halt foreclosure proceedings for borrowers in trial modifications. Treasury also now requires enhanced disclosures to borrowers that describe how evaluation for HAMP or a trial modification may happen at the same time as foreclosure proceedings, but that explain that the home will not be sold in a foreclosure sale while the borrower is being evaluated for HAMP or is in a trial period.[45]

- Treasury has strengthened a number of other disclosure requirements since HAMP began, including requiring increased disclosures to borrowers who were denied a HAMP modification describing the reason for their denial. Treasury also provided more guidance on the outreach efforts that servicers must make to borrowers who may be eligible for HAMP.

- The Dodd-Frank Wall Street Reform And Consumer Protection Act (P.L. 111- 203) made some changes to HAMP. These changes included a requirement that Treasury make a net present value test available on the internet, based on Treasury's NPV methodology, along with a disclaimer stating that specific servicers' NPV models may differ in some respects.[46] Treasury launched this online NPV calculator in May

2011, and it is available at https://check mynpv.com/. The law also requires that servicers provide borrowers with certain NPV inputs upon denying the borrowers for HAMP modifications; this differed from Treasury's existing guidance, which required borrowers to ask servicers to see certain NPV inputs within a certain time period if the borrower was denied a modification due to a negative NPV result.

Hardest Hit Fund

On February 19, 2010, the Obama Administration announced that it would make up to a total of $1.5 billion available to the housing finance agencies (HFAs) of five states that had experienced the greatest declines in home prices. This program is known as the Hardest Hit Fund, and several additional rounds of funding have been announced since its inception. The funding comes from the TARP funds that Treasury initially set aside for HAMP. Therefore, all Hardest Hit Fund funding must be used in ways that comply with the Emergency Economic Stabilization Act of 2008 (P.L. 110-343), which means that the funds must be used by eligible financial institutions and must be used for purposes that are allowable under P.L. 110-343.[47] The five states to receive funding in the first round of the Hardest Hit Fund are California, Arizona, Florida, Nevada, and Michigan.[48] The Administration set maximum allocations for each state based on a formula, and the HFAs of those states were required to submit their plans for the funds to Treasury for approval in order to be awarded funds through the program. The funding can be used for a variety of programs that address foreclosures and are tailored to specific areas, including programs to help unemployed homeowners, programs to help homeowners who owe more than their homes are worth, or programs to address the challenges that second liens pose to mortgage modifications. On March 29, 2010, the Administration announced a second round of funding for the Hardest Hit Fund. This second round of funding made up to a total of an additional $600 million available to five states that have large proportions of their populations living in areas of economic distress, defined as counties with unemployment rates above 12% in 2009 (the five states that received funding in the first round were not eligible). The five states that received funding though this second round are North Carolina, Ohio, Oregon, Rhode Island, and South Carolina. These states can use the funds to support the same types of programs eligible under the first round of funding, and are subject to the same requirements.[49]

On August 11, 2010, the Administration announced a third round of funding for the Hardest Hit Housing Fund.[50] This third round of funding makes a total of up to $2 billion available to 17 states and the District of Columbia, all of which had unemployment rates higher than the national average over the previous year. Nine of the states that are eligible for the third round of funding also received funding in one of the previous two rounds of Hardest Hit Fund funding.[51]

The states that received funding in the third round but not in either of the previous two rounds are Alabama, Georgia, Illinois, Indiana, Kentucky, Mississippi, New Jersey, Tennessee, and the District of Columbia. Like the first two rounds of funding, states must submit plans for the funds for Treasury's approval. Unlike the first two rounds of funding, states must use funds from the third round specifically for foreclosure prevention programs that target the unemployed.

Table 1. Hardest Hit Fund Allocations to States
(dollars in millions)

State	Funding
Alabama	$162.5
Arizona	$267.8
California	$1,975.3
Florida	$1,057.8
Georgia	$339.3
Illinois	$445.6
Indiana	$221.7
Kentucky	$148.9
Michigan	$498.6
Mississippi	$101.9
Nevada	$194.0
New Jersey	$300.5
North Carolina	$482.8
Ohio	$570.4
Oregon	$220.0
Rhode Island	$79.4
South Carolina	$295.4
Tennessee	$217.3
Washington, DC	$20.7
Total	$7,600.0

Source: http://www.financialstability.gov/roadtostability/hardesthitfund.html.

In September 2010, Treasury announced an additional $3.5 billion of funding to be distributed to the 18 states and the District of Columbia that were receiving funding through earlier rounds, bringing the total amount of funding allocated to the Hardest Hit Fund to $7.6 billion.

Table 1 shows the total allocation of funds, through all rounds of funding, for each state that is receiving funding through the Hardest Hit Fund.[52]

FHA Short Refinance Program

On March 26, 2010, the Administration announced a new Federal Housing Administration (FHA) Short Refinance Program for homeowners who owe more than their homes are worth. Detailed program guidance was released on August 6, 2010.[53] Under the program, certain homeowners who owe more than their homes are worth may be able to refinance into new, FHA-insured mortgages for an amount lower than the home's current value. The original lender will accept the proceeds of the new loan as payment in full on the original mortgage; the new lender will have FHA insurance on the new loan; and the homeowner will have a first mortgage balance that is below the current value of the home, thereby giving him or her some equity. Homeowners will have to be current on their mortgages to qualify for this program. Further, the balance on the first mortgage loan will have to be reduced by at least 10%. This program is voluntary for lenders and borrowers, and borrowers with mortgages already insured by FHA are not eligible.

The FHA Short Refinance Program is similar in structure to the Hope for Homeowners program (described later in this report), which was still active at the time that the FHA Short Refinance Program began but has since ended. However, there are some key differences between the two programs. First, Hope for Homeowners required that any second liens be extinguished. Under the new FHA refinancing plan, second liens are specifically allowed to remain in place. Incentives will be offered for the second lien-holder to reduce the balance of the second lien, and the homeowner's combined debt on both the first and the second lien will not be allowed to exceed 115% of the value of the home after the refinance. Second, under Hope for Homeowners, borrowers could be either current or delinquent on their mortgages and qualify for the program. Under the new FHA refinance plan, borrowers will have to be current on their mortgages. Finally, under Hope for Homeowners, borrowers had to agree to share some of their initial equity in the home with the government when the house was eventually sold. The FHA Short Refinance Program does not appear to require any equity or appreciation sharing.

The FHA Refinance Program began on September 7, 2010. As of the end of November 2011, FHA reported refinancing about 500 loans through the program.[54] Treasury has said that it will use up to $8 billion of the TARP funds originally set aside for HAMP to help pay for the cost of this program; additional program costs will be borne by FHA. The FHA Short Refinance Program is to be available until December 31, 2012, unless it is terminated before that date.

On March 10, 2011, the House passed H.R. 830, which, if enacted, would terminate the FHA Short Refinance Program and rescind unexpended funds. Borrowers whose loans had already been refinanced through the program would not be affected if this bill became law. CBO estimated that enacting H.R. 830 would decrease the federal deficit by $175 million.[55]

RECENTLY ENDED FEDERAL FORECLOSURE PREVENTION INITIATIVES

This sections describes federal foreclosure prevention initiatives that recently ended. However, some borrowers may be continuing to receive assistance through these programs if they began participating in the program prior to the program's end date. For information on earlier federal foreclosure prevention initiatives, see Appendix B.

Emergency Homeowners Loan Program

The Dodd-Frank Wall Street Reform and Consumer Protection Act (P.L. 111-203) included up to $1 billion for HUD to use to administer a program to provide short-term loans to certain mortgage borrowers who had experienced a decrease in income due to unemployment, underemployment, or a medical emergency, in order to help them make their mortgage payments.

HUD chose to target this funding to the 32 states (and Puerto Rico) that did not receive funding through the Administration's Hardest Hit Fund (described in the "Hardest Hit Fund" section of this report). HUD termed this program the Emergency Homeowners Loan Program (EHLP).[56] By statute, HUD was not able to enter into new loan agreements under EHLP after September 30, 2011.

The Emergency Homeowners Loan Program was administered through two different approaches. Under the first approach, state housing finance agencies that operate programs that were deemed to be "substantially similar" to the Emergency Homeowners Loan Program could use EHLP funds for their existing programs.

On April 1, 2011, HUD announced that it had deemed programs in five states (Connecticut, Delaware, Idaho, Maryland, and Pennsylvania) to be substantially similar to the EHLP and had approved those states' EHLP allocations to be used for their state programs. The EHLP programs in the remaining states used the second approach to administer the program.

Under the second approach, housing counseling organizations that are part of the NeighborWorks network[57] took applications for the program and performed certain other administrative and outreach functions (HUD retained responsibility for program monitoring and compliance, and for managing the note associated with the Emergency Homeowners Loan Program loan). Borrowers were able to begin applying for the program using this approach on June 20, 2011.

To apply, borrowers submitted a pre-application to a participating housing counseling agency.[58] After all pre-applications were received, qualified applicants were invited to submit a complete application. If there were more qualified pre-applications than funds available, then borrowers were to be chosen by lottery to submit full applications.

Borrowers originally had to submit pre-applications by July 22, 2011, to be considered for the program, although that deadline was later extended to September 15, 2011.[59]

To qualify for the EHLP, borrowers had to meet certain conditions, including the following:

- Borrowers must have had a household income of 120% or less of area median income prior to the unemployment, underemployment, or medical event that made the household unable to make its mortgage payments;
- Borrowers must have had a current gross income of at least 15% less than the household's income prior to the unemployment, underemployment, or medical event;
- Borrowers must have been at least three months delinquent and have received notification of the lender's intent to foreclose;
- Borrowers must have had a reasonable likelihood of being able to resume making full monthly mortgage payments within two years, and had a total debt-to-income ratio of less than 55%; and
- Borrowers must have resided in the property as a principal residence, and the property must have been a single-family (one- to four-unit) property.

The loans were to be used to pay arrearages on the mortgage as well as to assist the borrower in making mortgage payments for up to 24 months going forward. An individual borrower was eligible to receive up to a maximum of $50,000.

Borrowers were required to contribute 31% of their monthly gross income at the time of their application (but in no case less than $25) to monthly payments on the first mortgage, and were required to report any changes in income or employment status while they were receiving assistance.

The assistance ends when one of the following events occurs: (1) the maximum loan amount has been reached; (2) the homeowner regains an income level of 85% or more of its income prior to the unemployment or medical event; (3) the homeowner no longer resides in or sells the property or refinances the mortgage; (4) the borrower defaults on his portion of the first mortgage payments; or (5) the borrower fails to report changes in employment status or income. Loans made through the program were five-year, zero-interest, non-recourse loans secured by junior liens on the property.

The loans will have declining balances; the borrowers are not required to make payments on the loans for a five-year period as long as the borrowers remain in the properties as their principal residences and stay current on their first mortgage payments. If these conditions are met, the balance of the loan will decline by 20% annually until the debt is extinguished at the end of five years.

Table 2. Emergency Homeowners Loan Program Allocations to States
(dollars in millions)

State	Allocation	State	Allocation
Alaska	$3.9	New Hampshire	$12.7
Arkansas	$17.7	New Mexico	$10.7
Colorado	$41.3	New York	$111.6
Connecticut	$32.9	North Dakota	$1.3
Delaware	$6.0	Oklahoma	$15.6
Hawaii	$6.3	Pennsylvania	$105.8
Idaho	$13.3	Puerto Rico	$14.7
Iowa	$17.4	South Dakota	$2.1
Kansas	$17.7	Texas	$135.4
Louisiana	$16.7	Utah	$16.6
Maine	$10.4	Vermont	$4.8
Maryland	$40.0	Virginia	$46.6
Massachusetts	$61.0	Washington	$56.3
Minnesota	$55.8	West Virginia	$8.3
Missouri	$49.0	Wisconsin	$51.5
Montana	$5.7	Wyoming	$2.3
Nebraska	$8.3		
Total			$1,000.0

Source: U.S. Department of Housing and Urban Development, *Obama Administration Announces $1 Billion in Additional Help for Struggling Homeowners in 32 States and Puerto Rico*, press release, October 5, 2010, available at http://portal.hud.gov /portal/page/portal/HUD/press/press_releases_ media_advisories/2010/HUDNo.10-225.

However, the borrower will be responsible for repaying the loan to HUD if one of the following events occurs: (1) the borrower retains ownership of the home but no longer resides in it as a principal residence; (2) the borrower defaults on his or her first mortgage payments; or (3) the borrower receives net proceeds from selling the home or refinancing the mortgage. In the third case, if the proceeds of the sale or refinance are not sufficient to repay the entire remaining balance of the loan, the remaining balance will be considered to have been paid in full and the lien on the property will be released.

Table 2 shows the amounts that HUD designated for the Emergency Homeowners Loan Program for each state that was eligible for funding.

On March 11, 2011, the House passed H.R. 836, which would have terminated the EHLP and rescinded any unobligated program balances.

Any borrowers who had already received loans through the program would not have been affected if the bill had become law. CBO estimated that enacting H.R. 836 would have decreased the federal budget deficit by $840 million.[60]

Hope for Homeowners

Congress created the Hope for Homeowners (H4H) program in the Housing and Economic Recovery Act of 2008 (P.L. 110-289), which was signed into law on July 30, 2008. The program, which was voluntary on the part of both borrowers and lenders, offered certain borrowers the ability to refinance into new mortgages insured by FHA if their lenders agreed to certain loan modifications.

Hope for Homeowners began on October 1, 2008, and ended on September 30, 2011. FHA issued guidance stating that loans had to receive case numbers by July 29, 2011 in order to be eligible for Hope for Homeowners before the program ended.[61]

In order to be eligible for the program, borrowers were required to meet the following requirements:

- The borrower must have had a mortgage that originated on or before January 1, 2008.
- The borrower's mortgage payments must have been more than 31% of gross monthly income.
- The borrower must not have owned another home.
- The borrower must not have intentionally defaulted on his or her mortgage or any other substantial debt within the last five years, and he or she must not have been convicted of fraud during the last ten years under either federal or state law.
- The borrower must not have provided false information to obtain the original mortgage.

Under Hope for Homeowners, the lender agreed to write the mortgage down to a percentage of the home's currently appraised value, and the borrower received a new loan insured by the FHA. The home had to be reappraised by an FHA-approved home appraiser in order to determine its current value, and the lender absorbed whatever loss resulted from the write-down. The new mortgage was a 30-year fixed-rate mortgage with no prepayment penalties, and could not exceed $550,440. Homeowners paid an upfront mortgage insurance premium of 2% of the loan balance and an annual mortgage insurance premium of 0.75% of the loan balance, and any second lien-holders were required to release their liens. When the homeowner sells or refinances the home, he or she is required to pay an exit premium to HUD. The exit premium is a percentage of the initial equity the borrower has in the home after the H4H refinance; if the borrower sells or refinances the home during the first year after the H4H refinance, the exit premium is 100% of the initial equity. After five years, the exit premium is 50% of the initial equity.[62]

Under the original terms of the program, the lender was required to write the loan down to 90% of the home's currently appraised value. The upfront and annual mortgage insurance premiums were originally set at 3% and 1.5%, respectively, and second lien-holders were compensated for releasing their liens with a share of any future profit from the home's eventual sale rather than an upfront payment. Furthermore, homeowners were originally required to share a portion of both their equity and any appreciation in the home's value with HUD when the home was eventually sold or refinanced.

On November 19, 2008, HUD announced three changes to Hope for Homeowners in order to simplify the program and encourage participation. The authority to make these changes was granted in the Emergency Economic Stabilization Act of 2008 (P.L. 110-343).[63] These changes did the following: (1) increased the maximum loan-to-value ratio of the new loan to 96.5% of the home's currently appraised value, instead of the original 90%, in order to minimize losses to lenders; (2) allowed lenders to increase the term of the mortgage from 30 to 40 years in order to lower borrowers' monthly payments; and (3) offered an immediate payment to second lien-holders, instead of a share in future profits, in return for their agreement to relinquish the lien.

Congress authorized further changes to the Hope for Homeowners program in the Helping Families Save Their Homes Act of 2009 (P.L. 111-22), which was signed into law by President Obama on May 20, 2009. P.L. 111-22 changed the Hope for Homeowners program by allowing reductions in both the upfront and annual mortgage insurance premiums that borrowers pay; allowing HUD to offer servicers and H4H mortgage originators incentive payments for each loan that was successfully refinanced using Hope for Homeowners; and allowing HUD to reduce its share in any future home price appreciation (and giving HUD the authority to share its stake in the home's future appreciation with the original lender or a second lien-holder). P.L. 111-22 also placed the Hope for Homeowners program under the control of the Secretary of HUD and limited eligibility for the program to homeowners whose net worth did not exceed a certain threshold.

HUD used the authority granted in both of these laws to make changes to H4H from its original form. For example, HUD lowered the mortgage insurance premiums; set the maximum loan-tovalue ratio of the new loan at either 96.5% or 90%, based on the borrower's mortgage debt- and total debt-to-income ratios and credit score; offered immediate payments to certain second lien-holders to release their liens; eliminated the shared appreciation feature; and replaced the shared equity feature with the exit premium.[64]

The Obama Administration issued guidance for servicers on using Hope for Homeowners together with the Making Home Affordable program. This guidance required servicers who are participating in the Making Home Affordable program to screen borrowers for eligibility for Hope for Homeowners and to use that program for qualified borrowers prior to H4H's expiration. The Administration's guidance also offered incentive payments to servicers who used Hope for Homeowners, and to lenders who originated new loans under the program.

The Congressional Budget Office originally estimated that up to 400,000 homeowners could be helped to avoid foreclosure over the life of H4H.[65] In total, about 760 borrowers refinanced through the program.[66] Some have suggested that more borrowers and lenders did not use Hope for Homeowners because the program was too complex. The legislative and administrative changes described above were intended to address some of the obstacles to participating in the program.

OTHER EXISTING GOVERNMENT INITIATIVES

In addition to Making Home Affordable and Hope for Homeowners, a number of other programs have been created by federal, state, and local governments to attempt to stem the rise in foreclosures and help more homeowners remain in their homes. Although some of these programs are now obsolete, many continue to operate. (See Appendix B for a description of earlier foreclosure prevention programs that are generally no longer operational.) This section describes other recent, ongoing federal programs and policies to prevent foreclosure, and briefly outlines some state and local foreclosure prevention efforts.

Foreclosure Counseling Funding to NeighborWorks America

Another federal effort to slow the rising number of foreclosures has been to appropriate additional funding for housing counseling. In particular, Congress has recently appropriated funding specifically for foreclosure mitigation counseling to be administered by NeighborWorks America, a non-profit created by Congress in 1978 that has a national network of community partners.[67] NeighborWorks traditionally provides housing counseling to homebuyers and homeowners through its network organizations, and also trains other non-profit housing counseling organizations in foreclosure counseling.

The Consolidated Appropriations Act, 2008 (P.L. 110-161) provided $180 million for NeighborWorks to distribute for foreclosure mitigation counseling, which it has done by setting up the National Foreclosure Mitigation Counseling Program (NFMCP).[68]

NeighborWorks competitively awards the funding to qualified housing counseling organizations.[69] Congress directed NeighborWorks to award the funding with a focus on areas with high default and foreclosure rates on subprime mortgages.

The Housing and Economic Recovery Act of 2008 (P.L. 110-289) provided an additional $180 million for NeighborWorks to distribute through the NFMCP, $30 million of which was to be distributed to counseling organizations to provide legal help to homeowners facing delinquency or foreclosure.

Since HERA, Congress has continued to provide funding for the NFMCP through annual appropriations acts. The Omnibus Appropriations Act, 2009 (P.L. 111-8) included $50 million for NeighborWorks to distribute through the NFMCP, while the Consolidated Appropriations Act, 2010 (P.L. 111-117) and the Department of Defense and Full-Year Continuing Appropriations Act, 2011 (P.L. 112-10) each included $65 million. The Consolidated and Further Continuing Appropriations Act, 2012 (P.L. 112-55) provided $80 million for the

NFMCP. Table 3 shows the funding that has been provided for the NFMCP since its inception.

Table 3. Funding for the National Foreclosure Mitigation Counseling Program

Law	Date Enacted	Amount
Consolidated Appropriations Act, 2008 (P.L. 110-161)	December 26, 2007	$180
Housing and Economic Recovery Act of 2008 (P.L. 110-289)	July 30, 2008	$180
Omnibus Appropriations Act, 2009 (P.L. 111-8)	March 11, 2009	$50
Consolidated Appropriations Act, 2010 (P.L. 111-117)	December 16, 2009	$65
Department of Defense and Full-Year Continuing Appropriations Act, 2011 (P.L. 112-10)	April 15, 2011	$65
Consolidated and Continuing Appropriations Act, 2012 (P.L. 112-55)	November 18, 2011	$80

Source: P.L. 110-161, P.L. 110-289, P.L. 111-8, P.L. 111-117, P.L. 112-10, P.L. 112-55
Notes: The funds appropriated in P.L. 110-289 included funding for legal assistance for homeowners facing foreclosure.

Foreclosure Mitigation Efforts Targeted to Servicemembers

The federal government has made a number of efforts to prevent foreclosures specifically among members of the Armed Forces. The Servicemembers Civil Relief Act (P.L. 108-189), which became law on December 19, 2003, prohibits foreclosure completions on properties owned by servicemembers during a period of military service or within 90 days of the servicemember's return from military service.[70] The law also prohibits evictions of active servicemembers or their dependents, subject to certain conditions. The Housing and Economic Recovery Act of 2008 (HERA, P.L. 110-289) directed the Secretary of Defense to develop a foreclosure counseling program for members of the Armed Forces returning from active duty abroad. It also amended the Servicemembers Civil Relief Act to extend the prohibition on foreclosure completions to nine months after a servicemember's return from military service until December 31, 2010, after which the 90-day provision would go back into effect. The Helping Heroes Keep Their Homes Act of 2010 (P.L. 111-346) extended the nine-month prohibition on foreclosure completions until December 31, 2012.

State and Local Initiatives

In addition to federal efforts to prevent foreclosures, a number of state and local governments have implemented their own programs aimed at helping homeowners stay in their homes. Some of these efforts include supporting voluntary or mandatory pre-foreclosure counseling initiatives, establishing foreclosure mediation programs, imposing foreclosure moratoria, providing short-term loans to help homeowners at risk of foreclosure, enacting stronger reporting requirements on lenders' loan modification efforts, and initiating legal actions. Many states and localities have also implemented educational efforts to reach out to troubled homeowners. According to the Pew Charitable Trusts Center on the States, as of April 2008, 20 states had laws or regulations involving foreclosure mitigation, 24 states had statewide counseling efforts, 13 states had a foreclosure intervention hotline, and 9 states had developed loan funds to help homeowners refinance into more affordable mortgages or to provide short-term loans to borrowers facing foreclosure. Furthermore, at least 14 states had created foreclosure prevention task forces to attempt to address the problem of rising foreclosure rates.[71] Since that time, these numbers have likely increased as states have continued to develop their own responses to foreclosures.

PRIVATE INITIATIVES

While the government has initiated the mortgage modification programs described above, a number of private mortgage lenders and servicers have voluntarily attempted to implement their own foreclosure prevention initiatives. Many private lenders have engaged in ongoing individual loan modifications for some time, but have launched more targeted programs to help troubled borrowers in recent years. Many lenders also participate in federal programs such as HAMP. One example of private efforts to prevent foreclosures is the HOPE NOW Alliance, a voluntary alliance of mortgage servicers, lenders, investors, counseling agencies, and others that formed in October 2007.[72] The alliance is a private sector initiative created with the encouragement of the federal government to engage in active outreach efforts to troubled borrowers. Member organizations identify borrowers who may have difficulty making loan payments before they become seriously delinquent on their mortgages, and work with such borrowers to work out loan modifications or repayment plans that can keep the borrowers in their homes. HOPE NOW Alliance members have undertaken several initiatives to help troubled homeowners. One such initiative the alliance has supported is a hotline, operated by the Homeownership Preservation Foundation, that connects borrowers to HUD-approved housing counselors who can help homeowners contact their servicers and work out a plan to avoid foreclosure. The hotline serves as a first point of contact for troubled borrowers, and both HUD and non-profit organizations such as NeighborWorks America advocate its use.[73]

According to HOPE NOW's own reports, the alliance's members had executed close to 900,000 loan modifications in 2011 as of October 2011.[74] This number includes both modifications completed through the Home Affordable Modification Program (HAMP) and through servicers' proprietary programs. It does not include repayment plans or other types of workouts. (Under a repayment plan, it is possible that some borrowers could end up with higher, not lower, monthly payments. Therefore, in some cases repayment plans may not substantially reduce the risk that the assisted homeowners will eventually end up in default or foreclosure.) HOPE NOW also reports that the industry has completed a total of about 5 million mortgage modifications since 2007, including both HAMP and proprietary modifications.[75]

OTHER FORECLOSURE PREVENTION PROPOSALS

Some observers argue that the programs outlined above, which have already been implemented by various government and private organizations, have not been effective enough at stopping the rising foreclosure rate and keeping people in their homes. This section briefly outlines some existing proposals for further action to help prevent foreclosures.

Changing Bankruptcy Law

One method that has been suggested to help more homeowners remain in their homes is to amend bankruptcy law to allow a judge to order a mortgage loan modification as part of a bankruptcy proceeding. Bankruptcy judges currently have the authority to modify or reduce other types of outstanding debt obligations, including mortgages on second homes and vacation homes, but this authority does not extend to mortgages on primary residences. Opponents of such a change do not want judges to have such broad power to amend a contract after the fact. They argue that allowing these "cramdowns" would make lenders more hesitant to make mortgage loans in the future, since the threat of a loan being modified in this way could make mortgage lending more risky. Supporters of amending bankruptcy law say that, in addition to helping a borrower in bankruptcy avoid foreclosure through a court-mandated loan modification, such a change might also encourage lenders to work with borrowers to modify loans before the bankruptcy process begins in the first place. During the 111th Congress, provisions to amend bankruptcy law to allow judges to modify mortgages on primary residences were included in H.R. 1106, the Helping Families Save Their Homes Act of 2009, which passed the House on March 5, 2009. However, bankruptcy provisions were not included in the Senate's version of the bill, S. 896, which passed the Senate on May 6, 2009. A modified version of the Senate bill was signed into law (P.L. 111-22) on May 20, 2009, without the cramdown provision.

Foreclosure Moratorium

Some advocates have called for placing a temporary moratorium on foreclosure completions. Proponents of this idea argue that placing a freeze on foreclosure completions would give homeowners and lenders more time to work out sustainable loan modifications that would allow homeowners to remain in their homes and turn troubled mortgages back into performing loans that benefit the lenders. Opponents of a foreclosure moratorium argue that the government should not interfere with the right of a lender to complete foreclosure proceedings against a borrower who has defaulted on his or her loan. They note that delaying foreclosure proceedings through a foreclosure moratorium could result in greater losses for the lender if the ultimate outcome is still a foreclosure and the home's price has fallen further in the interim. Fannie Mae, Freddie Mac, and some private lenders have periodically instituted temporary foreclosure moratoria for mortgages they that they own to allow time for foreclosure prevention programs to be put into place or for other reasons.

ISSUES AND CHALLENGES ASSOCIATED WITH PREVENTING FORECLOSURES

There are several challenges associated with designing successful programs to prevent foreclosures. Some of these challenges are practical and concern issues surrounding the implementation of loan modifications. Other challenges are more conceptual, and are related to questions of fairness and precedent. This section describes some of the most prominent considerations involved in programs to preserve homeownership.

Who Has the Authority to Modify Mortgages?

In recent years, the practice of lenders packaging mortgages into securities and selling them to investors has become more widespread. This practice is known as securitization, and the securities that include the mortgages are known as mortgage-backed securities (MBS). When mortgages are sold through securitization, several players become involved with any individual mortgage loan, including the lender, the servicer, and the investors who hold shares in the MBS. The servicer is usually the organization that has the most contact with the borrower, including receiving monthly payments and initiating any foreclosure proceedings. However, servicers are usually subject to contracts with investors which limit the activities that the servicer can undertake and require it to safeguard the investors' profit. One major question that has faced foreclosure prevention programs, therefore, is who actually has the authority to make a loan modification. Contractual obligations may limit the amount of flexibility that servicers have to modify loans in ways that could arguably yield a lower return for investors. In some cases, loan modifications can result in less of a loss for investors than foreclosure; however, servicers may not want to risk having investors challenge their assessment that a modification is more cost-effective than a foreclosure. This problem can be especially salient in streamlined programs in which large numbers of loans are modified at once. With such streamlined programs, the cost-effectiveness of loan modifications depends on questions such as how many loans would have likely ended up in foreclosure without the modification, making it more difficult to say whether wholesale loan modifications are in the best interest of investors. One possible way to partially address the question of who can modify mortgages is to provide a safe harbor for servicers. In general, a safe harbor protects servicers who engage in certain mortgage modifications from lawsuits brought by investors. While proponents of a safe harbor believe that a safe harbor is necessary to encourage servicers to modify more mortgages without fear of legal repercussions, opponents argue that a safe harbor infringes on investors' rights and could even encourage servicers to modify mortgages that are not in trouble if it benefits their own self-interest.

P.L. 111-22, the Helping Families Save Their Homes Act of 2009, provides a safe harbor for servicers who modify mortgages consistent with the Making Home Affordable program guidelines or who used the since-expired Hope for Homeowners program. The legislation specifies that the safe harbor does not protect servicers or individuals from liability for any fraud committed in their handling of the mortgage or the mortgage modification.

Volume of Delinquencies and Foreclosures

Another issue facing loan modification programs is the sheer number of delinquencies and foreclosure proceedings underway. Lenders and servicers have a limited number of employees to reach out to troubled borrowers and find solutions. Contacting borrowers— some of whom may avoid contact with their servicer out of embarrassment or fear—and working out large numbers of individual loan modifications can overwhelm the capacity of the lenders and servicers who are trying to help homeowners avoid foreclosure. Streamlined plans that use a formula to modify all loans that meet certain criteria may make it easier for lenders and servicers to help a greater number of borrowers in a shorter amount of time. However, streamlined plans are more likely to run into the contractual issues between servicers and investors described above.

Servicer Incentives

Mortgage servicers are the entities that are often primarily responsible for making the decision to modify a mortgage or to begin the foreclosure process. Concerns have been raised that mortgage servicers' compensation structures may provide incentives for them to pursue foreclosure rather than modify loans in certain cases. Servicers' actions are governed by contracts with mortgage holders or investors that generally require servicers to act in the best interests of the entity on whose behalf they service the mortgages, although, as described above, such contracts may in some cases also include restrictions on servicers' abilities to modify loans. In addition to their contractual obligations, servicers have an incentive to service mortgages in the best interest of investors because that is one way that mortgage servicers ensure that they will attract continued business. However, some have suggested that servicers' compensation structures may provide incentives for servicers to pursue foreclosure even when it is not in the best interest of the investor in the mortgage. For example, servicers' compensation structures may not provide an incentive to put in the extra work that is necessary to modify a mortgage, and servicers may be able to charge more in fees or recoup more expenses through a foreclosure than a modification. Programs such as HAMP provide financial payments to servicers to modify mortgages, but critics argue that these may not be large enough to align servicers' incentives with those of borrowers and investors.[76] Recently, the Federal Housing Finance Agency (FHFA) and HUD have announced a joint initiative to consider alternative servicer compensation structures, although any changes would not take effect until at least 2012.[77]

Possibility of Re-default

Another major challenge associated with loan modification programs is the possibility that a homeowner who receives a modification will nevertheless default on the loan again in the future.

This possibility is especially problematic if the home's value is falling, because in that case delaying an eventual foreclosure reduces the value that the lender can recoup through a foreclosure sale. Data released quarterly by the Office of the Comptroller of the Currency (OCC) track the re-default rates of modified mortgages. Data from the third quarter of 2011 show that 23.5% of loans modified in the second quarter of 2010 were 30 or more days delinquent again three months after the modification, 33% were 30 or more days delinquent six months after the modification, and 37% were 30 or more days delinquent 12 months after the modification. The same data show that a smaller percentage of modified loans were 60 or more days delinquent: almost 11% of loans were 60 or more days delinquent three months after the modification, almost 20% were 60 or more days delinquent six months after the modification, and nearly 26% were 60 or more days delinquent 12 months after the modification.[78] Earlier reports from the OCC showed that mortgages modified in earlier quarters tended to have higher re-default rates; the decrease in redefault rates for loans modified in more recent quarters may have to do with an increased focus on modifications that reduce borrowers' monthly payments. The OCC has begun to include data in its quarterly report that show re-default rates according to whether the loan modification increased monthly payments, decreased monthly payments, or left monthly payments unchanged. The reports include such data for loans modified since the beginning of 2008. The third quarter 2011 report shows that, for loans modified in 2010, about 17% of loan modifications that resulted in monthly payments being reduced by 20% or more were 60 or more days delinquent twelve months after modification. This compares to a re-default rate of nearly 30% for loans where monthly payments were reduced by between 10% and 20%; about 37% for loans where payments were reduced by less than 10%; about 25% for loans where payments remained unchanged; and nearly 45% for loans where monthly payments increased. While loan modifications that lower monthly payments do appear to perform better than modifications that increase monthly payments or leave them unchanged, a significant number of modified loans with lower monthly payments still become delinquent again after the loan modification.[79] The OCC also reports that HAMP modifications appear to perform somewhat better than other types of modifications, possibly because of HAMP's focus on reducing monthly mortgage payments. For example, they report that about 13% of HAMP modifications completed in the second quarter of 2010 were 60 or more days delinquent six months later, while about 24% of other modifications from the same period were 60 or more days delinquent six months later.[80] Treasury's own data on the performance of HAMP modifications also show somewhat lower levels of re-default than are seen for other types of mortgage modifications to date. As of September 2011, Treasury reported that about 10% of permanent HAMP modifications were 60 or more days delinquent six months after modification, and about 19% of HAMP modifications were 60 or more days delinquent 12 months after modification.[81]

Distorting Borrower Incentives

Another challenge is that loan modification programs may provide an incentive for borrowers to intentionally miss payments or default on their mortgages in order to qualify for a loan modification that provides more favorable mortgage terms. While many of the programs described above specifically require that a borrower must not have intentionally missed payments on his or her mortgage in order to qualify for the program, it can be difficult to prove a person's intention. Programs that are designed to reach out to distressed borrowers before they miss any payments, as well as those who are already delinquent, may minimize the incentive for homeowners to intentionally fall behind on their mortgages in order to receive help.

Fairness Issues

Opponents of some foreclosure prevention plans argue that it is not fair to help homeowners who have fallen behind on their mortgages while homeowners who have been scraping by to stay current receive no help. Others argue that borrowers who got in over their heads, particularly if they intentionally took out mortgages that they knew they could not afford, should face consequences. Supporters of loan modification plans point out that many borrowers go into foreclosure for reasons outside of their control, and that some troubled borrowers may have been victims of deceptive, unfair, or fraudulent lending practices. Furthermore, some argue for foreclosure prevention programs because foreclosures can create problems for other homeowners in the neighborhood by dragging down property values or putting a strain on local governments. To address these concerns about fairness, some loan modification programs reach out to borrowers who are struggling to make payments but are not yet delinquent on their mortgages. Most programs also specifically exclude individuals who provided false information in order to obtain a mortgage.

Precedent

Some opponents of government efforts to provide or encourage loan modifications argue that changing the terms of a contract retroactively sets a troubling precedent for future mortgage lending. These opponents argue that if lenders believe that they could be forced to change the terms of a mortgage in the future, they will be less likely to provide mortgage loans in the first place or will only do so at higher interest rates to counter the perceived increase in the risk of not being repaid in full. Most existing programs attempt to address this concern by limiting the program's scope. Often, these programs apply only to mortgages that originated during a certain time frame, and end at a pre-determined date.

APPENDIX A. COMPARISON OF RECENT FEDERAL FORECLOSURE PREVENTION INITIATIVES

Table A-1. Comparison of Select Federal Foreclosure Prevention Programs

	Refinancing Programs			Modification Programs	
	Hope for Homeowners (H4H)	FHA Short Refinance Program	Home Affordable Refinance Program (HARP)[a]	Home Affordable Modification Program (HAMP)— Original	HAMP— Principal Reduction Alternative[b]
Program Basics					
Status	Created by P.L. 110-289. Modified by P.L. 111-22.	Obama Administration initiative.	Obama Administration initiative.	Obama Administration initiative.c	Obama Administration initiative to modify HAMP.
	Began on October 1, 2008.	Announced March 26, 2010; active since September 7, 2010.	Announced February 2009; active since April 1, 2009.	Announced February 2009, active since March 4, 2009.	Announced March 26, 2010; active since October 1, 2010.
	Ended on September 30, 2011.	Available until December 31, 2012.	Available until December 31, 2013.	Available until December 31, 2012.	Same as HAMP.
	762 loans refinanced through the program.	499 loans had refinanced through the program as of November 2011.	962,132 loans had been refinanced through HARP as of October 2011.	80,223 HAMP trial modifications and 750,748 HAMP permanent modifications were active as of November 2011.	15,875 trial PRA modifications and 36,454 permanent PRA modifications were active as of November 2011
Basic Premise	Allowed certain homeowners who owe more than their homes were worth to refinance into new, FHA-insured mortgages.	Allows certain homeowners who are current on their mortgages, but owe more than their homes are worth, to refinance into new, FHA-insured mortgages.	Allows certain homeowners who are current on their mortgages, but owe between over 80% of what their homes are worth, and whose mortgages are owned or guaranteed by Fannie Mae or Freddie Mac, to refinance into new, non-FHA insured mortgages.	Provides incentives to servicers to modify borrowers' mortgages so that monthly mortgage payments are no more than 31% of gross monthly income.	Expansion of HAMP to facilitate principal reductions on eligible mortgages.
	Reduced principal balance on first mortgage; maximum loan-to-value (LTV) ratio of new loan depended on borrower's circumstances.	Reduces principal balance on the first mortgage to no more than 97.75% of the home's value. The first mortgage must be reduced by at least 10%.	Does not reduce principal.	Principal reduction is allowed at servicer's discretion, but not required or specifically incentivized.	Requires participating HAMP servicers to consider reducing principal for eligible borrowers who owe over 115% of the value of their home. Provides incentives to lenders/investors specifically for reducing principal.

	Hope for Homeowners (H4H)	FHA Short Refinance Program	Home Affordable Refinance Program (HARP)[a]	Home Affordable Modification Program (HAMP)—Original	HAMP—Principal Reduction Alternative[b]
	Second liens had to be extinguished.	Second liens are allowed to remain; they must be re-subordinated, and total mortgage debt after the refinance may not exceed 115% of the home's value.	Second liens are allowed to remain; they must be re-subordinated.	Second liens are allowed to remain; they must be re-subordinated, and the Second Lien Modification Program provides incentives for modification or extinguishment of second liens.	Increases incentive payments available through the HAMP Second Lien Modification Program.
Program Details	Borrower refinanced into FHA-insured mortgage with a lower principal mortgage amount. Original mortgage holder absorbed loss resulting from write-down in mortgage value.	Borrower refinances into FHA-insured mortgage for no more than 97.75% of home's value. Original mortgage holder absorbs loss resulting from write-down in mortgage value.	Borrower can refinance into a new, non-FHA insured loan. The refinanced loan will not reduce the principal balance owed, but it can reduce the interest rate or move the borrower from an adjustable-rate to a fixed-rate mortgage, thereby lowering monthly payments or preventing a payment increase.	Servicers receive incentives to reduce eligible borrowers' mortgage payments to 38% of gross monthly income. Servicer can reduce payments through interest rate reductions, term extensions, and principal forbearance, and may reduce principal at their own discretion.	Requires servicers who are participating in HAMP to consider principal reduction for borrowers who owe at least 115% of the value of their homes.
				Government shares half the cost of further reducing payments to 31% of monthly income.	
	New mortgage amount could not exceed $550,440 (for a one-unit home).	New mortgage amount may not exceed FHA maximum loan limits.	New mortgage, like the original mortgage, cannot exceed Fannie Mae/Freddie Mac conforming loan limits.	Because the outstanding principal balance cannot exceed $729,750 (for a one-unit home) to participate in HAMP, the principal balance of loans modified through HAMP will necessarily not exceed this amount.	Same as HAMP.
	New mortgage had to result in a lower monthly mortgage payment than the original loan, but there was no minimum reduction in payment.	New total monthly mortgage payment (including second mortgage payments) must be no higher than approximately 31% of income.	The new mortgage must benefit the homeowner through a lower interest rate or a more stable mortgage product	The new mortgage payment must not exceed 31% of gross monthly income.	Same as HAMP. If principal is reduced, the amount of principal reduction will initially be treated

Table A-1. (Continued)

	Refinancing Programs			Modification Programs	
	Hope for Homeowners (H4H)	FHA Short Refinance Program	Home Affordable Refinance Program (HARP)[a]	Home Affordable Modification Program (HAMP)— Original	HAMP— Principal Reduction Alternative[b]
	Maximum loan-to-value ratios and total debt-to-income ratios depended on the borrower's delinquency status and credit score.d	New mortgage must result in a reduction of mortgage debt of at least 10% of the amount of the original outstanding principal balance, and must not exceed 97.75% of the home's value.	(for example, a fixed-rate loan instead of an adjustable-rate loan). Borrowers without mortgage insurance (MI) on the original loan are not required to get MI on the new loan.	Borrowers must successfully complete a three-month trial period before the modification becomes permanent.	as principal forbearance, and then will be forgiven in three equal parts over three years as long as the borrower remains current.
		Total household debt may not be more than approximately 50% in most cases.			
	Borrower paid upfront and annual FHA mortgage insurance premiums.e Borrower pays "exit premium" when the home is sold.f	Borrower pays upfront and annual FHA mortgage insurance premiums.	If the mortgage already had MI, that MI should be transferred to the new loan.	Mortgages may or may not have MI.	Same as HAMP.
	Second lien-holders had to release their liens.	Allows for existence of a second lien up to a total combined mortgage debt of 115% of home's value. If the second lien is not extinguished, the second lien-holder must agree to re-subordinate the lien.	Second liens are not explicitly addressed.	Second Lien Modification Program provides incentives for the modification or extinguishment of Second Liens.	Second Lien Modification Program still applies; incentives will be increased.
Incentives for Lenders/ Servicers/ Investors	HUD had authority to provide incentive payments to mortgage servicers and originators of new H4H mortgages.	No incentive payments related to first lien mortgage.	No incentive payments.	Incentives to servicers for making modifications. "Pay-for-success" incentives to borrowers and servicers if borrowers remain current. Incentives to lenders/investors in the form of half the cost of reducing the monthly mortgage payment from 38% to 31% of gross monthly income.	Incentives offered to lenders/investors based on the dollar amount of principal reduced.

	Hope for Homeowners (H4H)	FHA Short Refinance Program	Home Affordable Refinance Program (HARP)[a]	Home Affordable Modification Program (HAMP)— Original	HAMP— Principal Reduction Alternative[b]
	Incentive payments could be made to second lien-holders to facilitate the extinguishment of the lien.	Incentives will be made to second lien-holders to write down the balance of the second lien.	No incentive payments.	Incentives are offered for second lien-holders to modify or release their liens through the Second Lien Program.	Incentives will be increased for second lien-holders to write down the balance of the second lien.
	Performance of H4H mortgages were not be included in certain FHA evaluations of lenders' performance.	Performance of short refinances will not be included in certain FHA evaluations of lenders' performance.	No additional incentives.	Additional incentives are available for investors, borrowers, lenders, and servicers for certain other modification or foreclosure prevention activities.	Additional HAMP incentives continue to apply.
Borrower/ Mortgage Eligibility Requirements	Borrower could have an FHA-insured or non-FHA-insured mortgage g	Borrower must have a non-FHA-insured mortgage.	Borrower must have a mortgage that is owned or guaranteed by Fannie Mae or Freddie Mac.	Borrower must have a mortgage held by any participating lender or servicer.h	Same as HAMP.
	Borrower could be current or delinquent on his/her mortgage.	Borrower must be current on his/her mortgage.	Borrower must be current on his/her mortgage.	Borrower may be current or delinquent on his/her mortgage.	Same as HAMP.
	Borrower must have experienced a financial hardship.	No hardship requirement.	No hardship requirement.	Borrower must have experienced a financial hardship.	Same as HAMP.
	Borrower's total monthly mortgage payment must have been higher than 31% of gross monthly income. Borrower's net worth could not be greater than $1 million.	No minimum monthly mortgage payment specified.	Borrower owes between 80% and 125% of the value of the home.i	Borrower's total monthly mortgage payment must be higher than 31% of gross monthly income. Borrower must not have sufficient liquid assets to make monthly mortgage payments.	Same as HAMP. Borrower must owe at least 115% of the value of the home before servicers are required to consider principal reductions.
				The unpaid principal balance is no higher than $729,750 (for a one-unit property). This is the Fannie Mae/Freddie Mac conforming loan limit for high-cost areas.	
	Mortgage must have been originated on or before January 1, 2008.	No mortgage origination criteria specified.	Mortgage must generally have been delivered to Fannie Mae or Freddie Mac during or before the early months of 2009, but the actual dates depend on whether the loan is owned or guaranteed by Fannie or Freddie.	Mortgage must have been originated on or before January 1, 2009.	Same as HAMP.

Table A-1. (Continued)

	Refinancing Programs			Modification Programs	
	Hope for Homeowners (H4H)	FHA Short Refinance Program	Home Affordable Refinance Program (HARP)[a]	Home Affordable Modification Program (HAMP)— Original	HAMP— Principal Reduction Alternative[b]
Eligibility Requirements					
Property Eligibility Requirements	Home must have been the borrower's primary residence.	Home must be the borrower's primary residence.	Home not required to be primary residence.	Home must be the borrower's primary residence.	Same as HAMP.
	Property must have been single-family (1-4 unit) home[j]	Property must be single-family (1-4 unit) home.	Property must be single-family (1-4 unit) home.	Property must be single-family (1-4 unit) home.	Same as HAMP.
Lender/ Servicer Participation	Mortgage holders agreed to accept proceeds of new loan as payment in full on the original loan, and FHA-approved lenders agreed to make new H4H loans, on a case-by-case basis.	Mortgage holders agree to accept proceeds of new loan as payment in full on the original loan, and FHA-approved lenders agree to make new FHA-insured loans, on a case-by-case basis.	Fannie Mae- and Freddie Mac-approved lenders are authorized to participate.	Servicers who have signed HAMP participation agreements are required to participate; signing a participation agreement is voluntary.	Servicers who have signed HAMP participation agreements are required to participate in the program changes.

Sources: FHA Mortgagee Letter 2009-43; FHA Mortgagee Letter 2010-23; Fact Sheet on FHA Program Adjustments to Support Refinancings for Underwater Homeowners; Fact Sheet on Making Home Affordable Program Enhancements to Offer More Help for Homeowners; FHA Outlook, February 2010; FHFA Foreclosure Prevention and Refinance Report, November 2009/January 2010; Making Home Affordable Program: Servicer Performance Reports; Home Affordable Modification Program Guidelines; HAMP Supplemental Directive 09-01; Fannie Mae and Freddie Mac HARP guidance.

a. Fannie Mae and Freddie Mac have each issued their own specific guidelines for HARP.

b. Treasury's detailed guidance on HAMP, including the Principal Reduction Alternative and other related programs, can be found in the Making Home Affordable handbook, available at https://www.hmpadmin.com/portal/index.jsp.

c. While HAMP was created as an Obama Administration initiative, the funding for the program is provided through the Troubled Assets Relief Program (TARP). TARP was authorized in P.L. 110-343.

d. FHA Mortgagee Letter 2009-43. The maximum allowable LTV has changed since the program was first created.

e. Using statutory authority provided in P.L. 111-22, HUD has reduced the mortgage insurance premiums for H4H from their original levels.

f. Borrowers originally had to agree to share a portion of both their equity in the home and any house price appreciation with HUD when the home was eventually sold. P.L. 111-22 provided the authority to change these requirements. The exit premium is now a payment of a portion of the initial equity in the home after the H4H refinance.

g. FHA Mortgagee Letter 2009-43. When the program first began, only non-FHA-insured loans were eligible.

h. FHA-insured mortgages are eligible for FHA-HAMP, an FHA loss mitigation activity that shares many of the same features as HAMP. VA or USDA mortgages may or may not be eligible for HAMP, subject to the relevant agency's guidance.

i. Originally, HARP allowed homeowners to refinance if they owed up to 105% of the value of their homes. On July 1, 2009, the Federal Housing Finance Agency (FHFA) announced that it would increase the maximum loan-to-value ratio to 125%.

j. FHA Mortgagee Letter 2009-43. When the program first began, only 1-unit properties were eligible.

APPENDIX B. EARLIER FORECLOSURE PREVENTION PROGRAMS

Prior to the creation of the more recent foreclosure prevention programs described earlier in this report, several other foreclosure prevention programs were created or announced. Many of these programs were precursors to the programs that are in place today. This Appendix describes some of these programs, including *FHASecure*, Fannie Mae's and Freddie Mac's Streamlined Modification Program, and the FDIC's program for modifying loans that had been held by IndyMac Bank. Most of these programs are no longer active; exceptions are noted in the text.

FHASecure

FHASecure was a temporary program announced by the Federal Housing Administration (FHA) on August 31, 2007, to allow delinquent borrowers with non-FHA adjustable-rate mortgages (ARMs) to refinance into FHA-insured fixed-rate mortgages.[82] The new mortgage helped borrowers by offering better loan terms that either reduced a borrower's monthly payments or helped a borrower avoid steep payment increases under his or her old loan. *FHASecure* expired on December 31, 2008.

To qualify for *FHASecure*, borrowers originally had to meet the following eligibility criteria:

- The borrower had a non-FHA ARM that had reset.
- The borrower became delinquent on his or her loan due to the reset, and had sufficient income to make monthly payments on the new FHA-insured loan.
- The borrower was current on his or her mortgage prior to the reset. (Some borrowers with a minimum amount of equity in their homes could still be eligible for the program even if they had missed payments prior to the reset.)
- The new loan met standard FHA underwriting criteria and was subject to other standard FHA requirements (including maximum loan-to-value ratios, mortgage limits, and up-front and annual mortgage insurance premiums).

In July 2008, FHA expanded its eligibility criteria for the program, and borrowers had to meet the following revised eligibility requirements:

- The borrower became delinquent on his or her non-FHA ARM because of an interest rate reset or another extenuating circumstance, and had sufficient income to make monthly payments on the new FHA-insured loan.
- The borrower had no more than two payments that were 30 days late, or one payment that was 60 days late, in the 12 months preceding the interest rate reset or other extenuating circumstance.
- If the loan-to-value ratio on the FHA-insured mortgage was no higher than 90%, the borrower may have had no more than three payments that were 30 days late, or one payment that was 90 days late, prior to the interest rate reset or other extenuating circumstance.

- Borrowers with interest-only ARMs or option ARMs must have been delinquent due to an interest rate reset only (and not other extenuating circumstances), and must have been current on their mortgages prior to the reset; the revised eligibility criteria did not apply to these borrowers.
- The new loan met standard FHA underwriting criteria and was subject to other standard FHA requirements (including maximum loan-to-value ratios, mortgage limits, and up-front and annual mortgage insurance premiums).

FHASecure expired on December 31, 2008. In the months before its expiration, some housing policy advocates called for the program to be extended; however, HUD officials contended that continuing the program would be prohibitively expensive, possibly endangering FHA's single-family mortgage insurance program. HUD also pointed to the Hope for Homeowners program as filling the role that FHASecure did in helping households avoid foreclosure.[83] Supporters of extending FHASecure argued that the statutory requirements of Hope for Homeowners may have offered less flexibility in the face of changing circumstances than FHASecure, which could have been more easily amended by HUD.

When FHASecure expired at the end of 2008, about 4,000 loans had been refinanced through the program.[84] Critics of the program point to the relatively stringent criteria that borrowers had to meet to qualify for the program as a possible reason that more people did not take advantage of it.

IndyMac Loan Modifications

On July 11, 2008, the Office of Thrift Supervision in the Department of the Treasury closed IndyMac Federal Savings Bank, based in Pasadena, CA, and placed it under the conservatorship of the Federal Deposit Insurance Corporation (FDIC). In August 2008, the FDIC put into place a loan modification program for holders of mortgages either owned or serviced by IndyMac that were seriously delinquent or in danger of default, or on which the borrower was having trouble making payments because of interest rate resets or a change in financial circumstances.

The IndyMac program offered systematic loan modifications to qualified borrowers in financial trouble. The systematic approach means that all loan modifications follow the same basic formula to identify qualified borrowers and reduce their monthly payments in a uniform way. Such an approach is meant to allow more modifications to happen more quickly than if each loan was modified on a case-by-case basis.

In order to be eligible for a loan modification, the mortgage must have been for the borrower's primary residence and the borrower had to provide current income information that documented financial hardship. Furthermore, the FDIC conducted a net present value test to evaluate whether the expected future benefit to the FDIC and the mortgage investors from modifying the loan would be greater than the expected future benefit from foreclosure.

If a borrower met the above conditions, the loan would be modified so that he or she had a mortgage debt-to-income (DTI) ratio of 38%. The 38% DTI could be achieved by lowering the interest rate, extending the period of the loan, forbearing a portion of the principal, or a combination of the three. The interest rate would be set at the Freddie Mac survey rate for conforming mortgages, but if necessary it could be lowered for a period of up to five years in order to reach the 38% DTI; after the five-year period, the interest rate would rise by no more than 1% each year until it reached the Freddie Mac survey rate.

FDIC Chairman Sheila Bair estimated that about 13,000 loans were modified under this program while IndyMac was under the FDIC's conservatorship.[85] The FDIC completed a sale of IndyMac to OneWest Bank on March 19, 2009. OneWest agreed to continue to operate the loan modification program subject to the terms of a loss-sharing agreement with the FDIC.[86] Currently, OneWest is a participating servicer in HAMP, described earlier in this report.

Fannie Mae and Freddie Mac Streamlined Modification Plan

On November 11, 2008, James Lockhart, then the director of the Federal Housing Finance Agency (FHFA), which oversees Fannie Mae and Freddie Mac, announced a new Streamlined Modification Program that Fannie, Freddie, and certain private mortgage lenders and servicers planned to undertake.[87] Fannie Mae and Freddie Mac had helped troubled borrowers through individualized loan modifications for some time, but the SMP represented an attempt to formalize the process and set an industry standard. The SMP took effect on December 15, 2008, but has since been replaced by the Making Home Affordable plan, announced in February 2009 and described in an earlier section of this report.

In order for borrowers whose mortgages were owned by Fannie Mae or Freddie Mac to be eligible for the SMP, they had to meet the following criteria:

- The mortgage must have originated on or before January 1, 2008.
- The mortgage must have had a loan-to-value ratio of at least 90%.
- The home must have been a single-family residence occupied by the borrower, and it must have been the borrower's primary residence.
- The borrower must have missed at least three mortgage payments.
- The borrower must not have filed for bankruptcy.

Mortgages insured or guaranteed by the federal government, such as those guaranteed by FHA, the Veterans' Administration, or the Rural Housing Service, were not eligible for the SMP.

The SMP shared many features of the FDIC's plan to modify troubled mortgages held by IndyMac. Borrowers who qualified for the program had to provide income information that was current within the last 90 days to the mortgage servicer. Based on this updated income information, borrowers' monthly mortgage payments were lowered so that the household's mortgage debt-to-income ratio (DTI) was 38% (not including second lien payments). After borrowers successfully completed a three-month trial period (by making all of the payments at the proposed modified payment amount), the loan modification automatically took effect.

In order to reach the 38% mortgage debt-to-income ratio, servicers were required to follow a specific formula. First, the servicer capitalized late payments and accrued interest (late fees and penalties were waived). If this resulted in a DTI of 38% or less, the modification was complete. If the DTI was higher than 38%, the servicer could extend the term of the loan to up to 40 years from the effective date of the modification. If the DTI was still above 38%, the interest rate could be adjusted to the current market rate or lower, but to no less than 3%. Finally, if the DTI was still above 38% after the first three steps were taken, servicers could offer principal forbearance. The amount of the principal forbearance would not accrue interest and was non-amortizing, but would result in a balloon payment when the loan was paid off or the home was sold.

Negative amortization was not allowed under the SMP, nor were principal forgiveness or principal write-downs. In order to encourage participation in the SMP, Fannie Mae and Freddie Mac paid servicers $800 for each loan modification completed through the program. If the SMP did not produce an affordable payment for the borrower, servicers were to work with borrowers in a customized fashion to try to modify the loan in a way that the homeowner could afford.

Fannie Mae and Freddie Mac completed over 51,000 loan modifications between January 2009 and April 2009, when Fannie and Freddie stopped using the SMP and began participating in the Making Home Affordable program instead.[88] However, it is unclear how many of these loan modifications were done specifically through the SMP.

Federal Reserve Homeownership Preservation Policy

On January 27, 2009, the Federal Reserve announced the Homeownership Preservation Policy.[89] This plan provided guidelines, subject to Section 110 of the Emergency Economic Stabilization Act of 2008 (EESA), to prevent foreclosures on any residential mortgages that the Federal Reserve Banks might come to hold, own, or control, such as mortgage assets that they may receive as collateral for lending to troubled banks. In order to be eligible for a loan modification under the Homeownership Preservation Policy, a borrower would have to be at least 60 days delinquent (although the Fed could make exceptions for households experiencing circumstances that were likely to result in their becoming at least 60 days delinquent). If the expected net present value of a loan modification was greater than the expected net present value of foreclosure, the Federal Reserve Banks could modify mortgages by reducing the interest rate, extending the loan term, offering principal forbearance or principal forgiveness, or changing other loan terms. The modified mortgage would have to have a fixed interest rate, a term of no more than 40 years, and result in a mortgage debt-to-income ratio of no more than 38% for the borrower. The Fed must also have a reasonable expectation that the borrower would be able to repay the modified loan. If the borrower's mortgage debt was greater than 125% of the current estimated value of the property, the Fed would prioritize principal reductions over other types of loan modifications where possible. This policy applied to whole mortgages that the Federal Reserve Banks held, owned, or controlled. In the case of securitized mortgages in which the Fed had an interest, the Fed would encourage servicers to undertake similar loan modifications and support their efforts to do so.

End Notes

[1] For a more detailed discussion of the foreclosure process and the factors that contribute to a lender's decision to pursue foreclosure, see CRS Report RL34232, *The Process, Data, and Costs of Mortgage Foreclosure*, coordinated by Darryl E. Getter.

[2] U.S. Department of Housing and Urban Development, Office of Policy Development and Research, *An Analysis of Mortgage Refinancing, 2001-2003*, November 2004, p.1, http://www.huduser.org/Publications/pdf/ MortgageRefinance03.pdf.

[3] Congressional Oversight Panel, *December Oversight Report: A Review of Treasury's Foreclosure Prevention Programs*, December 14, 2010, page 10, available at http://cop.senate.gov/documents/cop-121410-report.pdf.

[4] For example, see Donald R. Haurin, Toby L. Parcel, and R. Jean Haurin, *The Impact of Homeownership on Child Outcomes*, Joint Center for Housing Studies, Harvard University, Low-Income Homeownership Working Paper Series, October 2001, http://www.jchs.harvard.edu/publications/homeownership/liho01-14.pdf, and Denise DiPasquale and Edward L. Glaeser, *Incentives and Social Capital: Are Homeowners Better Citizens?*, National Bureau of Economic Research, NBER Working Paper 6363, Cambridge, MA, January 1998, http://www.nber.org/papers/w6363.pdf? new_window=1.

[5] For a review of the literature on the impact of foreclosures on nearby house prices, see Kai-yan Lee, *Foreclosure's Price-Depressing Spillover Effects on Local Properties: A Literature Review*, Federal Reserve Bank of Boston, Community Affairs Discussion Paper, No. 2008-01, September 2008, http://www.bos.frb.org /commdev/pcadp/2008/ pcadp0801.pdf.

[6] Representative Spencer Bachus, "Remarks of Ranking Member Spencer Bachus During Full Committee Hearing on Loan Modifications," press release, November 12, 2008, http://bachus.house.gov/index. php?option=com_content& task=view&id=160&Itemid=104.

[7] Senator Chris Dodd, "Dodd Statement on Government Loan Modification Program," statement, November 11, 2008, http://dodd.senate.gov/?q=node/4620.

[8] For a fuller discussion of these types of mortgage products and their effects, see CRS Report RL33775, *Alternative Mortgages: Causes and Policy Implications of Troubled Mortgage Resets in the Subprime and Alt-A Markets*, by Edward V. Murphy.

[9] Even if the interest rate remains the same or decreases, it is possible for monthly payments to increase if prior payments were subject to an interest rate cap or a payment cap. This is because unpaid interest that would have accrued if not for the cap can be added to the principal loan amount, resulting in negative amortization. For more information on the many variations of adjustable rate mortgages, see The Federal Reserve Board, *Consumer Handbook on Adjustable Rate Mortgages*, http://www.federalreserve.gov/pubs /arms/arms_ english.htm#drop.

[10] Mortgage lenders are the organizations that make mortgage loans to individuals. Often, the mortgage is managed by a company known as a servicer; servicers usually have the most contact with the borrower, and are responsible for actions such as collecting mortgage payments, initiating foreclosures, and communicating with troubled borrowers. The servicer can be an affiliate of the original mortgage lender or can be a separate company. Many mortgages are repackaged into mortgage-backed securities (MBS) that are sold to institutional investors. Servicers are usually subject to contracts with mortgage lenders and MBS investors that may limit their ability to undertake loan workouts or modifications; the scope of such contracts and the obligations that servicers must meet vary widely.

[11] In a short sale, a household sells its home for less than the amount it owes on its mortgage, and the lender generally accepts the proceeds from the sale as payment in full on the mortgage even though it is taking a loss. A deed-in-lieu of foreclosure refers to the practice of a borrower turning the deed to the house over to the lender, which accepts the deed as payment of the mortgage debt. However, in some cases, the borrower may still be liable for the remaining outstanding mortgage debt when a short sale or a deed-in-lieu is utilized.

[12] Historically, one impediment to principal forgiveness has been that borrowers were required to claim the forgiven amount as income, and therefore had to pay taxes on that income. Congress recently passed legislation that excludes mortgage debt forgiven before January 1, 2013, from taxable income. For more information about the tax treatment of principal forgiveness, see CRS Report RL34212, *Analysis of the Tax Exclusion for Canceled Mortgage Debt Income*, by Mark P. Keightley and Erika K. Lunder.

[13] More information on the Administration's housing plan can be found at http://www.treasury. gov/initiatives/financialstability/programs/housing-programs/Pages /default.aspx.

[14] For more information on the Financial Stability Plan, see http://www.financialstability.gov /docs/fact-sheet.pdf. For more information on the American Recovery and Reinvestment Act of 2009, see CRS Report R40537, *American Recovery and Reinvestment Act of 2009 (P.L. 111-5): Summary and Legislative History*, by Clinton T. Brass et al.

[15] The third piece of the Administration's housing plan provided additional financial support for Fannie Mae and Freddie Mac in an effort to maintain low mortgage interest rates. The Department of the Treasury said that it would increase its Preferred Stock Purchase agreements from $100 billion to $200 billion for both Fannie Mae

and Freddie Mac, and would increase the size of their portfolios by $50 billion each. The funding for the increased preferred stock purchases was authorized by the Housing and Economic Recovery Act of 2008 (P.L. 110-289).

[16] Fannie Mae and Freddie Mac are government-sponsored enterprises (GSEs) that were chartered by Congress to provide liquidity to the mortgage market. Rather than make loans directly, the GSEs buy loans made in the private market and either hold them in their own portfolios or securitize and sell them to investors. The GSEs were put under the conservatorship of FHFA on September 7, 2008. For more information on the GSEs in general, see CRS Report RL33756, *Fannie Mae and Freddie Mac: A Legal and Policy Overview*, by N. Eric Weiss and Michael V. Seitzinger, and for more information on the conservatorship, see CRS Report RS22950, *Fannie Mae and Freddie Mac in Conservatorship*, by Mark Jickling.

[17] Borrowers can look up whether their loan is owned by Fannie Mae or Freddie Mac at http://making homeaffordable.gov/loan_lookup.html.

[18] HARP was originally scheduled to expire on June 10, 2010. The Federal Housing Finance Agency has extended the program three times. In March 2010, FHFA announced that it was extending the program until June 30, 2011. In March 2011, FHFA announced that it was extending the program by another year, until June 30, 2012. In October 2011, FHFA announced that it would extend the program until December 31, 2013. See the following Federal Housing Finance Agency press releases: "FHFA Extends Refinance Program by One Year," March 1, 2010, http://fhfa.gov/ webfiles/15466/HARPEXTENDED 3110%5b 1%5d.pdf; "FHFA Extends Refinance Program by One Year," March 11, 2011, http://fhfa.gov/webfiles/20399/HarpExtended0311R.pdf; and "FHFA, Fannie Mae and Freddie Mac Announce HARP Changes to Reach More Borrowers," October 24, 2011, http://fhfa.gov/webfiles/22721/ HARP_release_102411_Final.pdf.

[19] Federal Housing Finance Agency, "FHFA, Fannie Mae and Freddie Mac Announce HARP Changes to Reach More Borrowers," press release, October 24, 2011, http://fhfa.gov/web files/22721/HARP_release_102411_Final.pdf.

[20] Fannie Mae's detailed guidance on the program changes can be found at https://www.efanniemae.com/sf /guides/ssg/ annltrs/pdf/2011/sel1112.pdf. Freddie Mac's detailed guidance on the changes can be found at http://www.freddiemac. com/sell/guide/bulletins/pdf/bll1122.pdf.

[21] Federal Housing Finance Agency, *Foreclosure Prevention & Refinance Report: October 2011*, December 20, 2011, p. 5, available at http://www.fhfa.gov/webfiles/22853/Oct2011FPM 122011.pdf.

[22] HAMP shares many features of earlier foreclosure prevention programs, such as the Federal Deposit Insurance Corporation's plan to modify loans held by the failed IndyMac Bank, and Fannie Mae's and Freddie Mac's Streamlined Modification Program. These programs are described in detail in Appendix B.

[23] Treasury's guidance on HAMP for non-GSE mortgages is available in a handbook that is updated periodically to incorporate new guidance or changes to the program. That handbook is available at https://www.hmpadmin.com/portal/ index.jsp. HAMP guidance related to mortgages owned or guaranteed by Fannie Mae or Freddie Mac can be found on those entities' respective websites. In general, the HAMP guidance for GSE mortgages is similar to the guidance for non-GSE mortgages, but it is not always identical.

[24] Congressional Budget Office, *H.R. 839 HAMP Termination Act of 2011*, cost estimate, March 11, 2011, http://cbo.gov/ftpdocs/120xx/doc12097/hr839.pdf.

[25] Department of the Treasury, Section 105(a) Troubled Assets Relief Program Report to Congress for the Period February 1, 2009 to February 28, 2009, p. 1, available at http://www.financialstability.gov/docs/105 CongressionalReports/105aReport_0306 2009. pdf.

[26] U.S. Department of the Treasury, *Daily TARP Update for 01/10/2012*, http://www.treasury.gov /initiatives/financialstability/briefing-room/reports/tarp-daily-summary-report/TARP%20 Cash%20Summary/Daily%20TARP%20Update%20-%2001.10. 2012.pdf.

[27] Treasury's monthly reports on HAMP can be found at http://www.treasury.gov/initiatives_/financial-stability/results/MHA-Reports/Pages/default. aspx.

[28] U.S. Department of the Treasury, *Making Home Affordable Program Servicer Performance Report Through November 2011*, January 9, 2012, p. 2, http://www.treasury.gov/initiatives /financial-stability/results/MHA-Reports/ Documents/FINAL_Nov%20 2011%20MHA%20 Report.pdf.

[29] U.S. Department of the Treasury and U.S. Department of Housing and Urban Development, "Obama Administration Kicks Off Mortgage Modification Conversion Drive," press release, November 30, 2009, available at http://treas.gov/ press/releases/tg421.htm.

[30] U.S. Department of the Treasury, Making Home Affordable Program Performance Report Through April 2011, June 9, 2011. Servicer assessment results begin on page 14. All monthly reports can be found at http://www.treasury.gov/ initiatives/financial-stability/results/MHA-Reports/Pages/default.aspx.

[31] U.S. Department of the Treasury, *Making Home Affordable Program Performance Report Through July 2011*, September 1, 2011. Servicer assessment results begin on page 16.

[32] U.S. Department of the Treasury, *Making Home Affordable Program Performance Report Through October 2011*, December 7, 2011. Servicer assessment results begin on page 16.

[33] Servicer guidelines on 2MP are available at https://www.hmpadmin.com/portal/programs /second_lien.html.

[34] U.S. Department of the Treasury, *Making Home Affordable Program Servicer Performance Report Through November 2011*, January 9, 2012, p. 4, http://www.treasury.gov/initiatives /financial-stability/results/MHA-Reports/Documents/FINAL_Nov%202011%20MHA%20 Report.pdf.

[35] Servicer guidelines on HAFA are available at https://www.hmpadmin.com/portal/programs/ foreclosure_alternatives.html.

[36] Short sales and deeds-in-lieu are described in footnote 11. Under HAFA, the lender must agree to accept the proceeds of the short sale or the deed and property as full payment of the mortgage debt, and may not pursue borrowers for any remaining amounts owed on the mortgage. Short sales and deeds-in-lieu have a negative impact on a borrower's credit, but they may result in fewer negative consequences overall for the borrower than a foreclosure.

[37] Treasury has increased the amount of incentive compensation offered under HAFA to these amounts since the program was first announced.

[38] U.S. Department of the Treasury, *Making Home Affordable Program Servicer Performance Report Through November 2011*, January 9, 2012, p. 5, http://www.treasury.gov/initiatives /financial-stability/results/MHA-Reports/Documents/FINAL_Nov%20 2011%20MHA%20 Report.pdf.

[39] Originally, the forbearance period was three months. Treasury extended it to twelve months in Supplemental Directive 11-07, *Making Home Affordable Program – Expansion of Unemployment Forbearance*, July 25, 2011, available at https://www.hmpadmin.com/portal /programs/docs/hamp_servicer/sd1107.pdf. The change became effective on October 1, 2011.

[40] The original detailed guidelines on the Home Affordable Unemployment Program were released in Supplemental Directive 10-04 on May 11, 2010. These guidelines are available at https://www.hmpadmin.com/portal/docs/ hamp_servicer/sd1004.pdf. Updated guidance can be found in Treasury's Making Home Affordable Handbook, available at https://www. hmpadmin.com/portal/index.jsp.

[41] U.S. Department of the Treasury, *Making Home Affordable Program Servicer Performance Report Through November 2011*, January 9, 2012, p. 5, http://www.treasury.gov /initiatives/financial-stability/results/MHA-Reports/Documents/FINAL_Nov%20 2011%20 MHA%20Report.pdf.

[42] Detailed guidelines on the Principal Reduction Alternative were released in Supplemental Directive 10-05 on June 3, 2010. These guidelines are available at https://www.hmpadmin. com/portal/docs/hamp_servicer /sd1005.pdf.

[43] U.S. Department of the Treasury, *Making Home Affordable Program Servicer Performance Report Through November 2011*, January 9, 2012, p. 5, http://www.treasury.gov /initiatives /financial-stability/results/MHA-Reports/Documents/FINAL_Nov%202011%20 MHA%20 Report.pdf.

[44] This change is described in detail in Treasury's Supplemental Directive 10-01, issued on January 28, 2010, and available at https://www.hmpadmin.com/portal/programs /docs/ hamp_servicer/sd1001.pdf.

[45] These changes are described in detail in Treasury's Supplemental Directive 10-02, issued on March 24, 2010, and available at https://www.hmpadmin.com/portal/programs/docs/hamp_ servicer/sd1002.pdf.

[46] Servicers are allowed to use their own values for certain NPV inputs on the basis of their own portfolio experience, but such allowed changes are limited and must be approved by Treasury.

[47] Guidelines for HFAs' proposals for the first round of funding are available at http://www.makinghomeaffordable. gov/docs/HFA%20FAQ%20—%20030510%20 FINAL %20(Clean).pdf.

[48] See U.S. Department of the Treasury, "Help for the Hardest Hit Housing Markets," press release, February 19, 2010, available at http://makinghomeaffordable.gov/pr_ 02192010.html. See also "Housing Finance Agency Innovation Fund for the Hardest Hit Housing Markets ("HFA Hardest Hit Fund"): Frequently Asked Questions," available at http://www.makinghomeaffordable.gov/docs/HFA%20FAQ%20—%20030510%20 FINAL%20(Clean).pdf, for more information on the program and for maximum funding allocations for each state in the first round.

[49] See U.S. Department of the Treasury, "Administration Announces Second Round of Assistance for Hardest-Hit Housing Markets," press release, March 29, 2010, available at http://www.financialstability.gov/latest/ pr_03292010.html. This press release also includes the maximum funding allocation for each state in the second round.

[50] See U.S. Department of the Treasury, "Obama Administration Announces Additional Support for Targeted Foreclosure-Prevention Programs To Help Homeowners Struggling With Unemployment," press release, August 11, 2010, available at http://financialstability.gov /latest/pr_08112010.html.

[51] Except for Arizona, every state that received funding in one of the first two rounds of the Hardest Hit Fund also received funding in the third round.

[52] Descriptions of the programs that each state is funding through the Hardest Hit Fund are available at http://www.financialstability.gov/roadtostability/hardesthitfund.html.

[53] FHA Mortgagee Letter 2010-23, "FHA Refinance of Borrowers in Negative Equity Positions," August 6, 2010, available at http://www.hud.gov/offices/adm/hudclips/letters/mortgagee/.

[54] Federal Housing Administration, *FHA Outlook*, November 2011, available at http://portal.hud.gov/hudportal/ documents/huddoc?id=ol_current.pdf.

[55] Congressional Budget Office, *H.R. 830 FHA Refinance Program Termination Act of 2011*, cost estimate, March 7, 2011, http://cbo.gov/ftpdocs/120xx/doc12089/hr830.pdf.

[56] Details on the program can be found on HUD's website at http://www.hud.gov/offices/hsg /sfh/hcc/ehlp /ehlphome.cfm.

[57] NeighborWorks America is a HUD-approved housing counseling intermediary with a nationwide network of housing counseling affiliates. For more information on NeighborWorks in general, see the organization's webpage at http://www.nw.org/network /aboutUs/aboutUs.asp. For more information on NeighborWorks's foreclosure prevention activities, see "Foreclosure Counseling Funding to NeighborWorks America" later in this report.

[58] Information on applying for the EHLP can be found at http://nw.org/network/foreclosure /nfmcp/ehlp consumers.asp.

[59] U.S. Department of Housing and Urban Development, "HUD and NeighborWorks America Accepting Additional Applications for Emergency Homeowners' Loan Program," press release, August 29, 2011, http://portal.hud.gov/ hudportal/HUD?src=/press/press_releases_ media_advisories/2011/HUDNo.11-177.

[60] Congressional Budget Office, *H.R. 836 Emergency Mortgage Relief Program Termination Act of 2011*, cost estimate, March 7, 2011, http://cbo.gov/ftpdocs/120xx /doc12090 /hr836.pdf.

[61] See FHA Mortgagee Letter 11-20, "Termination of the Hope for Homeowners (H4H) Program," June 10, 2011, http://www.hud.gov/offices/adm/hudclips/letters/mortgagee /files/11-20ml.pdf.

[62] See FHA Mortgagee Letter 09-43, available at http://www.hud.gov/offices/adm/hudclips/letters /mortgagee/ 2009ml.cfm. Initially, borrowers had to share a portion of both their equity and any appreciation in the home's value with HUD when the home was sold or refinanced. P.L. 111-22 provided the authority to change this requirement.

[63] The decision to act on the authority granted in P.L. 110-343 and make these changes was ultimately made by the Board of Hope for Homeowners, which included the Secretary of HUD and the Secretary of the Treasury, among others. As described in the text, P.L. 111-22 placed the program under the control of the Secretary of HUD; the Board then took on an advisory role.

[64] For the most recent comprehensive guidance on Hope for Homeowners, including these changes, see FHA Mortgagee Letter 09-43, available at http://www.hud.gov/offices/adm /hudclips/letters/mortgagee/2009ml.cfm.

[65] Congressional Budget Office, Cost Estimate, *Federal Housing Finance Regulatory Reform Act of 2008*, June 9, 2008, p. 8, http://www.cbo.gov/ftpdocs/93xx/doc9366/Senate_Housing.pdf.

[66] See Federal Housing Administration, *FHA Outlook*, September 2010 and *FHA Outlook*, September 2011, both available at http://www.hud.gov/offices/hsg/rmra /oe/rpts/ooe /olmenu.cfm.

[67] Each year, Congress appropriates funding to HUD to distribute to certified housing counseling organizations to undertake various types of housing counseling, including pre-purchase counseling and post-purchase counseling. Congress also appropriates funding to NeighborWorks each year for neighborhood reinvestment activities, including housing counseling. The recent funding appropriated specifically for foreclosure mitigation counseling is separate from both of these other usual appropriations.

[68] For more information on the National Foreclosure Mitigation Counseling Program, see the NeighborWorks website at http://www.nw.org/network/nfmcp/default.asp#info.

[69] HUD-approved housing counseling intermediaries, state housing finance agencies, and NeighborWorks organizations are eligible to receive funds through the NFMCP.

[70] This law is a revision of the Soldiers' and Sailors' Civil Relief Act of 1940 (P.L. 76-861), which itself was a revision of the Soldiers' and Sailors' Civil Relief Act of 1918 (P.L. 65-103). Both earlier laws also included foreclosure protections for members of the military on or recently returned from active duty.

[71] The Pew Charitable Trusts Center on the States, *Defaulting on the Dream: States Respond to America's Foreclosure Crisis*, April 2008, http://www.pewcenteronthestates.org /uploaded Files/ PCS_DefaultingOnThe Dream_Report_FINAL041508_01.pdf.

[72] For a full list of current members of the HOPE NOW Alliance, see the HOPE NOW website at https://www.hopenow.com/members.php.

[73] The phone number for the HOPE NOW Alliance hotline is 888-995-HOPE (4673).

[74] The HOPE NOW Alliance, "Total Loan Mods for 2011 Nearing the One Million Mark," press release, December 7, 2011, http://hopenow.com/news/Total_Loan_Mods.pdf.

[75] The HOPE NOW Alliance, "Five Million Loan Mods Since 2007," press release, November 15, 2011, http://hopenow.com/press_release/files/Sept%202011%20 Data_5M%20Mods_ FINAL.pdf.

[76] For one discussion of the economics of mortgage servicing, see Section 3 of the Special Inspector General for the Troubled Asset Relief Program (SIGTARP) Quarterly Report to Congress, October 26, 2010, available at http://www.sigtarp.gov/reports/congress /2010/ October2010_Quarterly_Report_to_Congress.pdf.

[77] Federal Housing Finance Agency, "FHFA Announces Joint Initiative to Consider Alternatives for a New Mortgage Servicing Compensation Structure," press release, January 18, 2011, available at http://fhfa.gov /webfiles/19639/ Servicing_model11811.pdf.

[78] Office of the Comptroller of the Currency and Office of Thrift Supervision, *OCC and OTS Mortgage Metrics Report: Disclosure of National Bank and Federal Thrift Mortgage Loan Data, Third Quarter 2011*, December 21, 2011, pp. 32-33, http://occ.gov/publications /publications-by-type/other-publications-reports/mortgage-metrics-2011/ mortgage-metrics-q3-2011.pdf.

[79] Ibid., p. 39.

[80] Ibid., p. 37.

[81] U.S. Department of the Treasury, *Making Home Affordable Program Servicer Performance Report Through September 2011*, November 3, 2011, p. 3, http://www.treasury.gov/ initiatives/financial-stability/results/MHA-Reports/Documents/Sept%202011%20 MHA% 20Report_Final.pdf .

[82] FHA already offered refinancing options for homeowners who were current on their existing fixed- or adjustable-rate mortgages and continued to do so after the adoption of *FHASecure*.

[83] HUD Mortgagee Letter 08-41, "Termination of *FHASecure*," December 19, 2008, available at http://www.hud.gov/ offices/adm/hudclips/letters/mortgagee/2008ml.cfm.

[84] Congressional Budget Office, "The Budget and Economic Outlook: Fiscal Years 2009 to 2019," January 2009, available at http://www.cbo.gov/ftpdocs/99xx/doc9957/01-07-Outlook.pdf.

[85] Remarks by FDIC Chairman Sheila Bair to the National Association of Realtors Midyear Legislative Meeting and Trade Expo, Washington, DC, May 12, 2009. A transcript of these remarks is available at http://www.fdic.gov /news/news/speeches/archives/2009/spmay 1209.html.

[86] Federal Deposit Insurance Corporation, "FDIC Closes Sale of IndyMac Federal Bank, Pasadena, California," press release, March 19, 2009, http://www.fdic.gov/news/news/ press/2009/pr09042.html.

[87] The private mortgage lenders and servicers who participated in the Streamlined Modification Program were primarily members of the HOPE NOW Alliance, a voluntary alliance of industry members that formed to help homeowners avoid foreclosure. The HOPE NOW Alliance is described in detail in an earlier section of this report.

[88] Federal Housing Finance Agency, *Foreclosure Prevention Report: April 2009*, July 15, 2009, available at http://www.fhfa.gov/webfiles/14588/April_Foreclosure_Prevention71509F.pdf.

[89] Details of the Homeownership Preservation Policy can be found on the Federal Reserve's website at http://www.federalreserve.gov/newsevents/press/bcreg/bcreg20090130a1.pdf.

In: Melissa O. Murray and Willie T. Cole
Editors: Melissa O. Murray and Willie T. Cole

ISBN: 978-1-62257-294-6
© 2012 Nova Science Publishers, Inc.

Chapter 6

NATIONAL MORTGAGE SERVICING STANDARDS: LEGISLATION IN THE 112TH CONGRESS[*]

Sean M. Hoskins

SUMMARY

The United States single-family housing market has $10.5 trillion of mortgage debt outstanding. Servicers play an important role in this market. The owner of a mortgage loan or mortgage-backed security typically hires a servicer to act on its behalf. When loans are current, a mortgage servicer collects payments from borrowers and forwards them to the mortgage holders. If the borrower becomes delinquent, a servicer may offer the borrower an option that could allow the borrower to stay in his or her home, or the servicer may pursue foreclosure.

Following high foreclosure rates and recent allegations of abuse, mortgage servicing has attracted attention from Congress. In addition to hearings and congressional investigations, some in Congress have called for national servicing standards. The most comprehensive proposal, S. 824, the Foreclosure Fraud and Homeowner Abuse Prevention Act of 2011 (Senator Sherrod Brown et al.), and its companion bill in the House, H.R. 1783 (Representative Brad Miller et al.), contain provisions intended to protect investors and borrowers from improper servicing practices. S. 967, the Regulation of Mortgage Servicing Act of 2011 (Senator Jeff Merkley et al.), includes borrower protections in addition to those offered by S. 824 and H.R. 1783.

The servicing standards proposed in S. 824 and H.R. 1783 include provisions intended to ensure that servicers act in the best interest of investors who hold mortgage loans. The proposals would adjust the servicing compensation structure to better align servicer incentives with the incentives of the mortgage holder. Servicers would also be prohibited from purchasing services offered by their affiliates at inflated costs and passing the costs on to investors. In addition, servicers would be prohibited from choosing a loss mitigation option that would benefit their affiliates at the expense of other investors.

S. 824, H.R. 1783, and S. 967 have three major components for borrower protection. First, the three bills would require servicers to establish a single point of contact with the

---

[*] This is an edited, reformatted and augmented version of Congressional Research Service, Publication No. R42041, dated October 7, 2011.

borrower. The single point of contact would be a case manager who is assigned to each delinquent borrower and would manage communications with the borrower. Second, the three bills would prohibit servicers from dual tracking, which means initiating foreclosure on a borrower while simultaneously pursuing a loan modification. Servicers would instead be required to determine whether the borrower is eligible for an alternative to foreclosure before initiating foreclosure. Third, S. 824 and H.R. 1783 would set minimum experience, education, and training levels for loan modification staff and limit caseload levels for individual employees.

Legislation is not the only avenue to setting servicing standards. Regulatory agencies, such as the Consumer Financial Protection Bureau, the Board of Governors of the Federal Reserve System, and the Federal Deposit Insurance Corporation, may include some or all of the proposed standards in their rules on securitization and qualified residential mortgages pursuant to the Dodd-Frank Wall Street Reform and Consumer Protection Act (P.L. 111-203). Servicing standards could also be adopted through legal settlements between the servicers and the state attorneys general, as well as through enforcement actions taken by federal regulators in response to deficient servicing practices by some banks. If servicing standards are implemented by rule or by settlement agreements, they would apply only to those servicers under the regulators' purview or those who entered into the settlement agreements.

INTRODUCTION

In the United States, outstanding mortgage debt in the single-family housing market amounts to $10.5 trillion.[1] Mortgage servicers play an important role in this market. The owner of a mortgage loan or mortgage-backed security typically hires a servicer to act on its behalf in servicing mortgages. When loans are current, a mortgage servicer collects payments from borrowers and forwards them to the mortgage holders. If the borrower becomes delinquent, the servicer may pursue foreclosure or offer the borrower a workout option that may allow the borrower to stay in his or her home.

Examples of workout options include loan modifications, such as principal balance reductions and interest rate reductions, as well as repayment plans, which allow borrowers to repay the amounts they owe and become current in their mortgage payments. By contrast, mortgage liquidation options result in borrowers losing their homes. For example, in a short sale, the borrower sells the home and uses the proceeds to satisfy the mortgage debt, even if the sale proceeds are less than the amount owed on the mortgage. Foreclosure is similar to a short sale except that it is often involuntary. The home is repossessed and sold by the lien holder. If the sale price does not cover the amount owed, the borrower may have to pay the difference.[2]

Following high foreclosure rates and recent investigations of fraud and abuse, mortgage servicing has attracted attention from Congress. For example, congressional hearings, as well as state and federal investigations, have addressed allegations of "robo-signing," in which a small number of individuals sign a large number of affidavits and other legal documents that mortgage companies submit to courts and other public authorities to execute foreclosures.[3]

To protect borrowers and investors from abuse, some in Congress have called for national servicing standards. The proposed servicing standards include provisions to ensure that servicers act in the best interest of the holders of the mortgage loans and that delinquent borrowers are properly evaluated for loan modifications before foreclosure proceedings are initiated. The most comprehensive bill, S. 824, the Foreclosure Fraud and Homeowner Abuse Prevention Act of 2011 (Senator Sherrod Brown et al.), and its companion bill in the House, H.R. 1783 (Representative Brad Miller et al.), contain provisions to protect investors and borrowers. S. 967, the Regulation of Mortgage Servicing Act of 2011 (Senator Jeff Merkley et al.), also proposes reforms to the servicing industry.

In addition to the legislative proposals, there are other avenues through which servicing standards may be adopted. Some of the regulatory agencies responsible for implementing portions of the Dodd-Frank Wall Street Reform and Consumer Protection Act, such as the Consumer Financial Protection Bureau, the Board of Governors of the Federal Reserve System, and the Federal Deposit Insurance Corporation, are considering including some or all of the proposed standards in their rules on securitization and qualified residential mortgages. Servicing standards could also be adopted through legal settlements between the servicers and state attorney general offices, as well as through enforcement actions taken by federal regulators in response to deficient servicing practices by some banks. However, if servicing standards are implemented by rule or by settlement agreements, the standards would apply only to those servicers under the regulators' purview[4] or those who entered into the settlement agreements. Only legislation enacted by Congress would have universal coverage. Appendix A describes the non-legislative proposals.

This report analyzes the potential misaligned incentives in the servicer-mortgage holder relationship and the servicing standards that attempt to address each concern, the servicer-borrower relationship and the relevant servicing provisions, as well as the possible implications of reforming the servicing industry.

ARE SERVICER AND MORTGAGE HOLDER INCENTIVES MISALIGNED?

The Principal-Agent Problem and Mortgage Holders

Some experts argue that servicers face a host of competing incentives, not all of which encourage the servicer to act in the best interest of the loan holder. These incentives could encourage the servicer to pursue foreclosure when the investor would be best served by a loan modification, or they could encourage the servicer to offer a loan modification when the holders would have preferred foreclosure. The tension between what a servicer has incentives to do and what the note holder would prefer is an example of a principal-agent problem.[5] The servicer may make decisions about loans that maximize its income rather than maximize the return for the holders of the loans if the holders give the servicer too much flexibility to act.[6]

A principal-agent problem is unlikely when the servicer holds the loans in its own portfolio because, in this case, the principal is the agent and the interests are aligned from the start. The severity of the principal-agent problem differs for other types of mortgage holding arrangements:[7] investors in private-label securities (PLS)[8] and government-sponsored enterprises (GSEs).[9]

The principal-agent problem may be of most concern for investors in PLS because of their difficulty in effectively monitoring servicers and in structuring servicing contracts, which are called pooling and servicing agreements (PSA).[10] There are several ways in which private investors can monitor servicers. Prior to purchasing a share in a mortgage-backed security, investors can get one measure of the quality of a servicer by looking at rating agencies' evaluations of servicers' performances.[11] Nevertheless, the servicing rights may still be retained by the servicer affiliated with the loan originator[12] rather than shopped around to the best servicer available.

This reduces the investors' ability to influence the choice of a servicer. After the servicing rights have been awarded, investors can monitor the servicer through the trustee[13] that is hired by investors to act on their behalf. A trustee may replace the servicer if the servicer violates the PSA by failing to act in the best interest of the investor, but close monitoring of servicers may be costly and difficult. Servicers are not required to transparently report information on loan performance to trustees, and, close monitoring of servicers may not be explicitly stated in the PSA for some trustees.[14] Investors also have limited ability to encourage the trustee to monitor the servicer. Investors may have difficulty organizing their efforts to monitor because they may not know who the other investors are or may wish to free ride on the organizing efforts of other investors.[15] However, just because there are difficulties does not mean that they cannot be overcome. With billions of dollars at stake, investors have organized to file lawsuits against servicers and loan originators.[16]

In addition to facing minimal monitoring, servicers have some flexibility to determine what action to take with delinquent borrowers. To determine which option to pursue on a non-performing loan, servicers often perform a net present value (NPV) test. In an NPV test, servicers calculate the expected value of multiple loss mitigation and foreclosure options to determine which has the highest benefit for the owner of the loan. Servicers are often required by the loan holder to choose the option that has the highest NPV.

Servicers in PLS are generally given discretion[17] in choosing the variables involved in the NPV calculations, which may in theory enable rigging the NPV test to achieve an outcome that increases servicers' income even if better options might exist for investors.[18]

The GSEs have taken steps to address the principal-agent problem. Even before the Home Affordable Modification Program (HAMP),[19] the GSEs offered financial incentives to servicers for performing approved loan modifications. They quantitatively track servicer performance and recognize their top servicers.[20]

They also give specific guidelines to servicers for NPV tests.[21] Because the GSEs have assumed an even larger role in the housing finance system since the beginning of the most recent recession, servicers have an incentive to act in the GSEs' best interest in order to attract new business. Through these reputational, contractual, and financial incentives, the GSEs attempt to minimize the principal-agent problem.

During the housing boom of the mid-2000s, PLS gained a larger share of the market. Figure 1 shows the volume of mortgage-backed securities issued by Fannie Mae, Freddie Mac, and private-label investors. Fannie Mae and Freddie Mac have assumed a dominant role since the beginning of the most recent recession.

Given the limitations of monitoring servicers and their flexibility in choosing options for borrowers in default, it is possible that servicers may choose to maximize their income rather than serve the holders' interests. This is more of a concern for PLS, where the principal-agent problem is strongest, and less of a concern for loans held in servicer's portfolio, where incentives are aligned.

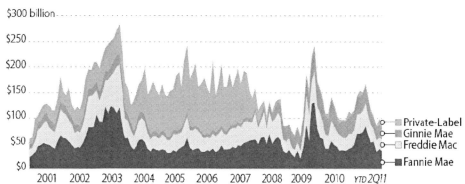

Source: Federal Housing Finance Agency, "Conservator's Report on the Enterprises' Financial Performance," Second Quarter 2011.

Figure 1. Volume of Mortgage-Backed Security Issuance.

Specific Conflict-of-Interest Situations

The principal-agent problem can be manifested in a variety of conflict-of-interest situations. The conflicts are of concern because they can exacerbate such problems as high foreclosure rates and the breakdown in securitization. The conflicts that arise typically have to do with servicer compensation, servicer affiliation with other entities, and servicer advances. Each is discussed below.

Servicer Compensation

Servicers have five primary sources of compensation. The largest form of compensation is the *servicing fee*. Servicers receive a percentage of the unpaid principal balance on the loans they are servicing. Depending on the type of loan, the fee can range from 25 basis points for a prime fixed-rate loan to 50 basis points for a subprime loan.[22] Second, servicers earn *float income*. Float income is the interest servicers earn by collecting payments from borrowers at the beginning of the month, earning interest on that money, and then forwarding the borrowers' payments at the end of the month. Third, servicers earn *fee income* from the fees that they charge delinquent borrowers. Other sources of fees include property valuation fees, credit report fees, and notary fees.[23] Fourth, servicers may receive *investment income* by retaining an ownership share in the investment that they are servicing. Fifth, servicers may receive *incentive payments* as part of HAMP or other government programs for each borrower that receives a permanent modification.

Some critics believe that this compensation structure leaves servicers unconcerned about maximizing the value of the underlying loan for investors.[24] They argue that servicers are likely to perform a loan workout only if doing so is more profitable for the servicer than foreclosure. This implies that a servicer will only perform a workout if it will earn enough revenue on the reperforming loan before it potentially redefaults to compensate it for the upfront cost of performing the workout. However, critics argue that, under this model, a servicer's decision is independent of the value of the loan and instead depends on the length of time before the loan redefaults and the size of the loan. Servicer compensation does not, therefore, incentivize the servicer to maximize the value of the loan to investors.

S. 824 and H.R. 1783 separate the servicing of borrowers that are current from the servicing of borrowers that are delinquent. Borrowers that are paying as scheduled would be serviced by the traditional primary servicer, whereas borrowers who are at least 60 days delinquent would have their servicing transferred to special servicers that specialize in minimizing losses for investors. The special servicer will be compensated through a fraction of the stream of payments from the entire pool.

The compensation structure for the special servicer is intended to make the servicer indifferent to the type of loss mitigation option and instead encourage it to maximize the NPV for investors. This could better align the interest of the special servicer with the interest of the investors. However, aligning servicer and investor incentives requires addressing both revenue and costs. The legislation addresses servicer compensation issues, but it does not address the costs borne by the parties when defaults occur. A servicer is often reimbursed for foreclosure expenses but not for the added cost of performing a workout option.[25] Some claim that this incentivizes servicers to perform foreclosures. It is unclear if the reforms will address this issue by requiring the same treatment of foreclosure and workout expenses.[26] Failure to address the costs of servicing distressed loans may still leave the incentive alignment issue unresolved.

Affiliate Relationships

Servicers are often affiliated with other entities such as providers of foreclosure services, loan originators, and securitizers. These affiliate relationships may also incentivize servicers to act in ways that are not in the investors' interests. Three types of affiliate relationships that critics cite as sources of potential conflict are described below, together with legislative and other proposed policy options that address each conflict.

First, servicers may be affiliated with organizations that provide foreclosure completion services, such as property preservation companies.[27] The opportunity to earn additional income for an affiliate may make the servicer more likely to choose foreclosure as an option. Even if servicers offer foreclosure services themselves, they are reimbursed on a first-priority basis once the house is liquidated.[28] This gives servicers an incentive to inflate the true cost of providing the additional services at the expense of investors. In other words, the opportunity to earn additional fees may, for decisions that are on the margin between foreclosing and offering a loss mitigation option, incentivize the servicer to choose foreclosure.[29] These additional fees are not required to be broken down in a transparent manner when reported to the trustee, making it difficult for investors to hold servicers accountable.[30]

Overcharging the investor for fees does not necessarily mean that incentives are misaligned with respect to the foreclosure decision. Fees to the servicer and its affiliates are just one component of the NPV test.[31] Foreclosure might still be the best option for the investor even if the investor pays more in fees. Overcharges may not be enough to tip the NPV test in some cases.

S. 824 and H.R. 1783 would limit servicers' ability to charge excessive fees for services that may be sold by an affiliate of the servicer. For example, if a borrower is no longer paying for his or her homeowner's insurance policy, the servicer is required to attempt to keep in place or reinstate the borrower's previous insurance policy. If that cannot be achieved, the servicer must provide force-placed insurance that is of similar cost and coverage as a standard homeowner's insurance policy. This proposal would prevent servicers from purchasing above-market rate insurance from an affiliate and passing the cost on to investors.

Other proposals to limit foreclosure fees have called for servicers' fees to be reasonably related to the cost of actually providing a service and to be disclosed more clearly in monthly statements to investors and borrowers.[32]

Second, servicers may be affiliated with loan originators or securitizers and lead to "representations and warranties" (rep and warrants) conflicts. Often in the case of mortgage-backed securities, the securitizer or loan originator will establish rep and warrants on the underlying loans that make up the pool for the security. A rep and warrants violation occurs when a loan is not of the type or quality that it was alleged to be at the time of the security's issuance.[33] When detected, the securitizer or originator may be required to purchase the loan out of the pool and place the loan on its balance sheet. The trustee is responsible for enforcing rep and warrant violations. Trustees, however, often do not have the loan-level information or ability needed to track violations, but servicers do have that information.[34] Servicers affiliated with the securitizer or originator that would need to repurchase the loan may, therefore, have an incentive to not report the violation. Rep and warrant issues, however, do not necessarily influence the decision of the servicer to offer a delinquent borrower a loss mitigation option or proceed with foreclosure given that this issues does not factor into the NPV test.

To address rep-and-warrant conflicts, some experts have suggested that an independent third party be responsible for protecting investors' interests and be given access to the loan-level information needed to detect rep and warrant violations.[35] The compensation of the third party would be structured to incentivize it to act in the best interest of the investors. However, private investors did, in some instances, hire third-party firms before the downturn in the housing market to perform due diligence on a pool of loans, and this proved to have limited effectiveness.[36] Other suggestions include increasing the penalties for violations beyond just repurchasing the loan.[37]

A third affiliate issue relates to second mortgages. During the housing boom of the mid-2000s, many borrowers took out a second mortgage to help finance the purchase of their home. Servicers of the first lien often retained ownership of the second lien.[38] A conflict of interest may arise if a servicer pursues options for a delinquent borrower that ensures that the second lien will be repaid. For example, a servicer whose affiliate owns the second lien may be less likely to agree to a short sale in which the price offered for the house will not cover the amount owed to the second lien holder even if a short sale may be the best option for the owners of the first lien.[39] The option that benefits the second lien holder may not necessarily benefit the first lien investors.

A recent study has found that borrowers have often continued to pay their second mortgage even if they could not afford to pay their first mortgage.[40] The study used a data sample of 1.4 million borrowers covering nearly all U.S. borrowers that had just one first and second lien. It found that the most important reason that borrowers stayed current on their second lien, which is often a home equity line of credit (HELOC), even if they were delinquent on their first lien mortgage was to maintain access to the credit offered by a HELOC. The study found limited evidence that servicers' conflicts of interest concerning second lien ownership could explain borrowers' behavior.

To address a possible second lien conflict, S. 824 and H.R. 1783 would prohibit a servicer or an affiliate of the servicer from owning a lien that is secured by a property if it is also servicing a different lien on the same property. For example, the servicer could not service the first lien but have its affiliate own the second lien on a home in the pool that it services. Others have put forward less stringent proposals that would require the servicer to disclose its ownership of a second lien and establish a formula to determine how much the subordinate lien should be reduced if the primary lien is also adjusted.[41]

Servicer Advances

When a borrower does not pay the full monthly amount that is due, servicers are often required to advance the principal or interest to investors. Servicers are typically reimbursed for these advances, but do not receive interest on their payments.[42] This gives servicers an incentive to minimize the amount of time that a loan is in default. Although servicers have the option to charge late fees to the borrower, servicers may still lose money on advances because the advances are basically a zero interest loan to investors.[43] This practice may be another reason why servicers might decide not to maximize the NPV of defaults and be concerned about the duration of delinquency or default. Some default periods could be profitable for servicers but other periods could be costly; all periods in which investors do not receive full payment are costly.

Often servicers will only have to advance payments to investors if the servicer thinks the advances are considered recoverable (usually through the sale of the house in foreclosure).[44] The GSEs will also limit advances to four months.[45] In addition, servicers are reimbursed for their advances soon after a loan modification. If reimbursement of advances after a loan modification occurs prior to the reimbursement after a foreclosure, then servicers would have an incentive to not foreclose.[46]

S. 824 and H.R. 1783 would prohibit servicers from advancing the delinquent principal and interest for more than three payment periods unless financing or reimbursement is made available to the servicer.

HOW ARE BORROWERS AFFECTED?

Mortgage servicing is not a consumer-facing market. Servicers are hired by investors and, therefore, are ultimately responsible to the investors. Servicers have an incentive to be concerned with the quality of their interaction with borrowers insofar as investors evaluate servicers by their customer service. For example, servicers may have little incentive to respond quickly to borrowers if investors do not value servicers that respond in a timely manner. Typically, borrowers cannot choose to switch servicers the way they can compare and choose goods and services in most markets. Critics say that the absence of this market-force mechanism makes borrowers vulnerable to servicer abuse.[47]

Single Point of Contact and Dual Tracking

S. 967, H.R. 1783, and S. 824 address the absence of a consumer-facing market by requiring servicers to assign a case manager to serve as a single point of contact to each borrower that seeks a loan modification. The case manager would manage communications with the borrower and be available to communicate by telephone and email during business hours. The case manager would also have the authority to decide if the borrower is eligible for a loan modification. If the borrower is deemed ineligible by the case manager, S. 967

would require an independent reviewer to confirm the eligibility status before the borrower is notified. The independent reviewer would be allowed to work for the same servicing company as the primary servicer so long as the reviewer was not under the same immediate supervision as the division that determines loan modifications.

The three bills further address the concerns stemming from the absence of a consumer-facing market by prohibiting dual tracking. Dual tracking occurs when servicers pursue a loss mitigation option while simultaneously initiating the foreclosure process on a borrower. Instead, servicers would be required to determine if the borrower is eligible for a loan modification before initiating foreclosure even if the foreclosure is otherwise authorized under the state's law.

Staffing Requirements

The servicing industry consolidated during the housing boom of the early 2000s. The top five mortgage servicers had a 60% market share by the end of 2009 compared with a 27% share for the top five servicers in 1999.[48] With relatively low delinquency rates, servicers could invest in automating their transaction processing systems and take advantage of economies of scale.[49] Servicers found little incentive to invest as heavily in the equipment and personnel required for loss mitigation. Critics argue that this left servicers understaffed when the delinquency rate spiked later in the decade.[50] **Figure 2** shows how the servicing market consolidated from 2004 to the first quarter of 2010. The rate of servicer consolidation slowed as the delinquency rate increased.

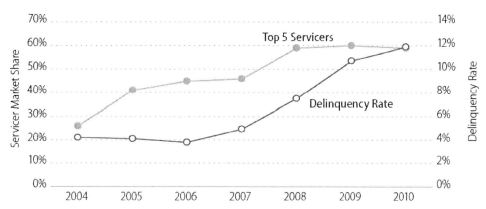

Source: Servicer market share data from Federal Housing Finance Agency, "Servicing Compensation Initiative pursuant to FHFA Directive in Coordination with HUD," February 2011; delinquency rate data from the Federal Reserve Bank of New York, "Quarterly Report on Household Debt and Credit," August 2011.

Notes: The delinquency rate measures the fraction of the total outstanding mortgage balance that is at least 30 days delinquent as of the first quarter of each year.

Figure 2. Servicer Consolidation.

To address concerns about staffing, S. 824 and H.R. 1783 mandate staffing requirements that set minimum experience, education, and training levels for loan modification staff. The legislation also proposes caseload limits for individual employees.

POTENTIAL IMPLICATIONS OF STANDARDS

Table 1 summarizes the issues and the reforms proposed by S. 824, H.R. 1783, and S. 967.

Table 1. Summary of Servicing Standards

Issues	Reform Proposals	S. 824 and H.R. 1783	S. 967
Misalignment due to compensation structure	Require a special servicer for delinquent borrowers	X	
Relationship with provider of foreclosure services	Limitation on fees charged to investors	X	
Rep and warrant conflicts	Third-party reviewer; increased penalty		
Ownership of 2nd lien	Prohibit owning 2nd lien	X	
Servicer advances	Limit servicer advances to three payment periods	X	
Absence of a consumer-facing market	Require a single point of contact; prohibit dual tracking	X	X
Understaffed servicers	Limitations on caseloads and requirements for training, education levels, and experience of staff	X	

Source: Table compiled by CRS.

The servicing standards may align servicers' incentives with investors' interests and protect borrowers from abuse, but could come at the expense of higher interest rates and closing fees for borrowers and lower returns for investors.[51] Just as servicers receive higher compensation for handling subprime mortgages that are more costly to service than prime mortgages, all borrowers could expect rates to increase as servicers would need to be compensated for the added cost of hiring and training more personnel to meet proposed regulations.[52] Servicers may experience reduced revenues as a result of the limitations on the fees servicers can charge and restrictions on ownership of second liens. Hence, borrowers might be required to pay higher rates or closing costs.

In addition, some believe that higher costs for servicers could accelerate the consolidation of the servicing industry and squeeze out community banks.[53] Servicers may satisfy the increased staffing requirements by taking advantage of the economies of scale offered by large call centers and automated transaction processing. If the proposals require that the special servicer for delinquent loans be from a different company than the primary servicer (as opposed to the special servicer being part of the same company as the primary servicer), then the servicing market may further segment into a few large primary servicers and smaller special servicers.

If special servicers are also subject to similar regulations about customer service, then they would be subject to the same pressures to consolidate as the primary servicers. If the lack of competition in the servicing industry was one of the factors driving the need for servicing standards, some may ask whether the standards are be self-defeating.

APPENDIX A. NON-LEGISLATIVE APPROACHES

In addition to the legislative proposals, servicing standards may be adopted through other avenues. One channel being considered is the rulemaking associated with the Dodd-Frank Act. Regulatory agencies responsible for implementing portions of the Dodd-Frank Act, including the Consumer Financial Protection Bureau, the Board of Governors of the Federal Reserve System, and the Federal Deposit Insurance Corporation, are considering including some or all of the proposed standards in their rules on securitization and qualified residential mortgages.[54] The Treasury Department, as part of its implementation of HAMP, requires participating servicers to establish a single point of contact.[55]

In addition, the Federal Reserve Board, the Office of the Comptroller of the Currency, and the Office of Thrift Supervision are taking enforcement actions against 14 servicers.[56] When examining the servicers, the agencies found "unsafe or unsound practices and violations of law, which have had an adverse impact on the functioning of the mortgage market."[57] The enforcement actions require servicers to establish a compliance program (subject to regulator approval) that includes some of the reforms already mentioned in this report. For example, servicers will have to improve their staffing and training as well as have a single point of contact to assure that communications are timely during the loan modification and foreclosure processes.[58] The regulatory agencies also plan to impose monetary sanctions.[59] The agencies' enforcement actions may have a significant effect because the 14 servicers represent more than two-thirds of the servicing market.[60] The actions taken by the regulatory agencies do not preclude other federal or state regulatory and law enforcement agencies from taking additional actions. For example, the state attorneys general are in settlement talks with the major mortgage servicers stemming from the investigations into fraud and abuse.[61]

The Federal Housing Finance Agency, which regulates Fannie Mae and Freddie Mac, has directed the GSEs to require their servicers to adopt servicer reforms. Through the Servicing Alignment Initiative, Fannie and Freddie will establish consistent policies and processes for servicing delinquent loans in four areas: borrower contact, delinquency management practices, foreclosure timelines, and loan modifications/foreclosure alternatives.[62] The initiative prohibits dual tracking during the first 120 days of delinquency but does not require (though it does encourage) designating a single point of contact. Because of the large role that Fannie and Freddie play in the housing market,[63] the reforms have the potential to significantly affect the servicing industry. FHFA is also working with the Department of Housing and Urban Development through the Servicing Compensation Initiative to reform the servicing compensation structure for Fannie and Freddie servicers.

If servicing standards are implemented by rule, by settlement agreements, or for Fannie and Freddie servicers, the standards would have a limited reach. Only legislation would have universal coverage.

APPENDIX B. DATA ANALYSIS OF PRINCIPAL-AGENT PROBLEM

Servicers are constrained in their dealings with delinquent borrowers by contractual agreements with the owners of the loans, but the contracts may be vague enough to allow servicers the flexibility to choose the workout option that is in their best interest. Servicers' relationships with affiliates, the requirement to advance payment or interest, and servicers' compensation structures may influence decisions about loss mitigation options. If the option that is selected contrasts with the interest of the investor, then the servicer might profit at the investors' expense. Because incentives influence servicer actions in conflicting ways, economic theory alone is insufficient to determine whether the net effect of servicers' incentives is to offer too many foreclosures, too many loss mitigation workouts, or the wrong type of workout. The potential principal-agent problem is reexamined in this section to see what data trends might suggest.[64] A comparison is presented of how loans are serviced when owned by the servicer versus when loans are serviced for a GSE or PLS. Assuming that a servicer that keeps its loans in portfolio is less likely to have a principal-agent problem, the loans serviced for GSEs should be serviced differently. The differences are expected to be even more exaggerated when comparing loans serviced for PLS to loans held in portfolio due to the stronger principal-agent problem in PLS.

A principal-agent problem may most strongly manifest itself when looking at the data on principal reductions. Servicers are compensated primarily on the unpaid principal balance of the loans they are servicing. Therefore, they have an incentive to not reduce the loan principal if other options are available. Figure B-1 shows the frequency with which principal reductions are performed when loans are held in servicers' portfolios and when serviced for a GSE or for a PLS. The data span the first quarter of 2009 to the first quarter of 2011. For example, of all the loan modifications performed in the fourth quarter of 2009 for loans held in a servicer's portfolio, 27.7% included a principal reduction.

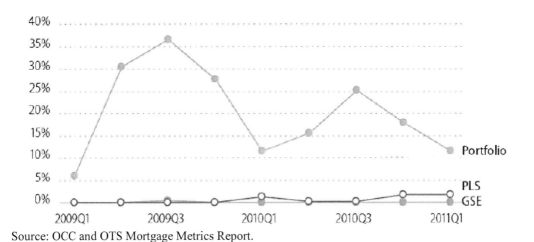

Source: OCC and OTS Mortgage Metrics Report.

Figure B-1. Frequency of Principal Reduction.

Loans held in portfolio saw more principal reductions than those owned by GSEs or PLS. The difference could be attributed to the principal-agent problem. However, alternative hypotheses may also explain the outcome. It is possible that the different mortgage holders own different types of loans.[65] Principal reductions may yield the highest NPV for portfolio loans but not for private investors' or GSEs' delinquent loans.[66] There may also be contractual differences facing servicers for each of the mortgage holders. Fannie and Freddie servicing guidelines do not allow for loan modifications involving principal reduction.[67] Servicers for private investors may also be limited by their pooling and servicing agreements in their ability to offer principal reductions.[68] Servicers for private investors may be less likely to reduce principal because they are concerned about being sued for choosing an option that an investor believes not to be in his or her best interest.[69] Investors may be more familiar with foreclosure or other forms of loan modification and therefore be less likely to question a servicer than if a principal reduction is offered to the borrower.[70]

Other forms of loss mitigation yield similar problems in attempting to isolate the impact of the principal-agent problem. Figure B-2 shows the frequency with which a principal deferral[71] is used in a loan modification. The use of principal deferral varies over time and the difference between its usage for loans held in portfolio versus loans serviced for GSE and PLS also varies. The amount of that variation that is attributable to the principal-agent problem is not captured in this model because there are too many differences across types of holders.

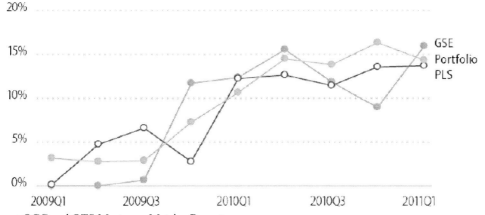

Source: OCC and OTS Mortgage Metrics Report.

Figure B-2. Frequency of Principal Deferral.

These two examples illustrate the difficulty in attempting to isolate the principal-agent problem in the data on loan modifications. The principal-agent problem cannot be measured without loan-level information as well as data on the limitations imposed by the pooling and servicing agreements.[72] Such detailed data are not available. Others have tried to determine if there is a causal link between securitization and increased foreclosures[73] (possibly due to a principal-agent problem), but the results are inconclusive.[74]

End Notes

[1] Board of Governors of the Federal Reserve System, *Household Finance: Mortgage Debt Outstanding*, June 2011, http://www.federalreserve.gov/econresdata/releases /mortoutstand /current.htm.

[2] See CRS Report R41572, *Incentives and Factors Influencing Foreclosure and Other Loss Mitigation Outcomes*, by Darryl E. Getter.

[3] See CRS Report R41491, *"Robo-Signing" and Other Alleged Documentation Problems in Judicial and Nonjudicial Foreclosure Processes*, by David H. Carpenter.

[4] Servicer regulation is often dependent on the servicer's parent company. A servicer may be an affiliate of a larger financial institution and the regulation of the servicer may depend on the regulation of the parent company. For example, if a servicer is affiliated with a bank holding company, it is regulated by the Federal Reserve Board. If the parent company is a national bank, it is regulated by the Office of the Comptroller of the Currency. In addition to federal regulations, servicers may be subject to state regulations. For an overview of U.S. financial regulation, see CRS Report R40249, *Who Regulates Whom? An Overview of U.S. Financial Supervision*, by Mark Jickling and Edward V. Murphy.

[5] Sheila Bair, "Opening Address at Summit on Residential Mortgage Servicing for the 21st Century," Washington, DC, January 19, 2011, http://www.fdic.gov/news/news/speeches /chairman/spjan1911.html.

[6] Office of the Special Inspector General for the Troubled Asset Relief Program, *Quarterly Report to Congress*, October 26, 2010, p. 160, http://www.sigtarp.gov/reports /congress /2010/October2010_Quarterly_Report_to_ Congress.pdf.

[7] There are also loans guaranteed by the federal government, but current legislation and academic literature does not focus on those loans so they will not be discussed in this report.

[8] In housing finance, a private-label security is "a mortgage-backed security or other bond created and sold by a company other than a government-sponsored enterprise (GSE). The security often is collateralized by loans that are ineligible for purchase by a GSE," Financial Stability Oversight Council, *2011 Annual Report*, p. 159, http://www.treasury.gov /initiatives/fsoc /Documents/FSOCAR2011.pdf.

[9] A government-sponsored enterprise is a "corporate entity that has a federal charter authorized by law but that is a privately owned financial institution," Financial Stability Oversight Council, *2011 Annual Report*, p. 156, http://www.treasury.gov/initiatives /fsoc/Documents /FSOCAR2011.pdf. For more on Fannie Mae and Freddie Mac, see CRS Report R40800, *GSEs and the Government's Role in Housing Finance: Issues for the 112th Congress*, by N. Eric Weiss.

[10] Pooling and servicing agreements (PSAs) are contracts negotiated between the investors and servicers to help guide the actions of servicers when borrowers are delinquent on their mortgage payments.

[11] Office of the Special Inspector General for the Troubled Asset Relief Program, *Quarterly Report to Congress*, October 26, 2010, p. 160, http://www.sigtarp.gov/reports /congress /2010/ October2010_Quarterly_Report_to_ Congress.pdf.

[12] Adam J. Levitin and Tara Twomey, "Mortgage Servicing," *Yale Journal on Regulation*, vol. 28, no. 1 (2011), p. 67.

[13] Working on behalf of the investors, "the trustee's role involves holding transaction cash flows in segregated accounts, notifying investors and rating agencies of covenant breaches and events of default, and managing servicing transfers if the original servicer is no longer able to function as servicer," Moody's, *Moody's Re-examines Trustees' Role in ABS and RMBS*, February 4, 2003, p. 1, http://www.moodys.com.ar/PDF/Research /Trustee's%20Role.pdf.

[14] U.S. Congress, Senate Committee on Banking, Housing, and Urban Affairs, Subcommittee on Housing, Transportation and Community Development, *Testimony of Laurie Goodman, Amherst Securities Group*, 112th Cong., 1st sess., May 12, 2011, p. 6.

[15] Adam J. Levitin and Tara Twomey, "Mortgage Servicing," *Yale Journal on Regulation*, vol. 28, no. 1 (2011), p. 58, 62.

[16] Carrick Mollenkamp, "Banks Pressed on Sour Home Loans," *The Wall Street Journal*, September 23, 2010, http://online.wsj.com/article/SB10001424052748704814204 575508143329644732.html.

[17] A recent white paper that studied the content of subprime securitization contracts found that servicers are often given general guidelines for modifying loans, such as follow customary servicing standards or service the loans as if they were held in your own portfolio. See John P. Hunt, *What Do Subprime Securitization Contracts Actually Say About Loan Modification? Preliminary Results and Implications*, Berkeley Center for Law, Business and the Economy, March 25, 2009, p. 9.

[18] Office of the Special Inspector General for the Troubled Asset Relief Program, *Quarterly Report to Congress*, October 26, 2010, p. 164, http://www.sigtarp.gov/reports /congress /2010/ October2010_Quarterly_Report_to_Congress.pdf.

[19] HAMP is part of the Obama Administration's Making Home Affordable program. HAMP provides financial incentives to participating servicers in order to encourage them to provide loan modifications to eligible troubled borrowers. See CRS Report R40210, *Preserving Homeownership: Foreclosure Prevention Initiatives*, by Katie Jones.

[20] Larry Cordell, Karen Dynan, and Andreas Lehnert et al., *The Incentives of Mortgage Servicers: Myths and Realities*, Federal Reserve Board, Finance and Economics Discussion Series, Working Paper 2008-46, September 8, 2008, p. 20, http://www.federalreserve.gov /pubs/feds/2008/200846/200846pap.pdf.

[21] Ibid., p. 18.

[22] A basis point is 0.01%. For example, a subprime loan with a $200,000 unpaid balance would yield (0.0050*200,000) $1,000 in annual income to the servicer. Servicers are compensated more for subprime loans because those loans often are more costly to service. Subprime borrowers default at a higher rate so servicers spend more to manage those defaults. Larry Cordell, Karen Dynan, and Andreas Lehnert et al., *The Incentives of Mortgage Servicers: Myths and Realities*, Federal Reserve Board, Finance and Economics Discussion Series, Working Paper 2008-46, September 8, 2008, p. 15, http://www.federalreserve.gov/pubs /feds/2008/200846/200846pap.pdf.

[23] Office of the Special Inspector General for the Troubled Asset Relief Program, *Quarterly Report to Congress*, October 26, 2010, p. 161, http://www.sigtarp.gov/reports /congress/2010/ October2010_Quarterly_Report_to_Congress.pdf.

[24] The model that follows is based on Adam J. Levitin and Tara Twomey, "Mortgage Servicing," *Yale Journal on Regulation*, vol. 28, no. 1 (2011), p. 72.

[25] Investors may be reluctant to reimburse servicers for added loss mitigation expenses because pursuing loss mitigation options that maximize the NPV is the expected function of the servicer. Investors may argue that performing appropriate loss mitigation options is what the servicer is already paid to do. See Larry Cordell, Karen Dynan, and Andreas Lehnert et al., *The Incentives of Mortgage Servicers: Myths and Realities*, Federal Reserve Board, Finance and Economics Discussion Series, Working Paper 2008-46, September 8, 2008, p. 19, http://www.federalreserve.gov/pubs/ feds/2008/200846/200846pap.pdf.

[26] It is also unclear what will happen if a delinquent loan reperforms. The special servicer may not have the incentive to make the loan reperform if doing so transfers the servicing rights back to the primary servicer.

[27] U.S. Congress, Senate Committee on Banking, Housing, and Urban Affairs, Subcommittee on Housing, Transportation and Community Development, *Testimony of Laurie Goodman, Amherst Securities Group*, 112th Cong., 1st sess., May 12, 2011, p. 7.

[28] Office of the Special Inspector General for the Troubled Asset Relief Program, *Quarterly Report to Congress*, October 26, 2010, p. 162, http://www.sigtarp.gov/reports /congress /2010/ October2010_Quarterly_Report_to_Congress.pdf.

[29] Fee income is only one source of servicer compensation. Even if the opportunity to earn additional fee income offered the incentive to foreclose, there are also incentives to not foreclose, such as the opportunity to earn additional revenue from the servicing fee (which is dependent on the unpaid principal balance; foreclosing on a home lowers the unpaid principal balance).

[30] U.S. Congress, Senate Committee on Banking, Housing, and Urban Affairs, Subcommittee on Housing, Transportation and Community Development, *Testimony of Laurie Goodman, Amherst Securities Group*, 112th Cong., 1st sess., May 12, 2011, p. 6.

[31] For an example of an NPV test, see Federal Deposit Insurance Corporation, *FDIC Loan Modification Program*, http://www.fdic.gov/consumers/loans/loanmod/FDICLoanMod.pdf.

[32] U.S. Congress, Senate Committee on Banking, Housing, and Urban Affairs, Subcommittee on Housing, Transportation and Community Development, *Testimony of Laurie Goodman, Amherst Securities Group*, 112th Cong., 1st sess., May 12, 2011, p. 6.

[33] Rep-and-warrants violations can occur for many reasons, such as misrepresentations of the income level of the borrower or the occupancy status of the house. U.S. Congress, Senate Committee on Banking, Housing, and Urban Affairs, Subcommittee on Housing, Transportation and Community Development, *Testimony of Laurie Goodman, Amherst Securities Group*, 112th Cong., 1st sess., May 12, 2011, p. 8.

[34] Ibid., p. 8.

[35] Ibid., p. 8.

[36] DBRS, *Review Services for the Secondary Mortgage Market*, August 14, 2007, http://www.dbrs.com/research /213821/dbrs-issues-report-review-services-for-the-secondary -mortgage-market.html.

[37] U.S. Congress, Senate Committee on Banking, Housing, and Urban Affairs, Subcommittee on Housing, Transportation and Community Development, *Testimony of Anthony Sanders*, 112th Cong., 1st sess., May 12, 2011, p. 7.

[38] For example, an executive with Bank of America testified during a congressional hearing that, "of the 10.4 million first liens Bank of America services 15% have a second lien with Bank of America." U.S. Congress, House Committee on Financial Services, *Testimony of Barbara Desoer, President, Bank of America Home Loans*, 111th Cong., 1st sess., April 13, 2009, p. 6.

[39] U.S. Congress, Senate Committee on Banking, Housing, and Urban Affairs, Subcommittee on Housing, Transportation and Community Development, *Testimony of Laurie Goodman, Amherst Securities Group*, 112th Cong., 1st sess., May 12, 2011, pp. 2-5.

[40] Amherst Mortgage Insight, *Strategic Default and 1st/2nd Lien Payment Priority*, February 17, 2011, p. 15.

[41] Sheila Bair, "Opening Address at Summit on Residential Mortgage Servicing for the 21st Century," Washington, DC, January 19, 2011, http://www.fdic.gov/news/news/speeches /chairman/spjan1911.html.

[42] Servicers may be reimbursed, but often not until the house is sold. Office of the Special Inspector General for the Troubled Asset Relief Program, *Quarterly Report to Congress*, October 26, 2010, p. 162, http://www.sigtarp.gov/ reports/congress/2010/October2010_ Quarterly_Report_to_Congress.pdf.

[43] Diane E. Thompson, *Why Servicers Foreclose When They Should Modify and Other Puzzles of Servicer Behavior: Servicer Compensation and its Consequences*, National Consumer Law Center, October 2009, pp. 23-24.

[44] Ibid., p. 23.

[45] Larry Cordell, Karen Dynan, and Andreas Lehnert et al., *The Incentives of Mortgage Servicers: Myths and Realities*, Federal Reserve Board, Finance and Economics Discussion Series, Working Paper 2008-46, September 8, 2008, p. 16, http://www.federalreserve.gov /pubs/feds/2008/200846/200846pap.pdf.

[46] Mortgage Bankers Association, *Residential Mortgage Servicing for the 21st Century*, White Paper, May 2011, p. 22, http://www.mbaa.org/files/ResourceCenter/ServicingCouncil/ResidentialServicingforthe21stCentury WhitePaper.pdf.

[47] U.S. Congress, House Committee on Financial Services, Subcommittee on Financial Institutions and Consumer Credit and Subcommittee on Oversight and Investigations, *Testimony of Raj Date*, 112th Cong., 1st sess., July 7, 2011, p. 2.

[48] Office of the Special Inspector General for the Troubled Asset Relief Program, *Quarterly Report to Congress*, October 26, 2010, p. 163, http://www.sigtarp.gov/reports /congress/ 2010/ October2010_Quarterly_Report_to_ Congress.pdf.

[49] A 2007 study found that mega servicers can service performing loans at a monthly cost of approximately $4/loan, large servicers at a cost of $6/loan, and small/medium servicers at $7/loan. See Federal Housing Finance Agency, *Servicing Compensation Initiative pursuant to FHFA Directive in Coordination with HUD*, February 2011, p. 8, http://www.fhfa.gov/webfiles/19719/FHFA_Servicing_Initiative_-_Background_and_Issues_2011- 02- 14_3pm_FINAL.pdf.

[50] See the discussion of the enforcement actions taken by the regulatory agencies in Appendix A.

[51] Adam J. Levitin and Tara Twomey, "Mortgage Servicing," *Yale Journal on Regulation*, vol. 28, no. 1 (2011), p. 89.

[52] For more on the potential costs of requiring a single point of contact and prohibiting dual tracking, see Mortgage Bankers Association, *Residential Mortgage Servicing for the 21st Century*, White Paper, May 2011, pp. 23-24, http://www.mbaa.org/tiles/Resource Center/ServicingCouncil/ResidentialServicingforthe21stCenturyWhitePaper.pdf.

[53] U.S. Congress, Senate Committee on Banking, Housing, and Urban Affairs, *Testimony of Jack Hopkins, President and CEO of CorTrust Bank*, 112th Cong., 1st sess., August 2, 2011.

[54] Comptroller of the Currency, Federal Reserve System, Federal Deposit Insurance Corporation, Federal Housing Finance Agency, Securities and Exchange Commission, Housing and Urban Development Department, "Credit Risk Retention," 76 *Federal Register* 24127, April 29, 2011.

[55] U.S. Department of the Treasury, *Supplemental Directive 11-04: Single Point of Contact for Borrower Assistance*, May 18, 2011, https://www.hmpadmin.com/portal/news/docs/2011 /hampupdate051811.pdf.

[56] The 14 servicers are Ally Bank/ GMAC, Aurora Bank, Bank of America, Citibank, EverBank, HSBC, JPMorgan Chase, MetLife, OneWest, PNC, Sovereign Bank, SunTrust, U.S. Bank, and Wells Fargo.

[57] Federal Reserve System, Office of the Comptroller of the Currency, Office of Thrift Supervision, *Interagency Review of Foreclosure Policies and Practices*, April 2011, p. 13, http://www.occ.gov/news-issuances/news-releases/ 2011/nr-occ-2011-47a.pdf.

[58] Federal Reserve System, Office of the Comptroller of the Currency, Office of Thrift Supervision, *Interagency Review of Foreclosure Policies and Practices*, April 2011, p. 13, http://www.occ.gov/news-issuances/news-releases/ 2011/nr-occ-2011-47a.pdf.

[59] The Federal Reserve System, *Press Release*, April 13, 2011, http://www.federalreserve.gov/newsevents /press/enforcement/20110413a.htm.

[60] Federal Reserve System, Office of the Comptroller of the Currency, Office of Thrift Supervision, *Interagency Review of Foreclosure Policies and Practices*, April 2011, p. 3, http://www.occ.gov/news-issuances/news-releases/ 2011/nr-occ-2011-47a.pdf.

[61] Brady Dennis, "State attorneys general tackle mortgage servicing," *Washington Post*, March 17, 2011, http://www.washingtonpost.com/business/economy/state-attorneys-general-tackle-mortgage-servicing/2011/03/17/ ABGmNCn_story.html.

[62] Federal Housing Finance Agency, *Frequently Asked Questions- Servicing Alignment Initiative*, April 28, 2011, p. 1, http://www.fhfa.gov/webfiles/21191/FAQs42811Final.pdf.

[63] See Figure 1.

[64] The data is taken from the OCC and OTS Mortgage Metrics Reports, which can be accessed at http://www.ots.treas.gov/?p=Mortgage%20Metrics%20Report. The reports contain data from eight national banks (Bank of America, JPMorgan Chase, Citibank, HSBC, MetLife, PNC, U.S. Bank, and Wells Fargo) and one thrift (OneWest Bank). Collectively, the nine institutions represent 63% of all first-lien residential mortgages outstanding in the United States. For more on the data, see *OCC/OTS Mortgage Metrics Loan-Level Data Collection: Field Definitions*, April 20, 2009, http://www.occ.gov/publications/publications-by-type/other-publications-reports/ mortgage-metrics-q2-2009/loan-level-data-field-defin-q2-2009.pdf.

[65] Loans held in servicers' portfolios reportedly tend to be nonconforming loans with increased risk characteristics and geographic concentration in weaker real estate markets, whereas GSEs have a greater percentage of prime loans. No background is given on PLS loans. Office of Comptroller of the Currency, Office of Thrift Supervision, *OCC and OTS Mortgage Metrics Report*, First Quarter 2011, p. 14,17, http://www.ots.treas.gov /_files/ 490078.pdf.

[66] For an analysis of why principal reduction may not be pursued, see Chris Foote, Kris Gerardi, and Paul Willen, *The seductive but flawed logic of principal reduction*, Federal Reserve Bank of Atlanta, March 9, 2011, http://realestateresearch.frbatlanta.org/rer/2011/03 /seductive-but-flawed-logic-of-principal-reduction.html.

[67] Office of Comptroller of the Currency, Office of Thrift Supervision, *OCC and OTS Mortgage Metrics Report*, First Quarter 2011, p. 27, http://www.ots.treas.gov/_files/490078.pdf; see Fannie Mae, *Fannie Mae Single Family 2011 Servicing Guide*, June 10, 2011, pp. 706-67, https://www.efanniemae.com/sf/guides /ssg/svcg/svc061011.pdf.

[68] One study noted that PSA bans on mortgage modification are rare, but the analysis is based on a relatively small sample of securitizations. See John P. Hunt, *What Do Subprime Securitization Contracts Actually Say About Loan Modification? Preliminary Results and Implications*, Berkeley Center for Law, Business and the Economy, March 25, 2009, pp.7-8.

[69] Larry Cordell, Karen Dynan, and Andreas Lehnert, et al., *The Incentives of Mortgage Servicers: Myths and Realities*, Federal Reserve Board, Washington, D.C., Working Paper 2008-46 of the Finance and Economics Discussion Series, September 8, 2008, p. 23, http://www.federalreserve.gov/pubs/feds/2008 /200846 /200846pap.pdf.

[70] However, there have been few instances of investor litigation in response to a servicer's loan modification decision. See Diane E. Thompson, *Why Servicers Foreclose When They Should Modify and Other Puzzles of Servicer Behavior: Servicer Compensation and its Consequences*, National Consumer Law Center, October 2009, p. 8.

[71] Principal deferral modifications are modifications "that remove a portion of the principal from the amount used to calculate monthly principal and interest payments for a set period. The deferred amount becomes due at the end of the loan term." In a principal reduction modification, a portion of the principal amounted is permanently forgiven. Office of Comptroller of the Currency, Office of Thrift Supervision, *OCC and OTS Mortgage Metrics Report*, First Quarter 2011, p. 10, http://www.ots.treas.gov/_files/490078.pdf.

[72] Regulators have reviewed servicers' foreclosure activities, but have not have not focused extensively on servicers' loan modification processes. See Federal Reserve System, Office of the Comptroller of the

Currency, Office of Thrift Supervision, *Interagency Review of Foreclosure Policies and Practices*, April 2011, p. 2, http://www.occ.gov/newsissuances/news-releases/2011/nr-occ-2011-47a.pdf.

[73] See Tomasz Piskorski, Amit Seru, and Vikrant Vig, *Securitization and Distressed Loan Renegotiation: Evidence from the Subprime Mortgage Crisis*, Chicago Booth School of Business Research Paper No. 09-02 , April 15, 2010.

[74] See Manuel Adelino, Kristopher Gerardi, and Paul S. Willen, *What Explains Differences in Foreclosure Rates? A Response to Piskorski, Seru, and Vig*, Federal Reserve Bank of Boston, Working Paper 10-2, http://www.bos.frb.org/ economic/wp/wp2010/wp1002.htm.

INDEX

A

abuse, x, 141, 142, 148, 150, 151
accounting, 34, 56, 57, 80
adjustment, 59, 85, 87, 88, 90
age, 60
agencies, x, 53, 59, 73, 111, 114, 120, 138, 142, 151
Alaska, 115
American Recovery and Reinvestment Act of 2009, 102, 135
amortization, 100, 134, 135
annual rate, 64, 79
appraisals, 24, 25, 60, 83, 103
Appropriations Act, 118, 119
ARM, 99, 131
assessment, 16, 62, 90, 122, 136, 137
assets, 15, 29, 31, 33, 40, 85, 90, 134
authority, ix, 94, 110, 117, 121, 122, 128, 130, 138, 148

B

balance sheet, 2, 5, 12, 19, 29, 48, 51, 53, 75, 87, 90, 147
bank holding companies, 49
banking, 6, 31, 34, 36, 46, 48, 49, 59, 60, 61
bankruptcy, 18, 33, 85, 121, 133
banks, viii, xi, 2, 3, 12, 13, 14, 19, 20, 23, 26, 29, 33, 34, 39, 44, 49, 61, 67, 76, 85, 88, 91, 134, 142, 143, 150, 157
bargaining, 89
barriers, ix, 35, 38, 55, 56, 82, 83
basis points, 57, 73, 145
beneficiaries, 24, 74
benefits, 16, 17, 22, 43, 52, 72, 74, 78, 82, 84, 85, 96, 122, 147
blogs, 36

blueprint, 39
bonds, 74
borrowers, vii, viii, ix, x, 1, 2, 3, 4, 5, 6, 8, 9, 10, 11, 12, 14, 15, 16, 17, 18, 19, 20, 21, 22, 23, 24, 25, 26, 31, 32, 33, 34, 35, 38, 42, 43, 44, 50, 51, 52, 53, 54, 55, 56, 57, 58, 59, 60, 71, 72, 73, 79, 82, 83, 84, 85, 86, 87, 88, 89, 93, 94, 97, 98, 99, 100, 101, 102, 103, 104, 107, 108, 109, 110, 111, 113, 114, 115, 116, 117, 118, 120, 121, 123, 124, 125, 126, 127, 128, 129, 131, 132, 133, 134, 135, 137, 138, 141, 142, 144, 145, 146, 147, 148, 150, 152, 154, 155
breakdown, 22, 145
break-even, 80
budget deficit, 116
Bureau of Labor Statistics, 45
businesses, 40, 65, 78
buyers, 55, 56, 78, 87

C

calculus, 85
call centers, 57, 150
candidates, 46
capital gains, 74
cash, 19, 33, 42, 46, 57, 73, 75, 77, 78, 83, 99, 154
cash flow, 19, 33, 46, 83, 154
census, 29, 45, 61, 66, 79
central bank, 74
challenges, ix, x, 58, 60, 86, 94, 97, 111, 122
Chicago, 30, 46, 158
cities, 54
collateral, 3, 6, 20, 63, 65, 78, 134
collateral damage, 3
commercial, 46, 48
commercial bank, 46, 48
communities, vii, viii, ix, 3, 28, 33, 38, 39, 47, 48, 50, 53, 56, 59, 93, 94, 97, 98

community, 48, 96, 97, 118, 150
compensation, x, 48, 51, 57, 58, 62, 85, 108, 123,
    137, 141, 145, 146, 147, 150, 151, 152, 155
competition, 24, 25, 69, 151
competitors, 20, 57
compliance, 43, 48, 56, 59, 114, 151
computer, 86
computer systems, 86
conference, 85, 91
conflict, 145, 146, 147
conflict of interest, 147
Congress, v, vii, ix, x, 1, 2, 3, 4, 6, 7, 8, 15, 18, 25,
    27, 31, 32, 34, 35, 36, 73, 82, 85, 90, 93, 94, 97,
    116, 117, 118, 121, 135, 136, 138, 139, 141, 142,
    143, 154, 155, 156
Congressional Budget Office, 21, 34, 118, 136, 138,
    139
congressional hearings, 142
Consolidated Appropriations Act, 118, 119
consolidation, 149, 150
construction, 63, 64, 66, 67, 77, 78, 79, 82, 88, 90
consumer price index, 31
consumer protection, 50
consumers, 11, 56, 78, 138, 155
consumption, vii, viii, 38
conversion rate, 57, 107
cost, viii, 2, 15, 16, 17, 19, 20, 23, 25, 34, 43, 46, 47,
    48, 56, 57, 60, 64, 69, 73, 78, 79, 82, 85, 86, 87,
    89, 102, 104, 105, 108, 113, 122, 127, 128, 129,
    136, 138, 145, 146, 147, 150, 156
cost effectiveness, 87
counseling, ix, 93, 114, 118, 119, 120, 138
covering, 72, 147
credit history, 32
creditors, 39, 59
creditworthiness, 50, 96
critical analysis, 82
criticism, 70
cure, 9, 17
current account deficit, 85
current prices, 68
customer service, 148, 151

D

danger, 17, 21, 26, 95, 132
database, 79
debt repayment, vii, 1, 3
defects, 103
deficiencies, 59, 60
deficiency, 56
deficit, 113

delinquency, 10, 43, 52, 55, 60, 61, 69, 96, 98, 118,
    128, 148, 149, 151
Department of Defense, 118, 119
Department of the Treasury, 53, 61, 132, 135, 136
depository institutions, 31, 36, 61, 74
depreciation, 47, 78
disclosure, 110
discounted cash flow, 33
dislocation, 39
disposable income, viii, 2, 3, 4, 22
disposition, 30, 36, 39, 48, 49, 56, 57, 60
distress, 63, 64, 67, 69, 76, 78, 87, 111
distribution, 8, 46, 47, 60
District of Columbia, 111, 112
Dodd-Frank Wall Street Reform and Consumer
    Protection Act, x, 36, 113, 142, 143
draft, 60
dual tracking, x, 142, 149, 150, 151, 156

E

economic damage, 39, 55
economic growth, 2, 65
economic losses, 39, 56
economic problem, vii, 1, 2
economic resources, 43
economic theory, 152
economics, 21, 36, 91, 139
economies of scale, 27, 149, 150
education, x, 142, 150
eligibility criteria, 22, 24, 108, 109, 131, 132
Emergency Economic Stabilization Act (EESA), 15,
    111, 117, 134
employees, x, 123, 142, 150
employment, 46, 109, 115
employment status, 115
encouragement, 120
enforcement, xi, 59, 62, 142, 143, 151, 156, 157
environment, 3, 19, 47, 57, 59, 67
equipment, 67, 78, 149
equity, viii, 2, 4, 5, 6, 8, 10, 11, 17, 20, 21, 23, 24,
    25, 30, 32, 40, 41, 42, 50, 54, 55, 65, 72, 79, 95,
    99, 100, 101, 103, 112, 113, 117, 130, 131, 138,
    147
erosion, 65
evidence, 15, 17, 29, 55, 66, 147
excess supply, vii, viii, ix, 26, 38, 58
executive branch, 97
exposure, 39, 43, 48, 51, 85, 87, 89

F

fairness, 12, 53, 55, 74, 122, 125
families, ix, 45, 81, 82, 83, 93, 96, 97, 98, 99
Fannie Mae, viii, 2, 3, 4, 8, 14, 15, 16, 18, 19, 20, 22, 23, 24, 25, 26, 28, 30, 31, 32, 33, 34, 39, 46, 50, 51, 59, 61, 70, 71, 79, 84, 87, 89, 102, 103, 104, 105, 122, 126, 127, 129, 130, 131, 133, 134, 135, 136, 144, 151, 154, 157
FDIC, 26, 35, 36, 77, 131, 132, 133, 139, 155
fear, 43, 73, 122, 123
federal government, vii, x, 1, 2, 3, 8, 11, 14, 20, 22, 33, 70, 94, 97, 102, 119, 120, 133, 154
Federal Housing Administration (FHA), ix, 43, 93, 112, 131
Federal Housing Finance Agency (FHFA), viii, 2, 4, 8, 14, 15, 16, 17, 18, 24, 26, 28, 30, 31, 33, 34, 35, 36, 37, 39, 46, 47, 49, 59, 60, 61, 62, 64, 70, 82, 84, 85, 102, 103, 123, 130, 133, 134, 135, 136, 139, 142, 143. 145, 149, 151, 156, 157
federal law, 49
Federal Register, 156
federal regulations, 154
Federal Reserve, v, x, 12, 21, 22, 23, 26, 27, 28, 29, 31, 32, 33, 34, 35, 36, 37, 46, 47, 49, 59, 60, 61, 62, 64, 70, 82, 84, 85, 134, 135, 142, 143, 149, 151, 154, 155, 156, 157, 158
Federal Reserve Board, 34, 35, 36, 59, 60, 135, 151, 154, 155, 156, 157
financial, vii, viii, 1, 2, 3, 5, 6, 8, 9, 12, 14, 18, 19, 20, 25, 26, 27, 31, 33, 36, 39, 40, 42, 46, 55, 61, 73, 74, 79, 81, 82, 86, 88, 89, 90, 91, 102, 104, 111, 123, 129, 132, 135, 136, 137, 139, 144, 154, 155
financial crisis, 81, 90
financial firms, 86
financial incentives, 14, 104, 144, 155
financial institutions, vii, viii, 1, 2, 3, 5, 6, 12, 20, 25, 26, 27, 31, 36, 39, 46, 61, 111
financial regulation, 154
financial resources, 55
financial sector, vii, viii, 1, 2, 19
financial shocks, 42
financial support, 102, 135
financial system, 2, 82, 102
fiscal policy, 63, 73, 74, 78
fixed costs, 20, 45, 47
flexibility, 51, 122, 132, 143, 144, 152
flooding, 5, 27, 28
force, 43, 54, 84, 146, 148
foreclosure, vii, viii, ix, x, 2, 4, 5, 6, 8, 9, 10, 12, 18, 26, 31, 32, 33, 34, 36, 38, 39, 44, 45, 47, 48, 52, 53, 55, 56, 57, 58, 59, 60, 61, 62, 66, 67, 68, 69, 74, 75, 76, 77, 78, 79, 82, 84, 86, 87, 88, 89, 93, 94, 95, 96, 97, 98, 100, 101, 102, 104, 105, 108, 109, 110, 111, 113, 118, 119, 120, 121, 122, 123, 124, 125, 129, 131, 132, 134, 135, 136, 137, 138, 139, 141, 142, 143, 144, 145, 146, 147, 148, 149, 150, 151, 153, 157
formation, 35, 67, 78, 79, 88
formula, 108, 111, 123, 132, 133, 148
fraud, 74, 83, 116, 123, 142, 151
Freddie Mac, viii, 2, 3, 4, 8, 14, 15, 16, 18, 19, 20, 22, 23, 24, 25, 26, 28, 30, 31, 32, 33, 34, 39, 46, 50, 51, 61, 70, 71, 79, 84, 87, 89, 102, 103, 104, 105, 122, 126, 127, 129, 130, 131, 132, 133, 134, 135, 136, 144, 151, 154
full employment, 79
funding, ix, 48, 49, 53, 93, 104, 105, 111, 112, 114, 116, 118, 119, 130, 136, 137, 138
funds, 22, 33, 54, 74, 78, 82, 90, 104, 105, 111, 112, 113, 114, 119, 120, 138

G

Georgia, 111, 112
goods and services, vii, 1, 3, 11, 148
government intervention, 70
governments, 58, 65
Great Depression, 40
Great Recession, 65, 66, 69, 74
gross domestic product (GDP), 22, 65, 73, 79
growth, 22, 44, 65, 73, 79, 88
GSEs, 3, 8, 12, 15, 17, 24, 25, 26, 29, 31, 35, 39, 43, 46, 47, 48, 49, 50, 51, 58, 60, 84, 87, 90, 91, 136, 143, 144, 148, 151, 152, 153, 154, 157
guidance, 27, 33, 36, 49, 60, 103, 110, 111, 112, 116, 117, 130, 136, 137, 138
guidelines, 33, 86, 104, 107, 108, 110, 123, 130, 134, 137, 144, 153, 154

H

Hawaii, 115
health, 37, 59, 74, 96
healthier market, viii, 2, 3
hiring, 150
holding company, 154
Home Affordable Modification Program (HAMP), ix, 12, 14, 52, 93, 103, 120, 126, 127, 128, 130, 144
Home Affordable Refinance Program (HARP), ix, 19, 50, 93, 102, 126, 127, 128, 130
home value, 40, 97, 98
homelessness, 96

homeowners, vii, viii, ix, x, 2, 3, 5, 6, 11, 14, 15, 18, 19, 21, 22, 24, 26, 30, 31, 35, 38, 39, 40, 42, 50, 51, 52, 53, 55, 57, 59, 63, 65, 69, 71, 72, 73, 74, 75, 78, 79, 80, 82, 83, 84, 85, 86, 87, 88, 89, 91, 93, 94, 95, 96, 97, 98, 99, 100, 101, 102, 103, 105, 109, 111, 112, 117, 118, 119, 120, 121, 123, 125, 126, 130, 139

homes, vii, viii, 1, 2, 3, 4, 5, 6, 8, 10, 14, 17, 26, 28, 30, 32, 38, 42, 43, 44, 45, 47, 52, 54, 55, 56, 58, 61, 63, 64, 65, 66, 67, 68, 72, 78, 79, 81, 82, 84, 87, 88, 95, 96, 97, 98, 99, 100, 101, 102, 103, 108, 111, 112, 118, 120, 121, 126, 127, 130, 131, 142

House, vii, viii, ix, x, 4, 38, 40, 59, 68, 76, 78, 79, 84, 90, 93, 97, 104, 113, 116, 121, 141, 143, 156

House of Representatives, ix, 90, 93

household income, 60, 68, 79, 84, 114

household sector, 39

housing, vii, viii, ix, x, 1, 2, 3, 5, 10, 11, 12, 15, 17, 19, 21, 22, 26, 27, 29, 32, 33, 36, 37, 38, 39, 42, 43, 44, 45, 47, 48, 49, 50, 51, 53, 58, 59, 60, 61, 63, 64, 65, 66, 67, 69, 70, 72, 73, 74, 75, 76, 77, 78, 79, 81, 82, 83, 85, 87, 88, 89, 90, 91, 93, 94, 96, 111, 114, 118, 120, 132, 135, 138, 141, 142, 144, 147, 149, 151, 154

Housing and Urban Development (HUD), 30, 36, 60, 81, 85, 89, 90, 113, 114, 115, 116, 117, 120, 123, 128, 130, 132, 135, 136, 138, 139, 141, 149, 151, 156

housing boom, 144, 147, 149

housing bubble, vii, 1, 2, 17, 26, 81, 83, 90

housing market, vii, viii, ix, x, 1, 2, 3, 5, 10, 11, 12, 15, 17, 19, 21, 26, 37, 38, 39, 43, 45, 47, 48, 49, 50, 51, 53, 58, 59, 61, 64, 66, 69, 70, 77, 78, 79, 81, 82, 87, 88, 89, 90, 93, 141, 142, 147, 151

I

imbalances, 26

improvements, 69, 73

incentive effect, 16

incidence, 55

income, vii, viii, 1, 2, 3, 4, 11, 19, 22, 30, 35, 40, 42, 44, 48, 51, 52, 53, 54, 57, 60, 61, 65, 73, 74, 76, 79, 80, 84, 85, 86, 98, 99, 100, 101, 104, 105, 107, 109, 110, 113, 114, 115, 116, 117, 126, 127, 128, 129, 131, 132, 133, 134, 135, 143, 144, 145, 146, 155

income distribution, 60

individuals, 22, 33, 43, 60, 68, 84, 95, 123, 125, 135, 142

industry, 56, 57, 73, 80, 89, 95, 121, 133, 139, 143, 149, 150, 151

inflation, 79

infrastructure, 12, 32, 57

frastructure, 49

institutions, 4, 6, 12, 14, 23, 26, 27, 29, 31, 46, 49, 56, 58, 59, 68, 74, 157

insurance policy, 146

interest rates, 2, 12, 20, 22, 34, 43, 54, 71, 73, 74, 81, 85, 95, 99, 100, 101, 102, 104, 125, 135, 150

interference, 97

intermediaries, 138

intervention, vii, 1, 2, 120

investment, viii, 2, 3, 11, 19, 22, 68, 77, 94, 145

investments, vii, 1, 74, 78

investors, ix, x, 3, 4, 6, 11, 12, 13, 14, 15, 17, 19, 22, 23, 26, 27, 28, 29, 30, 31, 32, 33, 35, 39, 45, 47, 48, 52, 57, 58, 61, 63, 68, 73, 74, 77, 78, 82, 85, 88, 90, 93, 104, 108, 109, 120, 122, 123, 126, 128, 129, 132, 135, 136, 141, 142, 143, 144, 145, 146, 147, 148, 150, 152, 153, 154

Iowa, 115

issues, ix, 12, 34, 35, 36, 37, 38, 39, 46, 47, 51, 53, 54, 55, 58, 59, 67, 75, 94, 122, 123, 146, 147, 150, 156

J

job creation, 65

joint ventures, 48

Jurisdictions, 58

K

kicks, 99

L

labor force, 67

labor force participation, 67

labor market, viii, 38, 44, 55

labor markets, 55

large-scale refinancing, viii, 2, 3, 5, 19, 21, 22

law enforcement, 151

laws, 60, 61, 117, 120, 138

laws and regulations, 60

lead, 10, 26, 86, 89, 147

legal issues, 34, 67

legislation, 18, 25, 34, 49, 73, 102, 123, 135, 143, 146, 150, 151, 154

legislative proposals, 143, 151

lending, x, 12, 43, 47, 50, 59, 65, 70, 94, 95, 121, 125, 134

liquid assets, 129
liquidity, 15, 136
litigation, 89, 157
loan principal, 152
loans, viii, x, 2, 3, 5, 8, 12, 14, 15, 16, 17, 18, 19, 20,
    21, 23, 24, 25, 26, 32, 33, 34, 35, 42, 43, 46, 48,
    50, 51, 52, 55, 56, 57, 58, 61, 62, 63, 66, 67, 69,
    71, 72, 73, 75, 79, 83, 84, 86, 89, 90, 94, 95, 97,
    98, 99, 100, 101, 102, 103, 104, 110, 113, 114,
    115, 116, 117, 120, 121, 122, 123, 124, 125, 126,
    127, 130, 131, 132, 133, 135, 136, 141, 142, 143,
    144, 145, 146, 147, 150, 151, 152, 153, 154, 155,
    156, 157
local government, 58, 63, 65, 78, 97, 102, 118, 120,
    125
locus, vii, 1, 2
Louisiana, 11, 115
lower prices, 47, 63

M

magnitude, 22, 53, 57, 74
majority, 45, 46, 103
management, 26, 27, 48, 51, 57, 60, 61, 151
market failure, 74
market share, 85, 149
Maryland, v, ix, 81, 114, 115
media, 32, 91, 115, 138
median, 31, 46, 52, 61, 84, 114
mediation, 120
medical, 52, 98, 113, 114, 115
methodology, 17, 110
metropolitan areas, 30, 45, 46, 49
Mexico, 115
Miami, 46
middle class, 84
migration, 55
military, 119, 138
Minneapolis, 32
mission, 15
Missouri, 115
models, 24, 25, 103, 110
modifications, x, 9, 14, 15, 17, 33, 39, 43, 52, 53, 55,
    56, 57, 59, 61, 62, 63, 70, 74, 75, 76, 78, 80, 81,
    82, 86, 87, 89, 94, 100, 101, 104, 105, 107, 108,
    109, 110, 111, 116, 120, 121, 122, 123, 124, 125,
    126, 128, 132, 133, 134, 135, 142, 144, 149, 151,
    152, 153, 155, 157
monetary policy, 39
Montana, 115
moral hazard, 9, 74
moratorium, 121

mortgage payments, viii, 1, 9, 11, 14, 23, 52, 53, 54,
    73, 80, 83, 84, 87, 98, 99, 100, 102, 103, 104,
    108, 109, 113, 114, 115, 116, 124, 126, 127, 129,
    133, 135, 142, 154
mortgage-backed securities, 11, 22, 32, 35, 52, 71,
    73, 81, 85, 122, 135, 144, 147
mortgage-backed security, x, 32, 141, 142, 154
motivation, 22, 83
multiple factors, 24

N

natural disasters, 11
negative consequences, ix, 93, 97, 137
negative effects, 39, 56, 59, 96
negative equity, 5, 6, 8, 10, 11, 17, 24, 32, 42, 52, 54,
    55, 71, 79, 100
non-housing¬related spending, viii, 2
nonprofit organizations, 48

O

Obama Administration, ix, 23, 33, 93, 111, 115, 117,
    126, 130, 136, 138, 155
obstacles, viii, 27, 38, 39, 43, 48, 50, 51, 56, 118
officials, 89, 132
Oklahoma, 115
Omnibus Appropriations Act,, 118, 119
open market operations, 12
operations, 43
opportunities, 4, 45, 54, 67
optimism, 69, 78
outreach, 107, 110, 114, 120
ownership, 31, 48, 62, 116, 145, 147, 148, 150

P

participants, 35, 47, 58, 77, 88, 89, 90
penalties, 116, 133, 147
pipeline, ix, 38, 47, 78, 87
PLS, 143, 144, 152, 153, 157
policy, viii, ix, 2, 3, 5, 11, 12, 14, 15, 17, 19, 22, 26,
    27, 29, 39, 43, 46, 49, 51, 54, 55, 64, 70, 74, 78,
    81, 82, 83, 85, 86, 87, 88, 89, 94, 132, 134, 146
policy options, 15, 146
policymakers, vii, viii, 37, 38, 39, 47, 48, 50, 53, 58,
    59, 64, 70, 73, 78, 79, 84, 97
pools, 28, 46, 47, 60
population, 84
portfolio, 12, 43, 47, 107, 137, 143, 144, 152, 153,
    154

positive correlation, 12
potential benefits, 55
precedent, x, 94, 122, 125
present value, 14, 18, 32, 53, 57, 104, 109, 110, 132, 134, 144
preservation, 146
President, viii, 2, 3, 14, 19, 22, 24, 32, 35, 75, 83, 102, 117, 156
President Obama, viii, 2, 3, 14, 19, 24, 75, 102, 117
prevention, ix, x, 34, 93, 94, 97, 102, 105, 111, 113, 118, 120, 122, 125, 129, 131, 136, 138
price changes, 65
price index, 64, 88
price signals, 45
prime rate, 95
private sector, 80, 89, 120
probability, 33, 54, 73, 76
profit, 48, 79, 117, 118, 120, 122, 152
profitability, 46
project, viii, 2, 4
property taxes, 61, 78
proposed regulations, 150
protection, x, 82, 84, 141
public officials, 84
public policy, 53
public service, 63
Puerto Rico, 114, 115

R

rating agencies, 144, 154
real estate, 26, 44, 48, 49, 58, 61, 76, 157
real income, 80
recession, vii, 1, 2, 43, 50, 63, 69, 70, 71, 78, 88, 89, 144
recovery, vii, viii, 1, 2, 5, 12, 22, 27, 31, 37, 38, 39, 46, 49, 56, 59, 63, 65, 66, 71, 72, 73, 78, 82, 88, 89, 90, 102
reform, x, 36, 84, 85, 89, 91, 110, 113, 138, 142, 143, 150, 151
reforms, 143, 146, 150, 151
regulations, 56, 57, 120, 151, 154
regulatory agencies, 143, 151, 156
regulatory requirements, 43
rehabilitation, 48
reimburse, 155
relative prices, 29
relief, 14, 33, 55
rent, 3, 4, 6, 26, 27, 29, 30, 31, 45, 47, 48, 49, 55, 61, 63, 66, 68, 77, 96
requirements, 43, 48, 51, 55, 56, 61, 71, 74, 75, 107, 110, 111, 116, 120, 130, 131, 132, 150
resale, 45

residential, 59, 154, 156
resilience, 55
resolution, 39, 56, 58, 89
resources, 35, 42, 50, 87, 90, 94, 97
response, xi, 15, 50, 54, 57, 70, 74, 78, 97, 99, 100, 107, 142, 143, 157
restrictions, 25, 61, 123, 150
restructuring, 60
retirement, 65
revenue, 12, 47, 57, 65, 97, 145, 146, 155
rewards, 83
rhetoric, 83
rights, 43, 48, 53, 56, 57, 72, 122, 144, 155
risk, 5, 9, 14, 17, 18, 20, 23, 24, 25, 27, 32, 33, 35, 39, 43, 47, 50, 51, 52, 57, 59, 61, 63, 72, 73, 74, 778, 79, 81, 85, 87, 89, 90, 94, 97, 98, 99, 120, 121, 122, 125, 157
rules, x, 72, 94, 103, 104, 142, 143, 151

S

safety, 50
sanctions, 14, 151
savings, 15, 16, 22, 25, 48, 53, 65
school, 63, 67, 96
scope, viii, 38, 49, 56, 89, 125, 135
Secretary of Defense, 119
Secretary of the Treasury, 138
securities, 17, 22, 26, 33, 70, 73, 74, 85, 122, 143
security, x, 32, 90, 141, 142, 144, 147, 154
self-employed, 100
self-interest, 122
Senate, 6, 22, 31, 32, 34, 35, 36, 37, 63, 81, 97, 121, 138, 154, 155, 156
services, x, 26, 62, 91, 141, 146, 147, 150, 156
settlement agreements, xi, 142, 143, 151
settlements, xi, 142, 143
shortfall, 75
short-term interest rate, 99
signs, 104
small businesses, 65
social costs, 53
South Dakota, 11, 115
speech, 26, 31, 34, 91
spending, vii, viii, 1, 2, 3, 4, 11, 12, 18, 19, 22, 30, 32, 35, 40, 52, 65, 82, 83, 105
spillover effects, 86, 96
stability, 33, 61, 136, 137, 139
stabilization, 52
staffing, 56, 150, 151
state, vii, xi, 1, 3, 8, 9, 11, 14, 17, 20, 26, 31, 48, 49, 50, 53, 54, 56, 58, 61, 67, 75, 76, 77, 78, 81, 94,

97, 102, 105, 111, 112, 114, 116, 118, 120, 137, 138, 142, 143, 149, 151, 154, 157
state laws, 49, 56
State of the Union address, viii, 2, 3, 19, 83
states, ix, 11, 28, 33, 34, 42, 47, 48, 49, 60, 79, 88, 93, 111, 112, 114, 120
statutes, 51
statutory authority, 130
stimulus, 22, 70, 83, 84
stock, ix, 38, 44, 45, 59, 65, 88, 136
stock price, 65
structure, x, 51, 57, 86, 90, 98, 113, 141, 145, 146, 150, 151
structuring, 143
subprime loans, 41, 95, 155
subsidy, 85
suppliers, 83, 85

T

tangible benefits, 96
target, 5, 9, 17, 21, 22, 26, 53, 55, 87, 111, 114
target population, 87
tax credits, 70
taxes, 28, 47, 57, 61, 135
taxpayers, 39, 52, 64, 72, 73, 78, 82, 84, 87, 89, 97
technical assistance, 50
tenants, 30, 46, 48, 60, 61
tension, 39, 51, 143
threats, 70, 78
thrifts, 13, 46, 61
time frame, 125
time periods, 49
Title V, 61
training, x, 142, 150, 151
transaction costs, 39
transactions, 28, 47, 56, 60, 77, 82, 109
Treasury, 14, 16, 17, 30, 43, 53, 56, 57, 61, 62, 74, 75, 81, 85, 86, 88, 89, 90, 105, 106, 107, 108, 109, 110, 111, 112, 113, 124, 130, 135, 136, 137, 151
Treasury Secretary, 85
trial, 14, 57, 61, 104, 105, 107, 108, 110, 126, 128, 133
turbulence, 15

U

U.S. Department of the Treasury, 33, 136, 137, 138, 139, 156
U.S. Treasury, 32
underwriting, 20, 25, 35, 43, 51, 52, 58, 69, 71, 131, 132
unemployment rate, 43, 60, 111
unions, 13
United States (USA), ix, x, 5, 11, 13, 22, 23, 32, 33, 37, 40, 41, 59, 62, 85, 93, 94, 141, 142, 157
USDA, 130

V

vacancies, 4, 66, 79
vacant homes, vii, viii, 3, 4, 6, 30, 38, 44, 52, 63, 66, 67, 82, 87
valuation, 24, 25, 60, 103, 145
variables, 144
variations, 29, 135

W

Washington, 36, 59, 60, 61, 62, 70, 112, 115, 139, 154, 156, 157
weakness, viii, 2, 38, 82
wealth, vii, viii, ix, 11, 12, 32, 38, 40, 59, 65, 69, 78, 79, 81, 96
White House, 82, 84
White Paper, 91, 156
wholesale, 122
windows, 83
Wisconsin, 115
workers, 53, 65
World War I, 64
wrongdoing, 88, 89

Y

yield, 28, 122, 153, 155